Mohammed
Marx
and Marhaen

The Roots of Indonesian Socialism

Mohammed Marx and Marhaen

The Roots of Indonesian Socialism

JEANNE S. MINTZ

FREDERICK A. PRAEGER, *Publishers*

New York • Washington • London

FREDERICK A. PRAEGER, *Publishers*
111 Fourth Avenue, New York 3, N.Y., U.S.A.
77-79 Charlotte Street, London W.1, England

Published in the United States of America in 1965
by Frederick A. Praeger, Inc., Publishers

Portions of this work have been adapted from *Marxism in Southeast Asia: A Study of Four Countries,* edited by Frank N. Trager with the permission of the publishers, Stanford University Press. © 1959 by The RAND Corporation.

Library of Congress Catalog Card Number: 65-14055

Printed in the United States of America

Acknowledgments

THE SOURCES USED IN THE PREPARATION OF THIS STUDY have been many and various. They include the academic literature in the field; newspapers and magazines from a number of countries; radio broadcasts, primarily those made over the official Indonesian short-wave radio station; and materials gathered over a period of years in interviews with some of the participants in the events described. Appropriate citations indicate the sources of the information used in all cases except some of those in the last category.

Since the late 1950's, politics in the Republic of Indonesia has developed along increasingly authoritarian lines. The result has been the arbitrary imprisonment of many persons known to oppose the central government. Those who support the central government but have some reservations about the regime's infallibility are constrained not only to express their doubts in secrecy but also to discuss information contradicting official government statements in secrecy as well. Under the circumstances, it would be a cruel breach of confidence to identify the individuals who supplied much of the information on which certain sections of the final chapters are based. I should like to express my gratitude to the many Indonesians who willingly and frankly discussed the current situation in their country with me, and I have attempted to repay their kindness by omitting their names or any identifying notes from the sections based on information they supplied.

Fortunately, my debts to others can be acknowledged more specifically. Throughout the writing of the manuscript, I was sin- gularly fortunate in having the warm encouragement and invalu- able criticism of Professor Rupert Emerson of Harvard University. I am also most grateful to the others, especially Peggy Durdin, formerly of *The New York Times,* and A. M. Halpern of the Council on Foreign Relations, who read portions of the manu- script and helped to improve it. None of them bears any responsi- bility for the book's inadequacies.

Approximately a third of the material in this study has ap- peared in roughly the same form as a chapter in a book spon- sored by The RAND Corporation, *Marxism in Southeast Asia: A Study of Four Countries* (Stanford: Stanford University Press, 1959). I am grateful to The RAND Corporation for permission to include this material in the present book.

J. M.

Contents

1. INTRODUCTION   3

2. THE SETTING: TRADITION AND CHANGE   11

3. INDONESIA'S FIRST MARXISTS   23
   The Indonesian Communist Party: First Phase, 1920-27 / The PKI and Its Foreign Links: 1920-27 / Minor Left-Wing Groups Before 1927

4. THE NEW GENERATION OF NATIONALISTS   47
   Contacts Abroad: PI and Liga / Contacts Abroad: The SDAP / Socialism, Indonesian-Style / Indonesie Klaagt Aan! *and the Mainstream of Nationalist Activity / The Comintern and Indonesian Nationalism: 1927-42*

5. THE JAPANESE OCCUPATION: THE LAST PHASE OF COLONIAL RULE   70

6. SOCIALISM IN THE REVOLUTION: IDEOLOGIES AND BEHAVIOR   80
   Pantja Sila / The Views of Hatta and the Sjahrir Socialists / The Religious Socialists / The Role of the PKI in the Revolution

7. FROM THE TRANSFER OF SOVEREIGNTY TO GUIDED DEMOCRACY: BACKGROUND TO THE POLITICAL STRUGGLE   100

Reactions to the International Scene / Domestic
Party Politics: The Background / The Haze Lifts
Briefly: The 1955 Election Results / Economics and
Party Politics

8. FROM THE TRANSFER OF SOVEREIGNTY TO GUIDED
DEMOCRACY: THE SOCIALIST PARTIES   126
PNI / Masjumi / PSI / Murba / PKI

9. THE MARCH TO GUIDED DEMOCRACY   157

10. GUIDED DEMOCRACY IN THEORY   165
The Basic Doctrine Expounded / The Constitution
of 1945 / Guided Economy / Indonesian Identity /
Indonesian Socialism

11. GUIDED DEMOCRACY IN ACTION   193
The Armed Forces / PKI / The President and the
Palace

12. CONCLUSION   217

SELECTED BIBLIOGRAPHY   229

INDEX   239

Mohammed
Marx
and Marhaen

The Roots of Indonesian Socialism

1

Introduction

POLITICALLY, THE REPUBLIC OF INDONESIA IS ONE OF THE most peculiar places in today's new world of emerging nations. Indonesia does not, like India, seek to establish a viable parliamentary democracy, nor is it, like Burma or Pakistan, prepared to acquiesce in the concentration of power in the hands of the military. The country operates under a system called "guided democracy," which in itself sounds like a contradiction in terms, and which also appears to be something of a contradiction in practice. Under guided democracy there are no free elections, the press is strictly controlled and many opposition leaders are summarily imprisoned. The concept of guided democracy has never received a popular mandate. On the contrary: It was imposed in the wake of two national elections in which four parties —none of them advocating guided democracy—received 80 per cent of the vote. The very introduction of guided democracy triggered a full-scale civil war. Nevertheless, and in spite of these contradictions, apparent or real, the regime has not only survived the civil war, but appears to command an adequate measure of popular support.

President Sukarno represents guided democracy as a form of political organization superior to parliamentary democracy, the latter having, in his view, demonstrated its inadequacy for Indonesia; as an outgrowth from indigenous traditions and forms of organization which had in themselves many characteristics that could be described as socialist; and as the culmination of the best socialist theorizing by Indonesians during the colonial period.

The socialism that guided democracy is designed to express is further identified as a unique Indonesian form, which the President calls marhaenism. Marhaenism, he says, is Marxism as practiced or applied in Indonesia. This special form of Marxism is the program that the present government, which purports to be a coalition of nationalist, religious, and Communist factions, is dedicated to carrying out.

Of the many seeming paradoxes splashed across the Indonesian political canvas, three are particularly glaring. First is the paradox of the Communist Party. Indonesia's Communist Party is the oldest in Asia and the largest outside the Soviet bloc, and its leaders hold high offices in government. However, the regime is not avowedly Communist, and the Indonesian Communist Party is alternately harassed and wooed by the authorities. Second is the paradox of the armed forces. The Indonesian armed forces are heavily represented in the highest councils of state, hold the reins of provincial and local government, and are actively engaged in the operation of nationalized business enterprises. But although the armed forces have all this access to power, they are not in fact as mighty as their accumulation of titles would seem to suggest, nor is the present government a full-fledged military regime. Finally, there is the paradox of the Indonesian Socialist Party. Although guided democracy is defined as the expression of a special Indonesian socialism, most of the important Socialist Party leaders are in prison, and the party itself has been outlawed. Still, in spite of these and other peculiar features of the Indonesian scene, apparently some kind of strange balance is being struck, for the regime not only continues to exist, but to some extent devises policy and carries it through.

This curious state of affairs provokes a whole range of inevitable questions. To begin with, what has guided democracy to do with socialism, Indonesian or other? Is this a new variation or adaptation of Marxist ideology? Is there any validity to President Sukarno's assertion that guided democracy and its collateral doctrines are a synthesis of the many forms of socialism found in Indonesia? Is guided democracy an invention that actually suits the

Indonesian situation in any ideological way? Or is the seeming viability of the regime purely the happenstance outcome of a balance of political forces—the Army on one side, the Communists on the other, with Sukarno shifting his weight between them—and is guided democracy, therefore, merely an institutionalization of President Sukarno's personal power? Is there anything permanent in the nature of the ideas that make up guided democracy? Are these ideas likely to outlive Sukarno and become a lasting feature of the Indonesian scene? What is the content of these ideas? Whence do they derive? What, if anything, is peculiarly Indonesian about them? Are the institutions of guided democracy in fact reflections of indigenous customs, or is this a myth created to justify the imposition of these institutions?

Of the numerous questions listed above, this study cannot deal equally fully with all of them, but will concentrate mostly on those that illuminate the socialist components and antecedents of the current Indonesian form of government. Our attention will be directed primarily to three basic questions: (1) What are the determinants of guided democracy? (2) Is guided democracy a derivation from Indonesian traditions? (3) Does it represent a synthesis of Indonesian socialist thought? This will lead us into a consideration of the following kinds of data, though not necessarily in the order given: the content of the ideas that make up guided democracy and its collateral doctrines of guided economy, Indonesian socialism, and Indonesian identity; how these ideas have been put into practice; the origins of these ideas—whether they are largely borrowed from some external sources, whether they derive from ideas that held sway in the decades before independence, or whether their roots lie in much older indigenous social practices—and finally the relationship of these ideas to the varieties of socialism avowed by virtually all Indonesian political leaders—the forms of socialism professed and practiced in Indonesia, and the extent of the Indonesian commitment to socialist doctrines.

To seek answers to these questions we must begin by examining the socialist ideas and institutions that have influenced the pattern of modern Indonesian political development. This will require covering a broad range of material both in time and along the political spectrum, for almost every significant organ of political expression in Indonesia—from the origin of its modern nationalist movement in the early years of this century to the present—has been or has claimed to be socialist. Necessarily, then, this work becomes in large part not only a study of socialism in Indonesia in the diverse forms in which it has existed and currently exists, but also, especially in the initial chapters, a study of much of Indonesia's modern nationalist movement.

Since socialism of one variety or another pre-empts most of the field of Indonesian politics, contemporary Indonesia is aptly described by the Socialist leader Sjahrir, when he says, "We in Indonesia are all socialists, or at least, socialistically inclined." [1] His words apply equally well to the leadership of the country's pre-World War II nationalist movement. Writing from a somewhat different vantage point, Ruslan Abdulgani, a leading figure in the present government, has described the position of socialism in Indonesia as "an essential ingredient of nationalism, since we believe that socialism offers our people the quickest escape from the poverties of their national heritage." [2]

But if all Indonesians are socialists, the question remains: What kinds of socialists are they? Socialism in Indonesia is woven of several threads. One is derived from the very structure of Indonesian society, particularly the traditional organization of village life in this essentially agricultural country. Another has its origin in an Indonesian adaptation of modern Islamic doctrine which developed into a religious socialism akin to the Christian socialism which was its contemporary in Western Europe. Both of these will be examined in the next chapter. Here we are concerned with the third strand, which has proved to be the dominant one in Indonesia: a complex intertwining of socialist con-

[1] Sutan Sjahrir, *Indonesian Socialism* (Rangoon: Asian Socialist Publishing House, 1956), p. 31.

[2] Ruslan Abdulgani, "Ideological Background of the Asian-African Conference," *United Asia*, VII (March, 1955), pp. 43-45.

cepts derived from a variety of Western sources in which Marxist-Leninist doctrine is the overriding element.

Socialist movements everywhere tend to be eclectic, but in Indonesia the degree of eclecticism is unusually high. Of the many Indonesians who call themselves Marxists, relatively few have actually studied and adopted the philosophical bases of Marxist theory. Indeed, until quite recently, few of them had ever been exposed directly to the writings of Karl Marx. It was not usually the gospel of Marx that penetrated Southeast Asia but rather the doxology according to Lenin, or even, as frequently happened in the British colonies, Marx as interpreted by Harold Laski. In the past ten years, there has been widespread dissemination in Asia of the works of such successful practitioners of contemporary Marxism as the leaders of the Chinese and Vietnamese Communist parties. But in the early days of the Indonesian nationalist movement, the socialist literature that reached Indonesia and fired the imagination of its leaders was a most heterogeneous mixture, including, for example, the works of Domela Nieuwenhuis, Henriette Roland Holst, the writings of Bakunin, and a good deal written about him. Many Indonesian socialists seem more familiar with the works of the Utopians and the pre-Marxist collectivists than with anything of later vintage. Nor is it always easy to determine which are the genuine and which are only the proclaimed sources of Indonesian socialist inspiration. This resembles the pattern with respect to the intellectual forebears of modern Indonesian nationalism. While Indonesian nationalist leaders generally cite the Japanese victory over Russia in 1905 and the Chinese Revolution of 1910 as the chief external stimuli of their own nationalist movement, the libraries of these same men are filled not with the writings of Sun Yat-sen, but with the works of Thomas Jefferson, less frequently Thomas Paine, and, invariably, numerous histories of the American Revolution.

Nevertheless, to the extent that certain Marxist ideas did penetrate into Southeast Asia, their popularity and appeal were enormous. The brand of Marxism that first made its way to Indonesia found a ready reception because of its explanation and description of colonialism. For those Indonesians who did read Marx, his characterization of European colonialism as "undisguised looting, enslavement, and murder" [3] had great attraction, as did the Marxist-Leninist definition of imperialism. Colonial nationalism found in Marxism as propounded by Lenin a ready-made theory that could explain the fact of foreign domination in terms emotionally and intellectually satisfying, that is, without loss of self-respect. Marxism as interpreted by Lenin gave a definition of imperialism which indicated that foreign domination was not an expression of an immutable relationship between white and nonwhite peoples, but only a particular historical phase bound up with the development of capitalism in Western Europe. And colonial nationalism in almost every instance has identified foreign rule and capitalism as synonymous.

The ideas introduced into Asia under the label of Marxism suggested not only the possibility but even the inevitability of foreign domination coming to an end. They offered a theory of political organization and struggle, coupled with the thesis that the Soviet Union was a bulwark against capitalism. Thus, while neither the ideology nor the strategy of most Asian groups calling themselves Marxist bears much resemblance to Western social-democratic or communist parties, the nationalist leaders of Asia expressed themselves and continue to express themselves in terms derived from the Marxist vocabulary.

Because twentieth-century colonial and postcolonial nationalism is almost inevitably steeped in a left-wing viewpoint, we will be concerned here with a far broader field than that of the parties, groups, and individuals calling themselves socialist or communist. Anti-imperialism can hardly mark the division between socialist and nonsocialist parties and programs in Indonesia. If one limits the parties to be studied to those committed to a program involving some degree of public ownership and control of the means

---

[3] Karl Marx, *Capital: A Critique of Political Economy* (New York: The Modern Library, 1932), p. 826. See also pp. 824, 827 for specific references to Dutch colonialism.

of production, the definition still covers the majority of the organs of political articulation in Indonesia, as it would almost anywhere in Asia. And even those parties and groups which use religion as a common denominator, as well as those which specifically claim to be anti-Marxist, have ideological elements that bear a strong resemblance to socialist political and economic principles.

Three words will figure very heavily throughout this study: Marxism, socialism, communism. This study will not seek to establish conclusive definitions for these terms, but there should be some indication of the sense in which they will be used here. Of the three, socialism will be used in the most inclusive sense but especially with reference to those groups and individuals whose ideologies are derived not only from Marxist-Leninist doctrine but from other sources as well. Marxism will be used to refer to all ideologies and movements that derive primarily from European Marxist sources. Communism will be used in the most exclusive sense, to identify those groups and individuals professing allegiance to official Communist ideology; it will also be used, with appropriate modifiers, for those groups and individuals who have identified themselves with the variations of Soviet Communism sometimes known as Trotskyism, and at other times and places referred to as national Communism. It should be noted that even if one could supply rigid definitions of these terms, in view of what has been said about the nature of socialism in Indonesia, this would do violence to the subject matter.

On this matter of language, a word should be said about materials translated from Indonesian. The Indonesian language[4] is

4 Indonesian is still a relatively young language, adopted as the national tongue in 1928 by a nationalist congress, but in general use only since 1942. A Language Commission, appointed in 1945, has the task of guiding its growth and expansion, particularly with reference to the development of precise, especially scientific, terminology.

No uniform system of spelling has been adopted as yet. This accounts for the occasional discrepancies in the spelling of Indonesian words quoted from different sources. As part of the effort to rid the language of any vestiges of Dutch influence, certain spelling changes were introduced after 1945. The only change that need concern us here is the substitution of the letter "u" for the

still a somewhat artificial one that has not been in use long enough to adapt itself to all the demands of modern life. Consequently, the language lends itself rather readily to obscurity under the most clear-cut of circumstances. When dealing with the abstractions of political ideologies, the peculiarly amorphous character of the language compounds whatever confusion of thought may exist. Furthermore, during the years of colonial rule, Indonesians developed to a high degree the capacity for expressing themselves in Delphic utterances as a precaution against the penalties imposed on "subversive" speech or writing. This characteristic means of expression was never wholly abandoned, and it has again come into its own under the present-day regime. Thus, in this country where political ideologies more often than not tend to be vaguely formulated, the limitations of the national language serve, if anything, to thicken rather than dissolve the mist that surrounds so much of Indonesia's political expression.

---

old "oe." Thus, references to prewar publications by Indonesians will occasionally be found with the author's name in the old spelling, as Soekarno for Sukarno.

2

The Setting:
Tradition and Change

THE INFLUENCE OF SOCIALISM IN INDONESIA UNDERSTAND-
ably took special forms under the impact of certain indigenous
conditions and of the nationalist movement.[1] The cultural tradi-

1 Among the chief historical sources are J. Th. Petrus Blumberger, *De Nationalistische Beweging in Nederlandsch-Indie* (Haarlem: H. D. Tjeenk Willink, 1931), and articles in *Encyclopaedie van Nederlandsch-Indie*, (8 vols., The
Hague: M. Nijhoff, 1917-1939); and L. M. Sitorus, *Sedjarah Pergerakan Kebangsaan Indonesia* (Djakarta: Pustaka Rakjat, 1951).

A somewhat less analytical account than that of Sitorus is found in A. K.
Pringgodigdo, *Sedjarah Pergerakan Rakjat Indonesia* (Djakarta: Pustaka Rakjat, 1949). A study of the nationalist movement in the decade before the Japanese occupation is given in J. M. Pluvier, *Overzicht van de Ontwikkeling der
Nationalistische Beweging in Indonesia in de Jaaren 1930 tot 1942* (The Hague:
W. Van Hoeve Ltd., 1953). The book of D. M. G. Koch, *Om de Vrijheid: de
Nationalistische Beweging in Indonesie* (Djakarta: Jajasan Pembangunan,
1950), offers some interesting observations by a Dutch journalist who was close
to the nationalist movement almost from its inception.

Among the standard works in English that contain valuable sections on the
nationalist movement are: Rupert Emerson, *Malaysia: A Study in Direct and
Indirect Rule* (New York: The Macmillan Company, 1937); J. S. Furnivall,
Netherlands India: A Study of Plural Economy (New York: The Macmillan
Company, 1944); and Bernard H. M. Vlekke, *Nusantara: A History of the
East Indian Archipelago* (Cambridge: Harvard University Press, 1945).

The social environment out of which Indonesian nationalism arose may be
examined in such works as A. D. A. de Kat Angelino, *Staatkundig beleid en
bestuurszorg in Nederlandsch-Indie* (2 vols. in 3; The Hague: Martinus
Nijhoff, 1930. An abridged edition of this work in English was published
under the title *Colonial Policy* [2 vols.; The Hague; Martinus Nijhoff, 1931.]);
B. J. O. Schrieke, several of whose studies have now been collected and published as *Indonesian Sociological Studies: Selected Writings of B. Schrieke*
(The Hague: W. Van Hoeve Ltd., 1955); W. F. Wertheim, *Indonesian Society
in Transition* (The Hague: W. Van Hoeve Ltd., 1956); and Robert Van Niel,

tions linked to communal landholding and *gotong rojong* or mutual assistance, the unique role of Islam in Indonesia, especially of Modernist Islamic doctrine, and the class structure of Indonesian society, particularly during the colonial period, all helped to mold the Indonesian view of socialism. Superimposed on these elements in the twentieth century were the general Asian awakening, the emergence of a Western-educated elite, a growing social and economic unrest, and a burgeoning nationalist movement. These factors helped to create an atmosphere receptive to socialist doctrine.

One of the relatively constant elements in the social climate was the primitive communism of a prefeudal, precapitalist variety that held sway in much of rural Indonesia. Until comparatively recent times, exclusive private ownership of land was a concept strange to most Indonesians. Land belonged to the community. While a kind of permanent family leasehold gradually emerged in the last century, land, according to *adat* (customary) law, could not be sold without the consent of the village. If a family moved away, after a specified period of time the land reverted to the community.[2] Although in the past forty years the amount of communal land has diminished sharply, the constellation of ideas and the general social outlook engendered by a village society organized on the basis of communal ownership of land still prevail throughout much of the countryside.

The traditional political organization of the villages, the *desa* system, is another significant element. The most important aspect of this system is the emphasis placed upon mutually acceptable

---

The Emergence of the Modern Indonesian Elite (The Hague: W. Van Hoeve Ltd., 1960).

The most complete, and indeed the indispensable, study of Indonesia's nationalist movement and its culmination in the Republic of Indonesia is found in George McT. Kahin, *Nationalism and Revolution in Indonesia* (Ithaca: Cornell University Press, 1952).

[2] Raymond Kennedy, *The Ageless Indies* (New York: The John Day Co., 1942), pp. 90-91. For a useful summary, see R. Supomo, "The Future of Adat Law in the Reconstruction of Indonesia," in P. W. Thayer (ed.), *Southeast Asia in the Coming World* (Baltimore: The Johns Hopkins Press, 1953).

decisions arrived at by compromise of all viewpoints expressed.[3] *Musjawarah,* the deliberations of the villagers, and *mufakat,* the unanimous decision that emerges from these deliberations, are the essence of social relations and community action. The concept of majority rule, of the majority point of view being imposed upon and accepted by a minority, is alien to village society. While final responsibility rests more or less in the hands of the village elders, agreement is reached through discussion and compromise; hence, responsibility tends to be shared as well. This shared decision-making is tied closely to another vital element of the village system: the concept of *gotong rojong,* or mutual assistance. *Gotong rojong* is the recognition of the common responsibility of the members of the community toward each other and toward the community as an entity. *Gotong rojong* is not just something to be invoked by an individual needing help; it has a more positive content. Things are done by the whole community for the whole community. *Gotong rojong* is the motivating force behind village projects embarked upon by all members of the community after agreement has been reached on the need. *Gotong rojong* was exploited with conspicuous success during the Indonesian Revolution, for the repair of railroads and the construction of roads, buildings, and irrigation systems.

Musjawarah and *gotong rojong* are in fact the key words which express the ancient and still-valid principles of social organization at the village level, and close to 90 per cent of Indonesia's population still lives in rural communities. Thus, when President Sukarno uses these terms as the symbols of guided democracy, he is invoking some of the most hallowed concepts of Indonesian life.

The tradition of reaching decisions through deliberation and the compromise of differing viewpoints is not limited to the sys-

[3] Some Indonesians prefer the term unanimity to describe this process and its end result. Whether one calls it compromise or unanimity, essentially the process consists of discussion in which varying points of view are aired, differences reconciled, and a unified view—which does not necessarily represent any single viewpoint—emerges.

tem of village organization, although this pattern of social behavior is most clearly seen in action at the village level. A cultural preference for compromise not only in decision-making but
in all social relationships pervades Indonesian life. Indirection,
not the head-on confrontation of opposing viewpoints, is generally the favored means of expression. One consequence of this in
the political sphere is the peculiarly blurred quality of much political debate. Arguments tend to be blunted because the proponents of a given view often back away from clear-cut expressions
of that view rather than risk offending their adversaries and
thereby running counter to this highly valued cultural precept.
This was true of much of the debate among prewar nationalist
leaders; it was true of much of the debate in the post war Indonesian Parliament. Another consequence of the preference for compromise has been the marked capacity of Indonesian political
leaders of widely varying opinions to seek and find satisfactory
middle ground for cooperation. One of the more recent examples
of this singular capacity for seeking compromise was the Musjawarah Nasional in the fall of 1957, to which Army officers in
active opposition to the central government—leaders of a rebellion in all but name—were invited and did participate.

Another deeply rooted cultural value of significance for political behavior is the widespread preference for slowness over
speed. To most Indonesians, rapid decisions or activity betoken
not the decisiveness so admired in many Western cultures but,
rather, a lack of wisdom. Indonesians are, by and large, a people
whose standard of values as applied to political behavior, as well
as to other aspects of life, is well summed up in the often-quoted
saying: "We do not eat the rice while it is hot." Political wisdom in Indonesia tends to consist of moving slowly and taking
great pains to avoid alienating any significant opposition, rather
than moving swiftly and decisively and presenting one's opponents with a *fait accompli.*

Generalizations of the sort just made are always risky and must
be approached with great caution and in full recognition of the
many exceptions that prevail. Nevertheless, in any consideration

of political doctrines and behavior, it is important to take into account the relevant culturally conditioned criteria for political behavior of the society under examination.

While such characteristics of the social landscape as *musjawarah* and *gotong rojong* remained more or less constant, other aspects of Indonesian life were undergoing basic changes from the beginning of the twentieth century. An increase in education, in contacts with the outside world through the introduction of cash crops, wage labor on plantations, and the gradual replacement of a barter economy by a money economy all resulted in new attitudes whose net effect was a loosening of family and village ties. Accompanying this process was a slight but significant shift in social values toward individualism. This same period was also marked by the beginnings of the modern nationalist movement and the revitalized role of religion as a force for change in Indonesian life.

Islam in Indonesia does not have a close resemblance to Islam as it is practiced elsewhere. For one thing, Islam, especially in Java, is only the latest addition to a body of ancient religious beliefs and practices on which layers of Hindu-Buddhism had already been superimposed. Therefore, while religion was and is one of the most important and binding elements in Indonesia,[4] it has been a flexible and dynamic force, not rigid in its adaptation to modern life. At the same time, Islam in Indonesia has never been a potent political or economic force on a national scale, although on the local level the *kiai*, the religious scholar or leader, generally enjoys considerable influence. There is, however, no powerful national church entwined with the repositories of nationwide political power.

The unique quality of Islam in Indonesia was further emphasized when, in the early years of this century, Indonesia's Moslem leaders were attracted to the Modernist Islamic movement, then developing in Cairo. The movement, which was as much social and political in character as it was religious, arose as a reaction to Western penetration into Moslem lands and cultures. In its re-

---

[4] Some 90 per cent of Indonesia's population is nominally Moslem.

ligious aspect, it was an attempt to return to the fundamentals of Islamic doctrine and practice, shorn of the saint worship and the animistic innovations in which medieval scholasticism had muffled the monotheism of the faith. The reformers sought to re- state their doctrine in the light of modern Western thought, to purify their practices and bring them closer to the fundamental precepts laid down in the Koran. Beyond the religious sphere, they wished to introduce some knowledge of Western science and history into the Islamic educational system and to modify the role of the religious scribes and other community leaders along the lines of the purified and modernized doctrine. Although the movement's founder had limited his political goal to a mild effort at Pan-Islamism, several important branches of the movement developed that were mainly concerned with incorporating into Islamic teachings principles of political and social justice de- rived from the West. In Indonesia, it was these teachings on po- litical and social reform which received special attention.[5]

The Indonesian protagonists of the Modernist movement were particularly concerned with modifying the role of the religious scribes, who exercised a vital influence on the Moslem commu- nity through their enforcement of elaborate social and judicial regulations. Fearing that the growing encroachment of the Dutch on village life was a threat to the Moslem social order, the Mod-

[5] The movement began in the second half of the nineteenth century under the leadership of an Afghan, Jamal-al-Din (1838-97). One of his chief disciples, Mohammed Abduh (1849-1905), an Egyptian, was the leader of the branch of the movement that found its way to Indonesia.

At the outset, much of the new doctrine was spread in Indonesia through the medium of the internationally distributed reformist journal *Al-Manar*, edited by a Syrian leader of the movement, Sheik Rashid Rida (1865-1935).

For the background out of which the Moslem reform movement emerged, see: C. Snouck Hurgronje, *Mohammedanism* (New York: G. P. Putnam's Sons, 1916). For the role of Modernist Islamic thought in Indonesia, see Harry J. Benda, *The Crescent and the Rising Sun: Indonesian Islam under the Japa- nese Occupation 1942-1945* (The Hague: W. Van Hoeve Ltd., 1958), especially chapter 2; C. A. O. Van Nieuwenhuijze, *Aspects of Islam in Post-Colonial In- donesia: Five Essays* (The Hague: W. Van Hoeve Ltd., 1958), chapter 2; and Kahin, *op. cit.*, pp. 44-49. For a detailed study of religion in contemporary Javanese village life, see Clifford Geertz, *The Religion of Java* (Chicago: The Free Press of Glencoe, 1960); chapters 10 through 12 contain valuable back- ground on the impact of the Moslem reform movement.

ernists were anxious to forestall further inroads by strengthening
their communities and bringing them into the modern world in
their own, Islamic, way. They therefore urged the adoption and
application of Western concepts of political and social equality
in place of the highly ritualized and often rigid code laid down
by the scribes. The Modernists also attempted to adopt and put
into practice Western techniques of organization. The most important early expression of the Modernist approach in Indonesia was the Mohammedijah, a movement founded in Java in
1912 by the religious leader Kiai Hadji Ahmad Dahlan. Although the Mohammedijah's initial purpose was to disseminate
the reformed approach to religion, it soon developed a more secular orientation through the establishment of a network of
schools, health clinics, women's organizations, and youth groups.

Because of the flexible nature of Islam in Indonesia, and especially because of the impact of the Modernist Islamic doctrine,
religion has played a significant role as a vehicle for Indonesian
nationalism and social development. Arriving at a time when Indonesian life was undergoing fundamental changes, the impact
of the new doctrine was enhanced, its spread from village to village ensured by religious leaders through long established channels of communication. In turn it was fed by the changing attitudes then beginning to emerge in rural Indonesia.

The turn of the century also saw the gradual emergence of
a modern nationalist movement, a movement initiated by some
of the small number of Indonesian students being educated in
Dutch schools in Holland and Indonesia. These students were
almost all members of families descended from the feudal aristocracy. Vis-à-vis the masses of the Indonesian people, they represented a social and intellectual elite by virtue of their Western-
style education as well as their social heritage. But the roads to
success were blocked to them under the colonial regime. Economic life in all spheres was dominated by the Dutch and other
Europeans; the minor functions of the middle class were performed by Chinese, Arabs, and Indians. There were practically
no indigenous landlords of significance, nor was there any Indo-

nesian middle class to speak of. The university students therefore, had no more reason to be tied to a "status quo" economic outlook than did the peasants and laborers. Furthermore, the students' advancement above a certain level in the colonial civil administration was practically impossible.

Proposals to broaden Indonesian participation in the civil service, first broached in 1867, still awaited action in 1914. The highest administrative rank open to an Indonesian, that of Regent, remained the province of a hereditary nobility descended from the ruling princes of certain of the pre-Dutch states. And even the Regent, whose relationship to the leading Dutch official, the Resident, was officially designated as that of a "younger brother," was limited in practice to exercising minor functions under the supervision of his Dutch superiors.[6] Educated Indonesians of less exalted birth were confined to much lower echelons of the civil service until well after World War I. Indeed, a year or so before Dutch rule ended in 1942, there were only 221 Indonesians among the 3,039 higher rank civil servants in the Netherlands East Indies Government.[7]

As part of their Westernized education, the students had been

[6] See Furnivall, *op. cit.*, pp. 90 ff.; pp. 266-69. The program to unify the Dutch and "Native Civil Service" was first offered only for Java (1867); in 1905, the proposal was extended to the whole archipelago. Both proposals were repeatedly shelved. In 1921 limited concessions were made to meritorious ruling Indonesian regents under the term *ontvoogding*, or emancipated, but this experiment proved unsatisfactory and was discontinued in 1931. Furnivall notes that the first Regent to be *ontvoogd* afterwards declared that he had never noticed any difference in his powers under the experiment.

Not only were the upper reaches of the civil service all but unavailable to Indonesians, but, in the ranks they did attain, their pay and benefits were always lower than those paid a Dutch civil servant performing the same work. In the period under discussion, the turn of the century, a reorganization of the two civil services was accomplished at the expense of the Indonesian one; from 1897 to 1904, the costs of the European Service rose by 1.5 million guilders while during the same period that of the Native Service fell by almost 1 million guilders.

[7] Kahin, *op. cit.*, pp. 34-35. Kahin notes further that in 1940, of the 13,172 upper middle-level civil service positions, Indonesians held 5,023, and of the 14,212 lower middle-rank positions, Indonesians held 8,830. Wertheim, *op. cit.*, pp. 147-49, indicates that most of the increase in middle-level posts held by Indonesians, which these figures represent, took place during the depression of the 1930's.

absorbing ideas associated with nineteenth-century European nationalism and liberalism. As their views took shape, they began
to evolve an articulate version of their own nationalism and to
advance beyond the simpler, largely negative ideas animating the
earlier revolts against Dutch rule. The inspiration of Western
education was greatly strengthened by two other factors in contemporary Asia. The first of these was, as Furnivall has pointed
out, the stirring of the East:

> The Chinese and Japanese went to war like Europeans; the Filipinos
> rose against Spain; the Chinese in the Boxer Rising braved the power
> of Europe; there was trouble in British India; events in Turkey were
> shaking the Moslem world; and in 1905 the victory of Japan over
> Russia started an impulse which was to transform the peoples in Neth-
> erlands India, as in other tropical dependencies, from the extreme of
> acquiescence to the extreme of self-assertion.[8]

In addition, there was the influence of Dutch educators and
liberally inclined members of the Netherlands East Indies Government, who, in their local capacity or upon returning to prominent positions in Holland, served to spark the "Ethical" colonial
policy (1900), which expressed official and popular Dutch conscience about the welfare of Indonesia.

Meanwhile, significant changes were also appearing in the
villages. In the late nineteenth century, sporadic outbreaks of
agrarian unrest had begun in Java. They continued to erupt
periodically until after World War I. While these peasant movements coincided in time with the first stirrings of the modern
nationalist movement, they were more the result of the social
disorientation that followed on the system of forced labor and
crop deliveries—the "Culture System"—than of the nationalist
fervor motivating the students. It is against the background of a
village democracy increasingly disturbed by the pressures of in-

---

8 Furnivall, *op. cit.*, p. 238. For discussion of the "Ethical Policy," see pp.
229 ff. "The public," says Furnivall, "might have been less sensitive to the appeal of these reformers to its conscience if circumstances had not at the same
time touched its pocket."

direct, and later of direct rule, and of a society whose members shared an increasing common poverty, that these peasant movements should be viewed.

The most significant of these movements was the Saminist, which, starting about 1890 in central Java, was considered by more than one observer as a manifestation of the natural communism of the Indonesian people. By 1907, this movement, named for its leader, Samin, had some 3,000 family heads enrolled in it. Fundamentally, the Saminist movement was a negativist peasant reaction to government interference. Members refused to pay taxes in kind or in labor, avoided contact with government employees, and generally wished "to be left free to lead their own lives." [9] In 1907, the Government arrested Samin and eight other peasant leaders and sent them into exile, but the movement apparently continued in strength until 1920.[10] The motivation and the techniques of Saminism and the other popular movements of the pre-World War I and wartime eras, most of the latter led by local religious figures, have a certain resemblance to the peasant uprisings of the early 1920's, led by dissident leaders of the official Communist Party, who preached a doctrine of "religious Communism."

Another change reshaping the Indonesian scene was the appearance of a degree of popular resentment against the Indonesian aristocrats who had been absorbed into the colonial civil service. In the growing bitterness against foreign authority, these men were assumed to be guilty of the sins of their employers.

[9] Kahin, *op. cit.*, pp. 43 ff. Although Furnivall does not discuss this movement, he supplies data that shed light on it. Displaced villagers were recruited by the "coolie agents" (pp. 355-56); the peasantry suffered during the depression of 1884 (p. 220), after which "plantation agriculture made rapid progress . . . at the expense of the natives"; progress in welfare at the end of the Culture System "was followed by stagnation and relapse" (pp. 222-23); "to sum up the general opinion (after the introduction of the Ethical System), the natives grow in numbers, and the other sectors of the community, the Europeans and the Chinese, in wealth" (p. 404).

[10] S. J. Rutgers, *Indonesie: het koloniale systeem in de periode tussen de eerste en de tweede wereldoorlog* (Amsterdam: Pegasus, 1947), II, 146. This was issued by a firm that publishes much Communist material.

Though many students were themselves of the aristocracy, their nationalist sentiments led them to identify themselves, if only in a paternalistic fashion, with the peasants and their grievances. They were joined by a handful of Indonesian merchants whose resentment, initially directed against the growing power of the Chinese traders, also came to embrace as well the feudal Indonesian rulers in the Dutch civil service.

The Chinese, since the last decade of the nineteenth century, had also become the object of indigenous grievances. Second only to Europeans, they had thrived in the capitalism of the colonial economy and received special privileges from the colonial rulers. Merchant, trader, miller, pawnbroker, middleman, as well as craftsman and farmer, the Chinese, for a period after 1900, came to be regarded as "a main cause of the diminishing welfare of the Javanese." [11] And the Chinese could and did serve also as scapegoats for inexpressible but nonetheless real anti-Dutch feeling: Anti-Chinese riots broke out in 1911-12; and the first Indonesian party of mass proportions and genuinely nationalist character, Sarekat Islam, had its origin in a trade association formed by Javanese batik merchants in 1909 in an attempt to halt Chinese incursions into the few areas of Indonesian commercial activity.

The intellectual ferment stirring the small educated class, the outbreaks of peasant defiance of governmental authority, the rising tide of resentment against the indigenous aristocracy and against the alien middle class—all these elements combined to

[11] Furnivall, *op. cit.*, pp. 239-42; 408-14. See also Victor Purcell, *The Chinese in Southeast Asia* (London: Oxford University Press, 1951), Part VII and particularly pp. 511 ff. For an account of the Chinese in the early part of the twentieth century, see P. H. Fromberg, "De Chineesche Beweging op Java," *Verspreide Geschriften* (Leiden: Leidsche Uitgeversmaatschappij, 1926). For a study of the legal position of the Chinese in Indonesia from the middle of the nineteenth century to the treaty on dual nationality between the Republic of Indonesia and the People's Republic of China in 1955, see Donald E. Wilmott, *The National Status of the Chinese in Indonesia,* Interim Reports Series, Modern Indonesia Project (Ithaca: Department of Far Eastern Studies, Cornell University, 1956).

make the atmosphere in Indonesia highly charged in the period under discussion. Marxism, then, did not burst upon the Indonesian scene as a revolutionary doctrine disturbing a tranquil, tropical paradise, but arrived at a time of significant change and growing tension.

3

Indonesia's First Marxists

IT IS GENERALLY AGREED THAT MARXISM WAS FORMALLY
introduced into Indonesia in 1914, with the founding of the Indies Social Democratic Association (Indische Sociaal Democratische Vereeniging). However, it is clear that some Indonesian
leaders had earlier become acquainted with the development in
Holland of a socialist party that was interested in Indonesian
affairs and specifically opposed the extension of Dutch rule by
force to those parts of the archipelago not previously subdued.
This was the Social Democratic Workers Party (Sociaal-Democratische Arbeiderspartij, or SDAP), founded in Amsterdam in
1894. This party had from the outset campaigned for an improved standard of living for the Indonesian people and had, as
early as March, 1901, while supporting the welfare provisions of
the new Ethical colonial policy, adopted a program advocating
the development of the Indonesian people toward ultimate self-
rule.[1] In the lower chamber of the Dutch Parliament, the party's
representatives championed increased political rights for Indonesians, an improved judicial system, an easing of the islands'
tax burden, better labor conditions, and the establishment of
some industries to speed up Indonesia's economic evolution.
Some knowledge of these activities reached Indonesian intellectual circles through the Dutch press and, more frequently,
through contacts with the handful of Dutch socialists residing in
Indonesia, several of them members of the SDAP.

[1] H. H. van Kol, "De Strijd der SDAP op Koloniaal Gebied," *Gedenkboek
ter gelegenheid van het vijf en twintigjaarig bestaan van de Sociaal-democratische arbeiderspartij in Nederland* (Amsterdam: Ontwikkeling, 1919), p. 89.

The first Indonesian nationalists to be drawn into the orbit of the SDAP in Holland were the exiled leaders of the Nationale Indische Partij,[2] Dr. Tjipto Mangoenkoesoemo and Soewardi Suryaningrat; the latter is better known as Ki Hadjar Dewantoro, the name he later adopted.[3] Both these men had been arrested for nationalist activities in Indonesia in 1913, but had been permitted to go to Holland, where they found a sympathetic welcome from the SDAP. Typical of the nationalist leadership of their times—and indeed of the decades that followed until the social upheaval brought on by World War II—they were both members of aristocratic families with no previous inclination toward socialism.

It was, however, with the founding of the above-mentioned Indies Social Democratic Association that socialism first took firm root in Indonesian soil. The Association was both an active political organization and the first socialist organization to be established in Southeast Asia. The founders were a group of Dutch socialists under the leadership of H. J. F. M. Sneevliet.[4] They were soon joined by some of the former members of the suppressed Nationale Indische Partij, along with other Eurasians and Dutch, and a few Indonesians. It was this group that later developed into the Perserikatan Komunis di Indonesia (PKI), or Indonesian Communist Union.

[2] Founded in 1912, with a membership of Eurasians and Indonesians, the NIP developed a program of racial equality, social and economic justice, and freedom.

[3] Ki Hadjar Dewantoro was the founder of the Taman Siswa school system, which played a vitally important role in building a generation of conscious nationalists emancipated from the bonds of much of the traditional education expounded in the villages and in the official government schools.

[4] H. J. F. M. Sneevliet, the man generally credited with playing the key role in establishing Indonesia's Communist movement, had been a member of the radical wing of the SDAP—the Tribunist group—which split off in 1909 to form the Sociaal-Democratische Partij (SDP), the forerunner of the Communist Party of Holland (CPH). In the 1930's, the CPH changed its name to Communist Party of the Netherlands (CPN). For the sake of simplicity, we will refer to the party throughout as the CPN. (See Blumberger, *Le Communisme aux Indes Néerlandaises*, p. 2; and Vlekke, *op. cit.*, pp. 338 ff.) Among the founders of the ISDV, along with Sneevliet, were H. W. Dekker, J. T. Brandsteder, A. Baars, and P. Bergsma.

The Indonesian Communist Party:
First Phase, 1920-27

During the early 1920's, the PKI was the largest and most significant Marxist Party in Indonesia.[5] Its history is filled with problems arising primarily from the dichotomy between Marxist ideology as represented by the Comintern on one side and the realities of Indonesian life on the other. Since these problems form the essential background not only of the development of the PKI itself but also of the role of ideas of Marxist origin in the larger stream of Indonesian nationalism, certain aspects of the PKI's early history bear examination here.

Originally composed of a handful of Indonesians working with the Dutch leaders of the Indies Social Democratic Association, the PKI grew from a small revolutionary faction operating within the country's first large-scale nationalist party, the Sarekat Islam (SI), to a mass-based party which by 1923 claimed to have some 50,000 members[6] and controlled a significant portion of the country's trade-union movement.[7] Even before the official founding of the PKI in May, 1920, the Communist leaders had tried to gain control of the SI by forming workers' groups within

[5] See Blumberger, *op. cit.*, and *De Communistische Beweging in Nederlandsch-Indie* (2nd rev. ed.; Haarlem: H. D. Tjeenk Willink, 1935); Sitorus, *op. cit.*; and Ruth T. McVey, *The Development of the Indonesian Communist Party and Its Relations with the Soviet Union and the Chinese People's Republic* (Cambridge: Massachusetts Institute of Technology, 1954).

[6] P. Bergsma, "A Letter from the Dutch East Indies," *World News and Views. International Press Correspondence*, London (hereafter referred to as *Inprecor*), III (September 27, 1923), 699.

[7] By the end of 1919, SI's central leadership had united 22 Indonesian trade unions, with a total membership of 77,000, under the direction of one of its own men. The Communists immediately sought to take control of this organization. Although Semaun, the key figure among the Communists, managed to have himself elected chairman of this trade-union federation, he found his attempts to control it blocked by the resistance of SI men who had retained the other top posts. Semaun then left to set up a rival trade-union federation, taking with him fourteen unions, including the highly important VSTP, the Association of Railway Workers, one of the oldest and most revolutionary of the trade unions. See *Vakbeweging* (Djakarta: Republic of Indonesia, Ministry of Information, May, 1947).

its branches. This technique succeeded to the extent that the PKI was able to rally to its banners a significant number of SI branches, but in many instances the victory was a hollow one, because many of these branches soon lost much of their peasant membership. Nevertheless, the PKI was able to build up a substantial following, primarily through the trade unions. Encouraged by this rapid rise, a faction of the PKI leadership attempted a coup late in 1926. This proved to be a crucial error. First of all, the PKI did not have enough organization and power to carry it off successfully. Furthermore, the coup was staged without taking practical account of the political and military realities of the time. The severity with which the authorities dealt with the PKI and its supporters destroyed its apparatus and drove it from the Indonesian scene as a political party for nearly a decade.

There were other reasons as well for the collapse of the PKI, aside from the gross misjudgments leading to the coup. From the outset, the Communists faced difficult problems in trying to adhere to the Comintern line regardless of its relevance to the domestic situation. In addition, the Communists failed to take sufficient account of the vigor of the prevailing mores, and in particular of the role of religion in Indonesian life. It was not a question of heresy; the Indonesian people are remarkably tolerant on matters of religion. But the peasants were rapidly alienated by the Communists' refusal to give religion any place in their world view; this appeared to many of them an attack on one of the most important elements in Indonesian life.

It is logical to suppose that on issues of the day there probably appeared to be few differences, in the eyes of the average peasant, between the Marxist-Leninist doctrine of the Communists and the Modernist Islamic socialism preached by Tjokroaminoto, Hadji Agus Salim, and other members of the SI's central leadership. In a society where capitalism and foreign rule were regarded as one and the same thing and considered the main enemy, initially it was not too difficult for religious nationalists and Communists to work together. For one thing, the central leadership of the SI, whose nationalist sentiments had originally been clothed in respectably religious terminology, was gradually drifting toward a more secular view of the world. Moreover, as the Communist faction within the SI grew stronger, the central leadership was forced to take a more radical stand on current issues, in an effort to maintain a hold on the rank and file. [8] All the same, the moderate SI leaders, adhering to their personal convictions, continued to appeal to moral and ethical standards based on religion and to rely on religious terminology to phrase their appeal.[9]

Throughout the struggle between the moderate central leadership of the SI and the Communists, which raged from 1916 to 1924 and occupied the center of the stage at each SI congress during that period, the SI leaders placed an emphasis on the role of religion that indicated their recognition of this issue's importance in the fight for control. Certainly the SI leaders were willing to exploit their opponents' formal atheism, and they did so on many occasions with conspicuous success. At times, the religious question appeared as a genuine issue dividing the leaders of the PKI and the central leadership of the SI; at times, it seems to have been primarily a matter of tactical behavior. Although the SI's central leadership was ultimately to lose much popular support because of its undue reliance on the appeal of religion alone, it is also true that the PKI's stand on religion was in large

[8] Furnivall notes that "Although the Indonesian labourer cared little for Karl Marx, and the great bulk of the party [SI] cared only for Nationalism, with Islam as its symbol, the leaders succumbed to the prestige of their European allies, and to their greater organizing capacity and better understanding of political tactics." See Furnivall, *Colonial Policy and Practice: A Comparative Study of Burma and Netherlands India* (Cambridge: Cambridge University Press, 1948), p. 235.

[9] An example of this is the often-quoted distinction which the SI's leaders made between "sinful," presumably Western, capitalism as opposed to other forms, presumably indigenous capitalism. (See Vlekke, *op. cit.*, p. 340; Pringgodigdo, *op. cit.*, p. 17; E. S. de Klerck, *History of the Netherlands East Indies* (Rotterdam: W. L. & J. Brusse, 1938), II, 534; and B. Alkema, *De Sarikat Islam* (Utrecht: G. J. A. Ruys, 1919), p. 49. Alkema lists the resolutions adopted at the SI's National Congress on October 21, 1917, including as point 3: "The SI will always fight against the domination of sinful capitalism."

measure responsible for alienating much of the mass support that the Communists had hoped to gain by utilizing the SI and its organization.

The problem of reconciling the fundamental and pervasive influence of religious beliefs on the majority of Indonesians with formal Communist atheistic ideology dogged the PKI throughout its existence in the 1920's, and still hampers it today. The Party's leaders tackled the question in various ways. At first, they firmly and openly repudiated religion; then, in one of their final efforts to keep from being expelled by the SI, they offered to take a neutral stand on the subject; [10] and on occasion they tried to utilize religion for the Party's own ends. Much as the SI had been expected to supply a mass organization through which the Communists could carry on their work, so Islam was tried in various times and places as a likely vehicle for Communist mass propaganda. For example, in the period after his exile but before his break with the PKI, the outstanding Communist, Tan Malaka, specifically recommended religion as a means of propaganda.[11] And for some time before this recommendation, it was evident that religion and religious leaders were being used to good effect by the Communists, especially in the Minangkabau area of Sumatra.[12]

That the struggle between the Communists and the central leadership of the SI extended down into the membership at large and that the root of the problem at the base, if not at the top, was the role of religion, was made clear in Tan Malaka's speech at the Fourth Comintern Congress at the end of 1922. There he stated with some eloquence the dilemma facing the Indonesian Communists in their efforts to apply the directives of the Third International to their domestic problems. Pointing out the diffi-

10 At the SI congress at Madiun in February, 1923. (See Blumberger, *Le Communisme aux Indes Néerlandaises*, p. 38).

11 Tan Malaka recommended the use of religion especially in such markedly orthodox Moslem areas as Solo, Jogjakarta, Atjeh, and Bandjermasin. See excerpts from his *Semangat Moeda* (Tokyo: 1926) in Blumberger, *De Communistische Beweging in Nederlandsch-Indie*, pp. 65-66.

12 Schrieke, "The Causes and Effects of Communism on the West Coast of Sumatra," *Indonesian Sociological Studies*.

culties raised for the PKI by the Second Comintern Congress resolution of 1920 opposing Pan-Islamism, he said:

> The Sarekat Islamists believe in our propaganda. They are with us "with their stomachs," but with their hearts they remain with the Sarekat Islam—with their heaven which we cannot give them. Therefore they boycotted our meetings, and we could not carry on propaganda any longer.[13]

After describing the then current *rapprochement* with the central leadership of SI, Tan Malaka warned that the question of Pan-Islamism was not settled and that it remained an important problem. He described the difference between historic Pan-Islamism and its current ideological content in the following manner:

> At present, Pan Islamism is a nationalist-liberation struggle, because Islam for the Moslems is everything; not only religion, but also the State, the economic system, the food, in fact everything. Thus, Pan Islamism now means the fraternity of all Mohammedan peoples and the liberation not only of the Arabian, but also the Indian, Javanese and all other oppressed Mohammedan peoples. This fraternity is called the liberation struggle against the British, French, and Italian capitalists, consequently against world capitalism. . . . This is our new task, and just as we are willing to support the national war, we shall also support the liberation struggle of the very active and energetic 250 million Mohammedans, who are subject to the Imperialist Powers. Therefore, I ask once more if we should support Pan Islamism in this sense, and in how far we are to support it.[14]

Nevertheless, whatever tack the Communists adopted, suspicion of their stand on religion still caused them heavy losses among their peasant following. Indeed, the antipathy aroused by the PKI's religious views was so strong in some areas where the Party had taken over the SI organizations that the local religious leaders were able to form rival organizations, known as Sarekat

[13] Tan Malaka, speech to the Fourth Comintern Congress, *Inprecor*, II (December 5, 1922), 875.

[14] *Ibid.*, pp. 875 f.

Hidjau (Green Association), which harried the Communists in the villages and in some instances engaged in armed clashes with the PKI's local affiliates.[15]

Having failed to win strong popular support within the SI, the PKI was frustrated in its attempts to wrest control of the organization from its original leadership. Thereupon, the Communists altered their strategy and began setting up Red SI branches in competition with the older organization. In 1921, these branches were re-formed into a new organization called Sarekat Rakjat (SR), or People's Association. This organization was originally intended to supply the mass base from which properly trained and approved candidates could "graduate" to membership in the PKI. In 1924, however, in what was to be a nearly fatal error, the PKI decided to abandon the predominantly peasant Sarekat Rakjat and to focus attention on building up strength within the labor movement. This policy represented the leaders' interpretation of what they understood to be the current "trade-union emphasis" of Communist doctrine. However, since the Party was already having difficulty in maintaining its following among the peasants, the new policy left the PKI leadership marching at the head of a revolutionary movement that lacked the mass peasant support formerly provided by the SR. At the same time, the Party rebuffed the renewed efforts of other nationalist organizations to reunite forces and to seek a new basis for cooperation. Both for abandoning their peasant supporters and for failing to form a united front with the bourgeois nationalist parties, the PKI not only suffered setbacks in its struggle for power, but also incurred the wrath of the leaders in Moscow.[16]

[15] Blumberger, De Communistische Beweging in Nederlandsch-Indie, p. 48, and Semaun, "International Imperialism and the Communist Party of Indonesia," Communist International, No. 17 (1926), pp. 75-82. In Semaun's article, the rival organization is called Sarekat Hindyu, and its members are charged with killing several PKI members.

[16] In March, 1925, the Executive Committee of the Comintern had directed the PKI to form a united anti-imperialist front with the non-Communist nationalists and to continue to work through the SR. (See article by "X," "The Revolutionary Movement in the East," Communist International, No. 18-19 (1926), pp. 97-115.

Having narrowly escaped disaster through its mishandling of the religious issue and its abandonment of the SR, the PKI proceeded to destroy itself by the coup in 1926. Despite the loss of much of its peasant following, the Party had managed to rebuild its strength, principally through control of a significant part of the labor movement. Misled by the appearance of strength suggested by the size of the unions under its domination, and swayed by the revolutionary ardor of a faction that had risen to prominence within the Party in 1924-25, the PKI in October, 1925, laid plans for a revolution to take place the following June. This was the fateful Prambanan decision, taken at a meeting of the Party's Executive Committee together with the leaders of the major Communist-controlled unions—a conference at which the revolutionary faction, led by Dahlan, Soekra, Alimin, and Musso, dominated the proceedings. However, increasingly severe measures by the authorities removed several of the leading participants from the scene; meanwhile, at a meeting early in 1926, a number of Party leaders from Java and Sumatra decided to drop their plans for revolt. This left the PKI with a leadership split on the issue of revolt and with a mass backing much smaller than the Prambanan conferees had counted on. The grandiose plans for revolution crumbled away into a poorly organized uprising in Java in November, 1926, followed by a similarly weak attempt in Sumatra some two months later, both crushed within a matter of days.[17]

Yet the events that led to this abortive coup are important, because they resulted in the schism that has divided the Communist movement in Indonesia ever since. The essentials of the story, as

[17] On the background of the rebellion and the conditions out of which it arose, see Harry J. Benda and Ruth T. McVey (eds.), *The Communist Uprisings of 1926-1927 in Indonesia: Key Documents*, Translation Series, Modern Indonesia Project (Ithaca: Department of Far Eastern Studies, Cornell University, 1960). For an interesting analysis of several facets of the revolt and its origins, see Harry J. Benda, "The Communist Rebellions of 1926-1927 in Indonesia," *Pacific Historical Review*, XXIV (May, 1955), pp. 139-52. Benda cites evidence to indicate that the revolts were not significantly inspired by adverse economic conditions, and points out that not only this but other revolutionary uprisings in Indonesia under colonial rule actually coincided with periods of unusual prosperity.

told by two leading contenders, are these: [18] Tan Malaka, one of Indonesia's leading Communists, who had been exiled some years earlier by the Dutch and was currently the Comintern's agent for Southeast Asia and Australia, opposed the Prambanan decision, as he had earlier opposed the Party's abandonment of the SR. Failing to carry his point in the months before the revolt was to take place, he had had circulated in Indonesia a document giving his reasons for opposing the plans. Tan Malaka's efforts to dissuade the local PKI leaders from supporting the revolution were apparently quite successful; his arguments are generally assumed to have been a decisive factor in causing many PKI leaders early in 1926 to drop the plans for a revolt. Thus, when the attempted coup ended in disaster, Alimin, Musso, and the other leaders who had pushed through the Prambanan decision and tried to carry it out over Tan Malaka's opposition, laid the blame for failure principally at his door. It was not until some time later, however, that this became the official Comintern version of the reasons for the revolt's failure.[19]

It was largely disaffection among the peasants that had led Tan Malaka to warn the Party against such a drastic step as revolt. The burden of his arguments, contained in *Massa Actie,* a pamphlet printed in mid-1926, was that the leadership of the Party no longer enjoyed sufficient mass backing to risk a major revolt and that the result might well be chaos. He pointed out that Moscow would be unlikely to offer any aid for a venture that had so little chance of success. He also questioned the strength of the Marxist training of PKI members who would have to assume positions of leadership in any attempt at revolt.[20] Earlier, when the PKI's mass support had been stronger, Tan Malaka had taken a more optimistic view of the Party's chances for successful revolt, provided proper attention was given to consolidating its sup-

[18] Tan Malaka, *Thesis;* and Alimin, *Analysis.* Summarized in Kahin, *op. cit.,* pp. 81-87.

[19] Rutgers, *op. cit.,* pp. 162 f.

[20] The original edition of this pamphlet is virtually unavailable except for one edition, printed in Djakarta in 1947, which Kahin indicates is a reprint of the 1926 edition published in Singapore.

port;[21] however, by the time the Prambanan decision was communicated to him, Tan Malaka felt that the PKI had missed the opportunity to strike with a possibility of success.

What kind of men were the Indonesian laborers and peasants who rallied to the PKI's banner and made their bid for power in that disastrous coup of 1926? Some 13,000 Indonesians were arrested in the days following the uprising; of these, 4,500 were imprisoned and more than 1,000 interned. Although the internees, who were concentrated at Boven Digoel, the camp in New Guinea, were labeled "Communists" by the authorities, it was clear even then to many observers that their crime and their motivation were essentially nationalist rebellion and not necessarily Communist revolution. Sjahrir, a later arrival in Boven Digoel, remarked of these prisoners of the 1926-27 uprising:

> [The majority were men] who followed the command of the PKI at that time . . . with the same sort of disposition that they would have followed any prince or venal quack or lunatic. The largest number of them were undeveloped villagers, and the percentage of illiterates was high. . . . [E]ven if a large majority of them were not Communists, they were still in favor of rebellion. However, I think that they did not even quite know what they wanted to represent thereby. . . . They are, simply and fundamentally, Indonesians. If one wishes to understand them, one must regard them in this light first of all, and only then can one really evaluate the so-called Communism that many of them profess. . . . One finds that it is a strange sort of Communism indeed, a mystical Hinduistic-Javanese, Islamic-Menangkabau, or Islamic-Bantem sort of Communism, with definite animistic tendencies. There are not many European Communists who could recognize anything of their Communism in this Indonesian variety.[22]

While Sjahrir's description was accurate as far as it went, other writers have shed additional light on the prevailing cultural dis-

---

[21] See *Toward the Indonesian Republic* (Canton and Tokyo: 1925) as quoted in Blumberger, *De Communistische Beweging in Nederlandsch-Indie*, pp. 62-67. In this pamphlet, Tan Malaka stressed the need for strengthening the Party and its cells in the armed forces as a preliminary to any violent action.

[22] Sjahrir, *Out of Exile* (New York: The John Day Company, 1949), pp. 73 f.

location and on some of the specific reasons that had started many of Sjahrir's fellow prisoners on the road to Boven Digoel. It is apparent from these analyses that the propaganda disseminated by the Communists had come to have a special meaning and had found a special place for itself in many parts of Indonesian society. True, as Sjahrir wrote, there was little resemblance to European Communism, but the appeal made by Communist leaders had clearly given a new tone to the dawning self-consciousness of Indonesian nationalism.[23]

Certainly the PKI leaders had not planned to depend for support on a following whose political orientation was practically limited to the negative slogans of anti-imperialism and anticapitalism. This was, however, the inevitable outcome of the leaders' attempt to build a mass party by seeking support without discrimination. There had, of course, been some attempts to school the rank and file in Marxist-Leninist teachings, and some sporadic gestures in the direction of holding Party membership to relatively small and well-instructed cadres. But none of these efforts—from the Dutch Communist leader Baars's lecture courses on "agitprop" work to the program, adopted in 1924, stipulating the training that aspiring Party members would have to undergo before acceptance—really took precedence in the eyes of the leaders over their drive for members. It is difficult to determine whether the PKI leaders were dizzied by the rapid success of their appeal to the masses or whether they were guided by their belief that the proper role of a colonial Communist Party with a mass base was, as in China, to move toward revolutionary action because "conditions were ripe." Certainly the PKI policy of seeking wide support fairly indiscriminately brought some strange figures into its ranks and caused the leaders considerable difficulty. For example, some unique "deviationists" became members of the Party, including groups calling themselves

---

[23] See, e.g., Schrieke, *Indonesian Sociological Studies,* esp. pp. 111 f., 149, and 160 f. It is very likely that Schrieke's comments on the lasting result of Communist propaganda in the area to which he confined his examination were applicable to other parts of Indonesia that had been similarly propagandized.

"religious Communists." In fact, some of the deviationists, among them Hadji Misbach at Solo, Soediro in Semarang, and Datuk Batuah in Sumatra, were even able to threaten the Party's control in a number of local branches.

While these groups were operating on the fringes of the PKI as well as harassing its central leadership, an attempt was made by the PKI leadership to give a more clearly identifiable Marxist-Leninist tone to the Party's program. Thus, starting with the congress of June, 1924, the symbols of international Communism were utilized more fully at public meetings. In addition, the program put forth at that meeting detailed plans for the establishment of a Soviet republic of Indonesia, including the use of the techniques of agitprop and the extension of the Party schools, still known in that pre-1926 era as Tan Malaka schools. Such measures did not, however, resolve the issue of the kind of Party organization the PKI leaders sought during this period, or to what extent their actions jibed with their expressions of views on the organizational question. In its earliest days, the Party was clearly intended to be a small elite group, operating as a cell within the mass-based SI.[24] However, the battle to gain control of the SI led the Communists to vie with the SI leaders in seeking mass support, and hence to subordinate the issue of the Marxist-Leninist training of these supporters. The brief experience of the PKI with the SR does not appear to have altered this organizational pattern. The fact that the Communist leadership of the local branches could be threatened by Hadji Misbach or Soediro and by other manifestations of non-Communist programs indicates that the Party's "intake" procedures were far more lax than its leaders were willing to admit at Comintern meetings. Thus, for example, in his report to the Sixth Comintern Congress, Semaun claimed that the 1926 uprising had failed in part

[24] This was apparently one of the first attempts by a Communist Party to infiltrate another Party and form cells within it as a means for developing its own propaganda and contacts among the masses. Sneevliet, in 1922, proposed this technique to the Chinese Communist Party. See Harold R. Isaacs, *The Tragedy of the Chinese Revolution* (1st rev. ed.; Stanford: Stanford University Press, 1951), pp. 58-59.

because of the elite nature of the Party organization; he maintained that the PKI had only 9,000 enrolled members at that time, contrasted with the 100,000 or more in the SI.[25] This account of the Party's size contradicts earlier boasts by PKI leaders about their strength and probably represents Semaun's effort to recast the history of the PKI and its errors in order to fit a new Comintern mold.

The PKI and Its Foreign Links: 1920-27

Reference has already been made to the links between the Indonesian and Dutch Communists and between the PKI and the Comintern. These merit further consideration. There is no doubt about the prime importance of individual Dutch Communist leaders in the establishment and first years of the Indonesian Party. However, as these men were in turn exiled by the Netherlands Indies Government, the link between the PKI and representatives of the Dutch Party weakened. Meanwhile, the tie between the Indonesian Communists and Moscow was strengthened in a variety of ways. The PKI was represented in the Comintern, and it participated in various Comintern agencies operating in the Far East and Southeast Asia. It was also of some importance that a number of Indonesians attended the Communist University of the Toilers of the East in Moscow.

The original quadrumvirate of Dutch Communists—Sneevliet, Brandsteder, Baars, and Bergsma—were in a sense the true fathers of Indonesian Communism. They provided the radical wing of the nationalist movement with a theoretical framework and a definition in Marxist terms of tendencies that had been developing in Indonesia for some time before their arrival. They also introduced their pupils to Communist strategy and tactics. And it was through Sneevliet that the PKI first established for-

---

[25] Semaun, "The Situation in Indonesia," Coreport to the Sixth Comintern Congress, *Inprecor*, VIII (October 4, 1928), 1243. Kahin, *op. cit.*, p. 84, offers figures that would reduce Semaun's claim of Party membership to "some 3,000 party members."

mal contact with Moscow in 1920.[26] Despite the importance of these men and their vital contribution to the birth of Indonesian Communism, it is interesting to note that their subsequent disappearance from the scene worked to the advantage of the PKI. As Semaun put it, "The very fact that the leadership of the party was in the hands of native comrades still further raised the prestige of the party in the eyes of the masses, for we must not forget that in a colonial country like Indonesia, the masses are somewhat prejudiced against the Dutch comrades." [27] This comment suggests one of the main reasons why the PKI's links with the CPN were never as strong as those with the Comintern. As Semaun indicated, the intensity of anti-Dutch feeling, which permeated much of the nationalist movement and especially its more extreme elements, automatically made any Netherlander a suspect figure, no matter what his political convictions or behavior. This was not the case in Holland, where Dutch and Indonesian Communists worked well together. By associating continually with a variety of Dutch people, Indonesians in Holland were more likely to distinguish between those Dutch who were regarded as political friends and those who were seen as foes. In Indonesia, however, the racist aspects of colonial rule diminished the possibilities for any real mass confidence in a leadership in which Dutch participation was visible. Semaun was highly conscious of this racial problem; in a pamphlet apparently intended for distribution to Dutch comrades and sympathizers, he noted that "a revolution in Indonesia without Communist leadership will develop into racial warfare," and that the Indonesian Communist Party had tried to solve this problem by attempting to "create affection for our white fellow-Communists." [28]

Two other reasons may be advanced for the relative weakness of the tie between the two parties. One was the lack of regular

[26] Sneevliet represented the Indonesian Communists at the Second Comintern Congress.

[27] Semaun, "The Situation in Indonesia," p. 1245.

[28] Semaoen [Semaun], *Hoe het Hollandsche Imperialisme het Bruine Millioenenvolk Aanzet tot een Massamoord op Europeanen in Indonesia* (Amsterdam: Brochurehandel der C. P. H., n.d.).

communication. There were few channels by which Indonesians below the top ranks could learn of the Dutch Party's activities and how these related to Indonesia's interests; in addition, the internecine warfare within the CPN during the 1920's served to confuse the picture, even for those Indonesian Communists who were informed on developments in Holland. Communication with Moscow was not without its difficulties, but at least the Comintern bureaus and organizations operating in Asia were a good deal closer than Holland. Furthermore, these Comintern bureaus were all seen as Asian groups, dealing with Asian problems, even as Moscow had the advantage of not being regarded as a Western capital.[29] Even where white Westerners were found on the Comintern staffs, the curse of paternalism, which always hung over the Dutch Party and its members in the view of most Indonesians, was apparently not felt, or at least not felt as keenly.

Finally, Indonesian relations with their Dutch comrades were severely damaged in the developments arising from the 1926-27 revolt. When news of the revolt first reached Holland, the initial reaction of the CPN was regarded as extremely weak, both by the Comintern and the PKI. Moscow immediately issued a strong denunciation of the Dutch Government and the Dutch Social Democrats.[30] The Dutch Communist Party's representative in the Netherlands Parliament, however, joined with the SDAP in backing a motion to send a committee of investigation to Java to inquire into the mass arrests and internments that had taken place in the wake of the revolt. Although De Visser, the repre-

---

[29] Although few Indonesians had more than a hazy idea of where Moscow is, or what the Russian peoples' racial origins are, the ideas and revolutionary slogans attributed to Moscow tended to make Russia seem like a fellow Asian country. Furthermore, to a handful of Indonesians, Russia had offered recognition on a footing of equality with representatives of Western countries, through participation in the Comintern. Finally—a point which is still significant today—few Indonesians had ever seen a Russian, but most of them had seen a number of Dutchmen, Englishmen, and Frenchmen; and this familiarity with the representatives of colonial powers had all too often not been conducive to mutual respect or liking.

[30] See *Inprecor*, VI (November 25, 1926), 1390, and (December 2, 1926), 1438. Musso returns to this theme in "How the Social Democrats Betray the Workers in Indonesia," *ibid.*, VIII (January 5, 1928), 13.

sentative in question, was Moscow's man, having come into power the previous year after the purge of the former leaders Wynkoop and van Ravesteyn, he obviously deviated from Moscow's position in his initial reaction to the Indonesian revolt. When attacked in the Comintern for his stand, De Visser claimed that the first reports of the revolt to reach the Dutch Communists had indicated that it was merely another "provoked struggle." However, he continued, "just as soon as the party recognized that the Javanese workers had gone over to an armed uprising, it did everything in its power to support them." [31] Nevertheless, the Indonesian Communists, who had already had their heated disputes with the former Communist leaders in Holland, accused the current leadership then and later of having failed to support the uprising in a proper fashion.

If relations between the Indonesian and Dutch Communists were not noticeably good, they were at least reasonably clear and public.[32] The same could not be said for the Comintern-PKI relationship during the period and over the events in question. The Prambanan leaders had sought the support of Moscow for their planned revolt and had timed the outbreak of the revolution to allow for that support to be received beforehand. Confusion arises because Moscow never made public its reaction to this request for support. To some observers, this silence suggests that the Comintern's reaction was negative, and Alimin's own silence about the Comintern's stand when he is defending himself and attacking Tan Malaka seems to point to the same conclusion.[33]

There is no doubt that before the PKI revolt the Indonesian Communist leadership had been criticized by Moscow. Stalin had accused it of "a deviation of the left" for the failure to apply

[31] De Visser, statement at the Sixteenth Session of the enlarged ECCI, December 6, 1926, *ibid.*, VI (December 30, 1926), 1635 f.

[32] In 1933 the CPN for the first time elected an Indonesian Communist, Roestam Effendi, as a member of the Dutch Parliament. The propaganda value of this move should not be underestimated. There are Indonesians who were not yet born when Effendi took his seat in the Dutch Parliament, who today point to that event as evidence that the only group in Holland that genuinely fought for Indonesian rights was the Dutch Communist Party.

[33] See, for example, Kahin, *op. cit.*, p. 83.

properly the "united-front-from-above" tactics of the Fifth Comintern Congress.[34] This criticism certainly lends credence to the view that the Comintern supported its agent Tan Malaka, who had been in Moscow in 1925 and who subsequently condemned the plan and the leaders of the proposed revolution. But Alimin and Musso, representing the "revolution-now" faction went to Moscow—probably in mid-1926—to plead for support. On this specific point the Kremlin is silent. That silence, and Alimin's later reticence about the event, however, do not necessarily justify the interpretation that Moscow's reaction to their appeal was negative. Quite the contrary: The evidence suggests that the Comintern probably did not oppose the plans for rebellion. Reference has already been made to endorsing actions taken both by the ECCI and the Profintern. And Bukharin, speaking at a session of the enlarged ECCI in late November, 1926, proclaimed: "From this rostrum we greet the proletarians and peasants of Indonesia, the broad working masses of this Dutch colony who are likewise engaged in a bloody struggle against capital. Our full support to the Indonesian people!" [35] Nor did this support end with the suppression of the revolt. Had Moscow wished to be negative or to repudiate the revolt, it could easily have done so after the arrest of members of both factions. Instead, the ECCI turned its attention to building up the importance of the revolt and defining the "tasks of Communists in Indonesia." [36]

[34] Speech, May, 1925, before the Communist University of the Toilers of the East, in *Marxism and the National and Colonial Question,* (Moscow: Foreign Languages Publishing House, 1940), p. 192. "X" (see above, fn. 16), reports similar criticism from the ECCI meeting of March, 1925. See also McVey, *Development of the Indonesian Communist Party,* p. 11.

[35] *Inprecor,* VI (November, 1926), 1429.

[36] See, e.g., "Leninist Teachings on the Colonial and National Revolutionary Movement and the Current Problems of the Revolutionary Movement in the East," *ibid.,* VII (January 13, 1927), 93-95, and, more important, VII (December 8, 1927), p. 1562.

Arnold C. Brackman, *Indonesian Communism: A History* (New York: Frederick A. Praeger, 1963), pp. 16-17, remarks that it would be logical to assume that Trotsky supported Alimin's plans whereas Stalin disapproved them. After noting that it is unlikely that the details will ever be disclosed, Brackman writes, "What we do know incontestably is that Alimin and Musso proceeded with their plans for revolution, that they enjoyed Stalin's confidence during

Why the Comintern took this stand is not so clear as the fact that it apparently did so. During the second half of 1926—the period of Musso and Alimin's visit—Stalin was publicly still optimistic about events in China, which could either aid or be aided by similar events in Indonesia. It may be that the Indonesian revolt was considered as reinforcement for the "revolutionary upswing" that he was still expecting, or even that it might provide a hedge in Indonesia against failure in China. In either case, the ECCI was to submit "the lessons of the Indonesian revolt to an extremely careful investigation," [37] and perhaps to find the scapegoat when it was ready. It is important to note that Musso, in particular, retained the support of Moscow until his death in 1948.

This issue of the Indonesian coup was still very much alive at the Sixth Comintern Congress in August, 1928, at which Musso, Tan Malaka, Semaun, and other Indonesians were present. The bitter and irreconcilable division that had split the Indonesian Communists almost immediately after the Prambanan decision continued to be ignored in Moscow. Though one delegate felt the failure of the uprising to have resulted largely from the split in the leadership,[38] Semaun analyzed the abortive coup and found the reason for its failure in less partisan and more "correct" Marxist-Leninist terms.[39] The Congress ended its sessions by refusing to pass judgment on the rival factions and by taking pains to list "the uprising in Indonesia, the deep ferment in India, the great Chinese revolution, which shook the whole Asiatic con-

---

the remainder of his rule, and that when the revolution in Indonesia materialized, they received a warm endorsement from the ECCI (although, of course, the ECCI may have had no alternative but to support a revolution waged in the name of Communism)."

37 *Inprecor,* VII (December 8, 1927), 1562-63.

38 Mauawar "(Report to the) Thirty-fourth Session, Moscow, August 17, 1928," *Inprecor,* VIII (October 17, 1928), 1325.

39 "The Situation in Indonesia," Coreport of Comrade Semaun, *ibid.,* VIII (October 4, 1928), 1243-47. Semaun apparently used the analysis of the ECCI as it appeared in *ibid.,* VII (December 8, 1927); cf. fn. 41. But he also appealed to revolutionary sentiment. "We believe," he said, "that it would be better to die fighting than to die without fighting, . . . and many of our members were . . . killed." *Ibid.,* VIII (October 4, 1928), 1246.

tinent . . . [as] links in one and the same international revolutionary chain, constituent parts of the profound general crisis
of capitalism." [40] Indonesian comrades did not rate as high as
Chinese, but they were still in excellent Comintern company.

Minor Left-Wing Groups Before 1927

While the PKI dominated the left wing during this period,
there were also several minor exponents of socialism on the scene.
Although none of these smaller parties or groups of leaders was
as significant as the PKI, they too were precursors of some of the
groups that were to come into their own in the years after the
disappearance of the PKI.

The scene of much of their activity was the *Volksraad*, the
advisory body for the Indies established in 1916 and convened
for the first time in May, 1918.[41] Here these parties had the opportunity of cooperating with the Indische Sociaal-Democratische Partij (ISDP), a Dutch Marxist group led by Cramer and
other Dutch Social Democrats.[42] Although these smaller nation-

[40] *Program of the Communist International* (New York, 1929), p. 20. Musso
was elected to the ECCI while Tan Malaka became candidate member. The
latter, identified by McVey as "Comrade Alphonso" at this congress, had engaged in vigorous and effective debate against Bukharin at a time when
Stalin was preparing to be rid of the latter. In this debate Tan Malaka was
called a Trotskyist, a label which stuck to him and his followers after his
eventual purge. For the debate, see *Inprecor*, VIII (September 4, September 25,
and October 4, 1928).

[41] In view of the present method of selecting the Indonesian parliament
under guided democracy, it is of interest that the *Volksraad* included both
elected and appointed members. Initially, half the members were appointed;
after 1927, the percentage of appointed members was reduced and only twenty-
two of the sixty members were appointed. The extensive right of appointment
"was intended to be used as a corrective of the election results." De Kat
Angelino, *Colonial Policy*, II, 412. Furnivall notes that in practice the Governor-General or other official charged with the duty of nomination often
appointed some of the government's "bitterest opponents, European or native." *Colonial Policy and Practice*, p. 250.

[42] Cramer had been one of the founders of the ISDV when it was established
in May, 1914; the ISDV had contained both orthodox and revisionist Marxists.
However, in 1917, when the extremist members of the ISDV, encouraged by the
news of the Russian Revolution, became increasingly emboldened, the less

alist parties did not really belong to the left wing of the nationalist movement, their contacts with the ISDP and especially their
experiences in the First and Second Radical Concentrations, the
two blocs formed successively under Cramer's leadership, helped
to give a Marxist flavor to the liberal nationalism of many of
these leaders. Although the program of this coalition was essentially nationalist rather than Marxist, it seems worthy of a brief
discussion here because, among other things, it is one of the
earliest attempts to apply the traditional Indonesian principle
of agreement through compromise to the facts of modern political party life.

The First Radical Concentration was formed during the second
session of the *Volksraad* at the end of 1918, when news of revolution and revolt was streaming in from different parts of the world
and there was a growing unrest in Holland. As Cramer put it,

> the current situation makes a concentration of the outspokenly demo-
> cratic native and European elements in this country necessary. The
> basis of this concentration is an urgent program of reforms, which are
> necessary because of the recent events in Europe.[43]

The members of the bloc were the ISDP, the SI, Insulinde, and
Budi Utomo.[44]

Cramer attempted to use the Radical Concentration to force
the conversion of the *Volksraad* into a provisional parliament.
His motion, introduced on November 25, 1918, came almost si-
multaneously with the news of a revolutionary outbreak in Holland; and, very shortly thereafter, without waiting to consult
higher authority, the Governor-General promised far-reaching

radical members of the party broke away to form the ISDP, which affiliated
itself with the SDAP in Holland.

[43] *Handelingen*, November 16, 1918, p. 211, quoted in Blumberger, article
on the Radical Concentration, *Encyclopaedie van Nederlandsch-Indie* (8 vols.;
The Hague: Martinus Nijhoff, 1917-1939), Supplement No. 5, 1927, p. 201.

[44] Insulinde: a predominantly Eurasian party. Budi Utomo: the earliest
and one of the smaller Indonesian nationalist groups, founded by a group of
medical students, mostly from aristocratic Javanese families, in 1908.

reforms. However, when the long-awaited revision of the colonial government's laws appeared in 1922, they proved a grave disappointment and led to the death of the First Radical Concentration.

Recognizing the need to direct the disillusioned nationalists into some channel that offered hope for success along parliamentary or at least constitutional lines, and conscious of the threat posed by the increasingly militant stand of the PKI and the ardent nationalists operating within the SI, Cramer, at the beginning of 1923, formed a Second Radical Concentration. This organization had a broader base than the original bloc and sought to include the entire nationalist movement, bringing in parties not represented in the *Volksraad,* as well as the labor movement. Leadership was still primarily in Cramer's hands, but members now included representatives of the PKI, who, not unexpectedly, came to play a major role in the bloc shortly after its inception. The bloc still continued to have constitutional reform as its goal; to this end, it published a militant manifesto in January, 1923, demanding an end to the exploitation of Indonesia by capitalists and a revision of the constitution along the lines originally proposed by the Governor-General.[45]

The Second Radical Concentration was even more short-lived than its predecessor. Almost from its inception it was divided, with Cramer, the ISDP, and the more moderate Indonesian parties ranged in opposition to the PKI and the parties and unions which leaned toward the Communists. This cleavage was distinguished, however, by the effort of several smaller Indonesian parties to seek some basis for cooperation on the traditional Indonesian grounds of compromise. Aware of the value of a unified organization that could work both within and outside the *Volksraad,* these minor parties attempted, in the words of one of them, to play the role of "a party of compromise between socialism and communism." [46] However, any basis for cooperation among

[45] Blumberger, article on the Radical Concentration.
[46] *Ibid.,* p. 203.

such disparate groups was destroyed when Semaun published a pamphlet that did not meet with the approval of the bloc's non-Communist leaders. The Second Radical Concentration then began to go downhill until its demise in June, 1923.

From these two attempts to seek reform by constitutional means, Indonesian nationalists learned several lessons. For one thing, the experience helped make it clear that tactics of cooperation and parliamentary action could have only limited results, if any. This lesson was to be of some significance when these same nationalists faced the central issue after 1927: the debate over cooperation or noncooperation. Another set of lessons had to do with Marxism and its interpretation by the Social Democrats. In the course of their cooperation with the ISDP, the nationalist leaders were exposed, to some extent, to the views and activities of the Second International and, more than that, to the thought that Marxism could travel more than one road. Finally, the parties in the First Radical Concentration were largely upper-class intellectual organizations whose leaders were firmly committed to the principle of legal, parliamentary procedure. When the Netherlands Indies Government failed to realize the concessions wrung from it by these leaders, the moderate group lost its chance of winning popular support even from the SI, much less from the more radical nationalist parties.

Meanwhile, another current was at work on the Indonesian scene. Operating outside the realm of political activity, but developing and broadening contacts at the mass level that would ultimately make it a major factor in the nationalist movement, was the Mohammedijah. In an attempt to practice the principles of social justice expounded in Modernist Islamic doctrine, the Mohammedijah emphasized education and social- and economic-welfare activities. It also indirectly encouraged the growth of nationalist sentiment in the many areas it reached.[47] Ultimately, of course, Mohammedijah was drawn directly into the political

---

[47] G. H. Bousquet, *A French View of the Netherlands Indies* (London: Oxford University Press, 1940), p. 5; see also Schrieke, *op cit.*, p. 154.

arena, first as a participant in the wartime Islamic federation established by the Japanese and later as a member organization of the Masjumi (Madjelis Sjuro Muslimin Indonesia, or Council of Indonesian Moslem Associations), the major Islamic political party of the postwar era.

4

The New Generation of Nationalists

IN 1927, A NEW SET OF LEADERS AND A NEW GROUP OF parties began to emerge. They represented colonial nationalism and were free, for the most part, of ties either to official Islam or to official Communism. Many of these new leaders who remained in the forefront during the 1930's are still among the principal figures of independent Indonesia today.

The new generation of nationalists differed from most of its predecessors in several ways, all of them representing a general broadening of intellectual horizons. For one thing, a majority of the new leaders were university-trained and formed part of a new intellectual elite that was gradually becoming an important and respected element in the Indonesian social structure. For another thing, most of these new leaders were Marxist-oriented in their thinking; but their Marxism, while dominating their outlook on economic and social matters, was, in the political sphere, subordinated to their nationalist principles. While the independent society they envisaged was based on some generalized socialist principles, the new leaders were unwilling to be deflected from their nationalist goals by either the Comintern or the Second International. Furthermore, the socialism embraced by these leaders, while tolerant of the views of the Islamic radicals, indicated a comparatively sophisticated acquaintance with the various schools of Western socialist thought.

The era after the collapse of the PKI also marked the first time that a significant number of the present generation of Indonesian leaders became acquainted with non-Communist European anticolonialists. This broadening of contacts, as well as much of the new leadership's experiences with the Third International during this period, in many instances took place while a number of the young nationalists were studying in Holland. Particularly important in this connection were the activities of the Indonesian student association, the Perhimpoenan Indonesia (PI), the League Against Imperialism (Liga), and the Dutch socialist movement.

Contacts Abroad: PI and Liga

Whether they joined Perhimpoenan Indonesia or not, the majority of Indonesian students in Holland were deeply influenced by the organization.[1] While the flavor of PI's politics was strongly Marxist, most of its members did not join the Dutch Communist Party but sought support for their nationalist goals from any anticolonial group. Nevertheless, the exiled PKI leaders as well as many Dutch Communists had a strong influence on the association and, up to a point, the non-Communist PI leaders worked closely with the PKI representatives. This cooperation culminated in the political accord signed on December 5, 1926, by Mohammad Hatta for PI and Semaun for the PKI. It was intended to serve as a preliminary to the establishment of a new nationalist party in Indonesia, to be led by returned PI members.[2] The agreement stated that PI was to assume top leadership and full responsibility for the nationalist movement in Indonesia, while the PKI and its affiliates were not to oppose PI's leadership as long as it continued to seek independence for Indonesia. The ac-

[1] PI was established in 1922 as the successor to a previous student organization that had been less political in character.

[2] Earlier plans to form such a party had been deferred because of the strength of the PKI. By the time the accord was signed, however, shortly after the unsuccessful uprising of 1926 in Java, it was apparently clear to the PI's non-Communist leaders that the PKI would now cease to exist in the open as a political force.

cord was intended to forestall any disputes over control of this new party, but it was a short-lived agreement. Semaun repudiated it the following year, stating that he had committed an error in signing this political contract and had come to the conclusion that an obligation of this sort would mean the liquidation of the independent role of the PKI.[3]

Although firm evidence is lacking, it is possible to speculate with some degree of assurance about the factors that precipitated Semaun's repudiation of the accord at this particular time. The most probable explanation is that his repudiation was an early application of the new Comintern line eschewing cooperation with nationalist groups—a reaction to the defeats in Indonesia and in China and a prelude to the line laid down at the Sixth Comintern Congress. In any case, despite the repudiation of the accord and until the hardening of the new Comintern line late in 1929, the non-Communist PI leaders continued to maintain their contacts with the Indonesian Communists in Holland, with the Communist Party of the Netherlands, and with the Third International's subsidiary organs.

PI's principal line of communication with the Third International at this time was through the League Against Imperialism, which had been set up by the Comintern in 1926. As a front organization, it was at first a heterogeneous collection of persons and parties that had attracted to its ranks a number of Asian nationalists of various political persuasions. The tie between the League and Moscow must have been fairly obvious despite the membership of numerous Social Democratic parties and groups. This tie, however, and the League's obvious connections with various Comintern organs, such as the International Red Aid, were, if anything, probably regarded with some approval by the Asian nationalists, since the International Red Aid especially had vociferously advertised its support for the colonial nationalist movements. Even among those Indonesian nationalists who may

3 Blumberger, *Le Communisme aux Indes Néerlandaises*, p. 161. Semaun's repudiation of the accord appeared in the Dutch Communist paper *Tribune* on December 12, 1927. See also Brackman, *op. cit.*, p. 18, on the background to the agreement.

have felt some uneasiness over the League's tie with the Comintern, support from any source was welcome, and, at the outset, the League had a respectably large number of non-Communist affiliates.

Cooperation between PI and the League was therefore extremely close at first. Hatta was a member of the League's Executive for some time, and together with other PI delegates as well as Semaun, who represented the PKI, Hatta took an active part in the League's first major conference in Brussels in February, 1927. Responding to his speech outlining the situation in Indonesia,[4] the League adopted a resolution expressing sympathy and support for the Indonesian liberation movement and calling upon the Dutch Government to give the Indonesians the right of self-determination, to annul the expulsions and death sentences arising out of the recent revolt, and to accord a general amnesty.[5] The League also proposed sending a delegation to Indonesia to make contact with the nationalists there—a proposal that came to nothing because of the Netherlands Indies Government's refusal to permit the League's representatives to enter the country. When, late in 1927, the Dutch authorities arrested and imprisoned the leaders of PI in Holland, the League vied with the Dutch Socialists in energetic protests, although it was the efforts of the latter that reportedly made a deeper and more widespread impression on the Dutch people.[6]

Meanwhile, the divergent tendencies within the League were leading to the splitting of its leadership into two camps: the Communists on the one side, and the non-Communist nationalists

---

[4] In that speech, Hatta referred to the 1926 revolt in Java as a national insurrection of the Indonesian people against the tyrannical oppression under which they suffered; the PKI's role was not stressed. (See "Special Report on the International Congress against Colonial Oppression in Brussels," *Inprecor*, VII [February 25, 1927], 328.)

[5] Blumberger, *Le Communisme aux Indes Néerlandaises*, p. 157.

[6] See, e.g., the pamphlet written by a Dutch socialist attacking the government's trial of these leaders: J. E. W. Duijs, *De Vervolging Tegen de Indonesische Studenten Mohammad Hatta, Mr. Ali Sastroamidjojo, Raden Mas Abdul Madjid Djojoadhiningrat en Mohammad Nazir Pamontjak. Vergedigings-Rede, Gehouden in de Zitting de Arr. Rechtbankte s'Gravenhage op 8 Maart 1928* (Amsterdam: Ontwikkeling, 1928).

from a variety of colonial countries, together with the European Social Democrats, on the other. This division in turn sharpened the dissension between the non-Communist PI leaders in Holland and the PKI representatives. The showdown came after the Sixth Comintern Congress in 1928, when the League, applying the new doctrine of united front from below, renounced cooperation with the bourgeois nationalist movements in the colonial countries. As a result of this new policy, the non-Communist members began to withdraw. Relations between the League and PI deteriorated rapidly, and PI left the League in the summer of 1929.[7]

Contacts Abroad: The SDAP

While it did not alter the essentially Marxist orientation of PI's non-Communist leaders, this experience did tend to turn the attention of some of them to the other major socialist body in Holland, the SDAP. As noted above, this party had a long history of activity on behalf of Indonesia, and, during the 1920's and 1930's, was increasing its activities in the colonial field. In 1933, the SDAP set up a colonial bureau and a colonial press service, Persindo, headed by L. N. Palar, an Indonesian nationalist who had been active in the SDAP.[8] While going much further in their demands for the abolition of colonialism than did the Second International as a whole, the SDAP still failed to win much

[7] Details on the history of PI and the League can be found in Blumberger, *Le Communisme aux Indes Néerlandaises*. For an analysis of these relations by a leading participant, see Mohammad Hatta, "Het Anti-Koloniale Congres te Brussel in het licht der Wereldgeschiedenis"; "Het Brusselse Congres Tegen Imperialisme en Koloniale Onderdrukking en onze Buitenlandse Propaganda"; and especially "Een Nabetrachting van het Tweede Congres der Liga Tegen Imperialisme en voor Nationale Onafhankelijkheid te Frankfurt," in *Verspreide Geschriften* (Amsterdam: C. P. J. van der Peet, 1952), pp. 160-86.

[8] Persindo and the CPN rival press bureaus were in competition for space in the Indonesian nationalist press. The CPN, though harshly critical of the "bourgeois nationalists" of Indonesia in Holland, avoided such criticism in the selection of Communist material sent to Indonesia. Thereupon Persindo, indicating the source of such material, forwarded to Indonesia the critical CPN articles. As a result, the Communist press bureau soon fell into disrepute.

favor with Indonesian nationalists. This was in part because it was difficult to give a moderate socialist program the appeal necessary to win mass support. For example, the resolution on colonialism adopted by the SDAP in January, 1930, while demanding independence and the right of self-determination for all peoples, recognized the "realities" of the existing situation. Basing its demand for colonial independence on socialist principles, the party's resolution then stated that, *as long as* foreign authority continued to exist, this authority should be conducted on the basis of a policy directed toward national independence for colonial peoples.[9] This tacit recognition of colonialism, contrasted with the Comintern's appealing and militant slogans demanding the immediate abolition of colonialism, was denounced vigorously by most Indonesian nationalists as well as by the Communists. So was the next point in the resolution, which recommended that foreign rule be exercised under the supervision of the League of Nations, in which the dominated nations would have their representatives. In the minds of most Indonesian nationalists, these points overshadowed the resolution's unconditional recognition of the right of national independence.

In any case, however much the approach of the SDAP may have appealed to moderate Indonesian intellectuals, few nationalist leaders would have been willing to risk the loss of popular support that siding with the SDAP would have meant. Nevertheless, after the Seventh Comintern Congress in 1935, when the Communists ceased stressing the fight for colonial independence in favor of collective security, it was the SDAP which was, in vain, the major protagonist of the Indonesian cause in the Dutch Parliament and press. Earlier, the SDAP had carried on a vigorous campaign in Holland over the *Zeven Provincie* incident in

[9] Daan van der Zee, *De Wereld Vrij: Socialistische Beschouwingen over het Koloniale Probleem* (Amsterdam: Arbeiderspers, 1931), pp. 156-61. For a detailed history of the SDAP's stand on the Indonesian question, especially in the Dutch Parliament, see the same author's *De SDAP en Indonesie* (Amsterdam: Arbeiderspers, 1929). For an analysis, see Hatta, "De Tweede Internationale en de Onderdrukte Volken"; and "De Koloniale resolutie der Tweede Internationale," in *Verspreide Geschriften*, pp. 445-61.

1933,[10] while it concurrently sought, through the non-Communist trade-union federation, to establish a basis for cooperation with Indonesia's organized labor movement.[11] Thus, while few Indonesian nationalists were openly affiliated with the SDAP, there is no doubt that the party and especially some of its leaders in the fight against colonialism, like Troelstra and Stokvis, had a strong influence on the political orientation of many Indonesians in the post-1926 generation of leaders.

10 The *Zeven Provincie* incident, the mutiny of the crew of a Royal Dutch Navy cruiser off the coast of Sumatra, was popularly supposed to have been an isolated event remote from the mainstream of Indonesian nationalist activities. However, information given the author by an Indonesian imprisoned for complicity in the affair indicates that the mutiny was not the reaction of disgruntled Indonesian seamen but the outgrowth of plans laid by the socialist trade union to which the Indonesian crew members belonged. Like all Indonesian labor organizations of that era, the sailors' trade union was primarily a political organization; despite its public protestations to the contrary, the Dutch Indies Government was apparently aware of this connection between the mutineers and the nationalist movement and promptly arrested a number of Indonesians known to be active in the sailors' union or in the trade-union federation with which it was affiliated. In Holland, the entire affair caused considerable furor, especially since the mutiny had been ended by a Dutch naval aircraft dropping a bomb on the ship. In the public meetings on the incident and in the ensuing Parliamentary debates, the SDAP's activities drowned out the minor public protests of the Communists. In Indonesia, the *Zeven Provincie* affair was quickly played down by the authorities, but a visitor to the island some years later remarked on the uneasiness still visible in Dutch circles—an uneasiness that was attributed to overtones of the incident. (See Geoffrey Gorer, *Bali and Angkor* [Boston: Little, Brown & Co., 1936], p. 6.) As for the Third International, the mutiny was seen as a "part of the current tide of colonial revolution." (See Wang Ming, "The Revolutionary Movement in the Colonial and Semi-Colonial Countries and the Tactics of the Communist Parties," *Communist International*, XII, No. 17-18 [September 20, 1935], 1323-33.) The fact that the sailors' trade union involved was linked to the Socialist (NVV) rather than to the Communist trade-union federation was not mentioned.

11 The Dutch Socialist Trade Union Federation (Nederlandsch Vakbeweging Vereeniging) sent a delegation to Indonesia to establish contact with the Indonesian labor movement in the mid-1930's; in 1938 the SDAP sent Palar to report on the Indonesian labor unions and to work out a more satisfactory basis for cooperation. There is some evidence that this mission was favorably received by Indonesian nationalists. The latter expected the Dutch unionists' aid in support of a demand for an Indonesian Parliament. The SDAP later (February 10, 1940) waged an unsuccessful battle in the Dutch Parliament for this. (See Pringgodigdo, *op. cit.*, p. 145; and Pluvier, *op. cit.*, pp. 145 f.)

Socialism, Indonesian-Style

Nevertheless, the Marxism that came to Indonesia via returning PI members was for the most part not the Marxism of the SDAP. Instead, the leaders of the new parties, study groups, and clubs that began to emerge in this era developed a new brand of socialism that was a synthesis of the ideas absorbed in Holland reformulated in terms derived from and relevant to Indonesia's social traditions. At the outset, some of the mass-based parties reflected in their membership and their programs the fact that there was still considerable sympathy among Indonesian nationalists for the now disorganized PKI. The disillusionments arising out of the shift in the 1928 Comintern line and the PI's experience in the League Against Imperialism were still to come. Some returning PI leaders, including Sjahrir and Hatta, were convinced that one of the essential lessons of the 1926-27 revolt— a lesson that constituted the heart of Tan Malaka's opposition to the timing of the revolt—was the need to educate a cadre group in depth. Without such provision, they felt, a mass party for independence could be destroyed whenever the colonial authorities chose to remove the usually thin layer of top leadership.

Reflecting on this period a quarter of a century later, Sjahrir offered a plausible explanation for the Communist content and orientation of nationalist doctrine in that era and in the programs of the Partai Nasional Indonesia (1927) and its successor parties such as Partai Indonesia (1931). In his opinion, the outlawing of the PKI, the lack of any openly Socialist or Communist Party in Indonesia from 1926 until 1945, and the persistent suspicion that European Social Democracy was not genuinely committed to anticolonialism favored the influence of Moscow.

The brand of socialism which gained influence in politically awakening Indonesia was of the radical and revolutionary type, which was generally considered to be represented by the Third International. . . . Hence, from its very beginning the Partai Nasional Indonesia was infused with revolutionary minded socialist tendencies, and in its propaganda, this party freely borrowed from the concepts and terminology of official communism: the Comintern . . . it adopted almost entirely the theory on Imperialism of the Communist International.[12]

Indonesie Klaagt Aan! and the Mainstream of Nationalist Activity

The eclectic nature of the socialism of the Partai Nasional Indonesia (PNI) as well as its strong reliance on the Comintern for the theoretical framework of its views on capitalism and imperialism are best seen in *Indonesie Klaagt Aan!* (*Indonesia Accuses!*), one of the major pieces of nationalist writing of that era. This was the famous defense speech made in 1930 by Sukarno, the founding leader of the new nationalist party.[13] In addition to indicating the extent of his borrowings from Marxist-Leninist theory, the work also shows the variety of other sources contributing to Sukarno's knowledge of socialism and contains one of the first expositions of the doctrine of Marhaenism, which in recent years has been incorporated into the philosophy of the postwar PNI and utilized by other parties as well. Sukarno's speech is important not only for what it suggests about his political orientation and resources, but also because his views represented the views of a good part of the nationalist leadership of that era.

Recognizing the hopelessness of avoiding further imprisonment, Sukarno in his defense speech was clearly dictating a document that he fully intended to be widely disseminated among the Indonesian people. One of his major points was to emphasize that his attacks on capitalism and imperialism were not attacks on the

12 Sjahrir, *Indonesian Socialism*, pp. 29 f.

13 Sukarno, one of the few top nationalist leaders of the era to have been educated solely in Indonesia, had been arrested in December, 1929, and later tried and sentenced, together with 3 of his colleagues, on the charge of fomenting public disorder and recommending the overthrow of the Netherlands Indies authority. The PNI, taking a militant stand for complete political and economic independence and advocating the strategy of noncooperation, had become the most powerful nationalist organization in the country, with a membership of more than 10,000 within 2 years of its establishment.

Netherlands Indies Government as such, because, he said, "capitalism and imperialism are not synonymous with Dutch or Dutchmen or other foreigners. Capitalism and imperialism are systems. Capitalism and imperialism are not identical with a regime. We have often stressed that both capitalism and imperialism are international in character." In explaining why it was necessary for his party to develop a theoretical framework within which to operate, Sukarno quoted at length from Kautsky on the education of the masses and then pointed out that "a mass action without theory . . . is a mass action without soul, without will, while it is this will which is the motivating power of such an action." [14] In addition, he stated:

> The Partai Nasional Indonesia is convinced that national independence is the most important condition in the efforts to reconstruct Indonesian society; thus all efforts of the Indonesian people must be directed toward achieving national independence. . . . The proletariat can break the resistance of the capitalist classes against the turnover of private property into public property by acquiring political power. Essentially, according to our convictions, the same applies to colonized peoples, to peoples dominated by foreign imperialisms. And it is the acquisition of this political power which the PNI advocates.

In attempting to show that the PNI was neither Communist nor the heir of the PKI,[15] Sukarno pointed out that, although it

[14] Soekarno [Sukarno], *Indonesie Klaagt Aan! Pleitrede voor den Landraad te Bandoeng op 2 December 1930, Gehouden door Ir. Soekarno.* These excerpts are taken from a photostatic copy of an edition published in Dutch for Het "Fonds Nasional" der Federatie van Indonesische Politieke Vereenigingen (PPPKI), n. pl., 1931.

[15] On this point he had the support, whether he knew it or not, of several of his fellow Indonesians in Moscow. (See the characterization of the PNI as a petty bourgeois party in the reports to the Sixth Comintern Congress by Semaun and Mauawar, *Inprecor*, VIII [October 4, 1928], 1247, and [October 17, 1928], 1326.) On the other hand, PI, the Indonesian Students' Association in Holland, although by then largely under Communist domination, regarded the PNI with somewhat more approval. Hatta noted in an unsigned article in the PI journal that "on the ruins of the PKI and SR's there has been formed a new mass movement. . . . In these difficult times, only a few people believed in the possibility of a new mass movement. Among these pioneers were the founders of PNI: Ir. Soekarno, Mr. Sartono, Dr. Tjipto Mangoen-

was like the PKI in opposing imperialism and considering mass action the means by which to acquire power,

> [the PNI] is a revolutionary nationalistic party and its mass-character, its *kromo-ism*, its *marhaen-ism*, are not the result of any communistic principles but exist because the Indonesian community makes it necessary for the PNI to subscribe to such a *marhaenism*. It is a necessity, just as European society makes it necessary for European socialists to adhere to proletarianism. The Indonesian community is a *kromo-istic* community, a community which consists of small peasants, small wage-earners, small seamen, in short . . . in all fields, a *kromo* or a *marhaen*.[16] A national bourgeoisie strong enough to take up arms against imperialism does not exist as yet. The Indonesian movement must be oriented toward the *kromo*, the *marhaen*. In their hands lies Indonesia's fate, and from the organization of the *kromo* and the *marhaen* must we draw our strength. The movement which keeps apart from the common people, which merely carries on "salon" politics, etc., cannot conduct politics seriously.

This speech soon became the bible of the nationalist movement. It was in this speech that Sukarno staked out the ideas basic to his philosophy and built the strong foundations for the succeeding decades of his national leadership. At the same time, he gave to this PNI a tradition and an outlook that were to be of considerable value to the party of the same name organized after the war.

To a large extent, the launching of the PNI as a mass party initiated and dominated the "second wave" of the nationalist movement. Up to World War II, the PNI principles of national-

---

koesoemo, Soedjadi, Mr. Iskaq, Ir. Anwari, Dr. Samsi, Mr. Soejoedi and Mr. Soenario. . . . [This new party differs from the PKI only in that] the ultimate aim of the PNI is national independence." ("De Groei van de P. N. I. en de Regeeringsteereur in Indonesia," *Indonesia Merdeka*, January-February, 1930, pp. 1 f.)

16 Both *kromo* and *marhaen* originally meant peasant, although *marhaen* has come to mean proletarian or worker as well. *Kromo* is a kind of stock term for a Javanese farmer. *Marhaen*, according to the *Ensiklopedia Indonesia* (3 vols.; Bandung: W. Van Hoeve Ltd., 1954-1956), is derived from the name of a peasant in the Sunda region of Java.

ism and Marxism served as the ideological norm for political activity. However, no one sector of the nationalist leadership attained exclusive hegemony over the movement. A number of sub-issues, which could not properly be described as either left or right and which were at the time integral to Indonesian politics, brought into existence ardent nationalist organizations that deviated in program and structure from the model set by the PNI. These variations on the basic theme of independence are too numerous to allow for detailed discussion here; however, the essential differences among them should be noted in typical examples.

TRIBUTARY STREAMS: CADRE PARTIES

One set of variants was represented by those who based their activity on cadre rather than on mass membership. Such was the Club Pendidikan Nasional Indonesia (Indonesian National Education Club), to which Hatta and Sjahrir devoted their efforts from the time of their return from Holland until they were arrested in 1934. In their opinion, a party with a limited trained membership could avoid the fatal blow that governmental suppression usually dealt to mass-based parties with a small leadership. Hatta and Sjahrir chose to work slowly and carefully, building up an elite group, thoroughly trained in nationalist principles, that would be able to continue to spread their doctrine in ever-widening circles even after some arrests occurred.

It has been suggested that this organizational concept was the product of its authors' adoption of the Leninist concept of a vanguard revolutionary party. However, in discussing this period, both leaders have maintained that their plan of organization was derived from the situation in Indonesia rather than from any external, doctrinaire sources. Whether or not Lenin influenced these men in this respect, their ideological equipment from that time on arose largely from socialist roots acquired initially in Holland. Their party very soon gave evidence of a socialist orientation, and its program was based on the principles of "sovereignty of the people and collectivism." [17]

Another example of cadre structure was the Partai Repoeblik Indonesia (Pari), founded in Bangkok by Tan Malaka in early 1927.[18] This crypto-Communist organization functioned originally as an underground apparatus, with its leaders engaged in infiltrating mass nationalist organizations. During the first years of Pari's activity in Indonesia, Tan Malaka was still a Comintern representative despite his opposition to the policies and the leaders responsible for the PKI failure in 1926-27. His aides, who built up the organization in Indonesia, were apparently able to attract considerable personal support for their leader among the men they recruited. Later, during the Japanese occupation and in the first years of the Indonesian Revolution, the leaders of Pari, among them Sukarni and Adam Malik, were clearly committed to Tan Malaka's national Communist views. They were firmly opposed to the Third International's representatives, the PKI, on the numerous occasions when the two groups battled each other politically and physically during this period, although in program there were actually few basic differences between them.

Similar in almost every respect to Pari was the Communist un-

17 Ali Sastroamidjojo, "Survey of the Indonesian National Movement," *Indonesian Life*, I (March-April, 1947), 6. The article claims that this was the first time these principles were introduced by a political party in Indonesia. More likely this was the first time the principles were explained and outlined in detail rather than merely presented in slogans. The eclectic nature of Hatta's approach to socialism can be seen, for example, in his article "Marxisme of epigonenwijsheid?" ("Marxism or the Wisdom of the Epigones?"), *Nationale Comentaren*, Nos. 10, 11, 12, 13, 14 (1940), and reprinted in Hatta, *Verspreide Geschriften*, pp. 117-41.

18 Kahin, *op. cit.*, pp. 85-87; see pp. 313-19 for details on Partai Murba, the postwar party founded by Tan Malaka in 1948, much of whose leadership was drawn from Pari. Tan Malaka gave to the word *murba*, normally translated as proletariat, a special definition: "people who have nothing except brain and body. . . . different from the Western proletariat. The Indonesian Murba is not yet completely separated from the family, as in the West. . . . [T]he struggle and the enemy of the Indonesian Murba are different from [those] of the Western proletariat." The meaning of *Murba* is not unlike the meaning of the phrase "workers of hand and brain," which was used in the West during the 1930's.

derground organization established by Musso in 1935.[19] Generally referred to as the "illegal PKI," this party instructed its members to join the non-Communist nationalist parties and to encourage the formation of an anti-Fascist front.

In the years following the PKI debacle of 1926-27, there had also been a few brief and more open attempts by the outlawed Communists to re-enter political life. The first of these short-lived revivals was the Sarekat Kaum Buruh Indonesia (SKBI), or Association of Indonesian Workers, established in 1928 allegedly as a nonparty group that was to confine its activities to the economic field and specifically to union organization. Despite Communist protestations about the nonpartisan, nationalist character of this organization, soon after its founding the SKBI's leaders were embroiled in a struggle for control with a group of "revolutionary nationalists"—a battle in which the latter lost out. Actually, the SKBI was apparently established by a group of Surabaya Communists led by Soenarjo and Marsoeki. Their aim was to infiltrate the various unions in order to gain control—a return to the early PKI strategy used in the attempt to take over the SI. SKBI had some success in its single year of operation, and, among other things, became affiliated with the League Against Imperialism. In July, 1929, the government arrested the leaders and outlawed the organization.[20] Other attempts to re-establish the Communist movement during the "third period" of the Comintern were equally unsuccessful.[21] Nevertheless, it was apparent that a large number of PKI sympathizers was still to be found, particularly in and around the major cities on Java. As Kahin notes, much of Sukarno's following in PNI and Partai In-

[19] Musso had returned from Moscow to Indonesia and remained in Java, under an assumed name, for about a year.

[20] Reesema, "The Terror in Indonesia," *Inprecor*, IX (August 16, 1929), 883. See also "Manifest uitgegeven op 2 Januari 1930, n.a.v. de Razzia tegen de P.N.I.," *Indonesia Merdeka*, VIII (January-February, 1930), 13 f.

[21] According to McVey, in 1928, propagandists J. Waworoentoe, C. Wentoek, and K. Kamoe, students at the Communist University of the Peoples of the East, were sent to Indonesia apparently to help reorganize the movement there, but were interned by the authorities in March, 1929. (See McVey, *op. cit.*, pp. 19 f.)

donesia (Partindo) probably came from former members of the
SR and the trade unions in which the Communists had previously played a dominating role.[22]

These three cadre organizations under one guise or another,
but with a relatively stable leadership, survived the 1930's, played
a role during the Japanese occupation, and emerged during the
revolution and after as the Socialist Party (PSI), the Communist
Party (PKI), and the Murba Party, respectively.

COOPERATION VERSUS NONCOOPERATION

Another major issue that divided nationalists during this period hinged on certain strategic conceptions necessary to achieve
independence: Could independence be gained by working with
or opposing the Dutch colonial and home government, by parliamentary or extraparliamentary means, or by a combination of
both? Some parties, among them Budi Utomo, and some of the
regional parties, such as the Pasundan and the Serikat Sumatra,
favored cooperation with the colonial government and hence
were willing to participate in the *Volksraad*. Other parties,
such as the PNI, its successor, Partindo, and the PSII, advocated
a policy of noncooperation. In addition, despite the fact that the
issue of cooperation is necessarily one of fundamental and usually divisive import in indigenous nationalist movements, there
were parties, like the Surabaya Study Club, which had a mixed
membership of those for and against cooperation.[23] The cleavage
on this question did not parallel any left or right division in socio-
economic or political philosophy, nor did all the parties maintain their respective positions unchanged throughout the period
under examination.[24] The foundations of the debate over cooper-

[22] Kahin, *op. cit.*, p. 91.

[23] Mohammad Hatta, *(Statement on)* *The Conception of the President*
(1957), p. 2.

[24] For example, Parindra, which was formed in 1935 out of a fusion of
several small moderate parties and was generally characterized as both "moderate" and "cooperative" (see Sastroamidjojo, *op. cit.*, p. 7), was, on July 11,
1941, the sole party in the *Volksraad* to vote against the establishment of an

ation underwent a metamorphosis in the late 1930's for a variety of reasons, but the issue remained a major one up to the time of the arrival of the Japanese.

The debate over the strategy of cooperation versus noncooperation and the desire to build a mass party also affected the religious nationalists. Sarekat Islam had survived its earlier conflict with the Communists. In 1929 it changed its name to Partai Sarekat Islam Indonesia (PSII), but its influence as a nationalist organization had gradually diminished while its emphasis on religion increased. Five years later two opposing camps of leaders split the organization. One group, led by Sukiman and Abikusno Tjokrosujono, insisted on a policy of noncooperation while seeking to rebuild the mass-based organization with the aid of the religiously conservative local leadership. The other, led by Hadji Agus Salim, rejected this policy for one of limited cooperation while retaining the Modernist Islamic socio-religious program.[25] The latter emphasis tended to restrict the membership of the party, although it was not intended to resemble a cadre organization.

In spite of these differences, Indonesian leaders nonetheless drew on other Indonesian resources in efforts to advance the cause of independence. Three times during this period—the last time just before the arrival of the Japanese—Indonesian nationalists, utilizing traditional patterns of compromise, succeeded in bringing about large-scale nationalist unity. The first of these federations was the PPPKI (Permufakatan Perhimpunan Politik Kebangsaan Indonesia, or Union of Political Associations of the Indonesian People). It was formed in late 1927 by six nationalist parties—including some for and some against cooperation—and through the initiative of PNI and SI (later PSII). The price of this unity, however, as Hatta later wrote, was that "in the PPPKI it was forbidden to touch upon principal differences of opinion between its members such as religious belief and noncoopera-

---

Indonesian militia on the grounds that this long-sought nationalist goal would be acceptable only if preceded by political reform. (See Vlekke, *op. cit.,* p. 390.)

25 Kahin, *op. cit.,* p. 94 f.

tion." [26] Though the federation was doubtless weakened by these differences among its component members, such differences were not considered a deterrent to continuing the united effort for independence on the basis of compromise. PPPKI was suspended in 1933 mainly because of Dutch action against the noncooperating parties in the federation.

Six years later a substantially enlarged federation was again organized, this time principally on the initiative of Parindra. Known as Gapi (Gabungan Politik Indonesia or Federation of Indonesian Political Parties), it included eight major nationalist parties. Gapi adopted a four-point program calling for self-determination, national unity based upon political, economic, and social democracy; a democratically elected Indonesian Parliament; and cooperation between the Indonesian people and the Netherlands in face of the Fascist threat. In the next two years, Gapi succeeded in uniting an unprecedented number of nationalist groups; its final effort was to form the all-embracing Indonesian People's Council (Madjelis Rakjat Indonesia). The war, not the Dutch, then interrupted this surge toward independence.

The Comintern and Indonesian Nationalism: 1927-42

As we have seen, the nationalist movement in the late 1920's and in the 1930's developed in response to peculiarly Indonesian issues. It was supported by a generalized political philosophy drawn from both wings of European Marxism and from Western secular and Islamic religious nationalism. It remains to note more specifically the relationship between the Comintern and Indonesian nationalists during this period.

With the exception of the SKBI and Pari, there seems to have been little Comintern activity in Indonesia during the early years following the Sixth Comintern Congress. However, the abrupt shift in policy introduced in 1935 at the Seventh Comintern Congress by the so-called Dimitrov doctrine had important repercussions in Indonesia and, ultimately, in Indonesian political

---

26 Hatta, *The Conception of the President*, p. 3.

circles in Holland as well. Actually, the revision of strategy to accommodate to the change in the party line had begun in Indonesia, as elsewhere, some months before the official promulgation of the "People's Front" doctrine. Much of what went on from 1935 to the outbreak of the war has been obscured by the clandestine nature of the establishment and activities of the "illegal PKI." There is some evidence, however, in official PKI postwar statements and publications that the illegal PKI was the beginning of their party's participation in the Popular Front.[27] It now appears that members of the illegal PKI did, in the prewar period, penetrate into various nationalist parties, where they were largely successful in cloaking their political loyalties while advancing their program. Few Indonesians then or for some time after World War II seemed to be aware of the link between these individuals and international Communism.

The Communists found the task of building up an anti-Fascist, anti-imperialist front in the years after 1935 simplified by the developing character of Indonesian nationalism itself. Nationalists of whatever inclination could and did argue the merits of cooperation with the Dutch Government without losing nationalist standing. The Soetardjo Petition,[28] introduced in the *Volksraad* of 1936 by a group of moderate nationalists espousing cooperation with the Dutch Government, serves as a case in point. This petition, a mild document, sought to win Dutch consent for a conference to plan Indonesian self-rule within the boundaries provided by the existing Netherlands Constitution. (The PI in Holland, already under a large measure of Communist control, supported this parliamentary move.) The petition was passed by a majority vote in the *Volksraad,* but, though the official rejection was not formally delivered until 1938, it was soon clear that neither the Dutch Government nor Parliament would approve it. This stubborn policy weakened the status of the moderate na-

---

27 See McVey, *op. cit.,* p. 21.

28 So called for its first signer, Soetardjo, who was chairman of the PPBB (Persatuan Pegawei Binnenlandsche-Bestuur, or Civil Servants' Association) and a leading figure among the moderate nationalists.

tionalists, who had in this instance been led by Parindra, and helped further to convince other nationalists of the superior merit of a noncooperative policy. The net effect of this episode was to encourage all sectors of the nationalist movement to seek greater unity and to adopt a more militant—in this sense a leftist —nationalist program. A campaign for internal consolidation along the national front was begun; a nationalist press bureau was established, and steps were taken to unify the nationalist school system.[29]

While the militant nationalists who had opposed cooperation in the past now resumed the leadership of the movement, they did not employ the strategy of noncooperation that might logically have been expected. Instead, they reacted against another political current that had gradually been growing in significance on the Indonesian scene during the early 1930's: the expanding Dutch Nazi movement and its offshoots.[30] The Dutch organizations most prominent in Nazi and Nazi-oriented activities were also those most vehemently opposed to the nationalist movement and its social welfare ventures. As a result, there were wings of the nationalist movement whose programs coincided with the objectives of the Communists in building up an anti-Fascist front. While some nationalist leaders were undoubtedly apprehensive over the growing threat of international Fascism, it would have been rather difficult for them to win popular support for an anti-Fascist front, which required cooperation with like-minded Dutch individuals and organizations, had it not been for the visible evidence supplied on the scene by the Dutch Fascist organizations.

When a new party, Gerindo (Gerakan Rakjat Indonesia, or Indonesian People's Movement), was established in the spring of 1937, it took the stand that cooperation with the Dutch was necessary in the present international situation since, in this

29 S. H. Tajibnapis, "De Laatste Tien Jaren voor de Japanese Bezetting," *De Brug-Djambatan,* I (April, 1946), 12 f.

30 See e.g., Alexandre von Arx, *L'Evolution Politique en Indonesie de 1900 à 1942* (Fribourg: Artigianelli-Monza, 1949); and Furnivall, *Netherlands India,* p. 255.

time of crisis, "the most important fact is . . . the crisis of democracy." [31] This new party obviously reflected both the revolutionary-nationalist and the Communist strains, and included in its leadership a number of prominent nationalists: Sartono, who had been active in the PNI and Partindo; Wikana, who was closely connected with the "illegal PKI," and Amir Sjarifuddin, who, at a later date, claimed to have been a Communist since the mid-1930's.[32] Certainly, Gerindo's program bore a strong resemblance to the Comintern line, from its demand that the East-West controversy be abandoned as the basis of colonial nationalism and replaced by a demarcation line based on democracy versus antidemocracy, to its declaration of willingness to participate in the *Volksraad* in light of the current international situation.

Gerindo, while powerful, proved a relatively short-lived organization. It faded from the scene after a decision to join Gapi,[33] reached at the party's second congress (August 1-2, 1939), led many of its leaders to concentrate their efforts on the latter organization. Thus far there is no evidence that Communists in Indonesia publicly espoused the line that Western Communists adopted between August, 1939, and June, 1941, in conformity with the Nazi-Soviet pact.

On the other hand, Gapi, like Gerindo, stressed two themes that made it possible for revolutionary nationalists and Communists to remain in the same organization: the formation of an anti-Fascist front and the demand for commitments from Holland for increasing measures of self-rule and self-determination. Anti-Fascist sentiment, certainly on the elite level, could win a following more, perhaps, in reaction to the vigorous Dutch Nazi movement in Indonesia than out of sympathy for the fate of Holland as such, though there were numerous evidences of support for Holland's predicament after May, 1940, from noncooper-

[31] J. A. Verdoorn, *The National Movement in Indonesia.* Reprinted in collection of documents issued by Republic of Indonesia, Ministry of Information. (Jogjakarta: n.d. [probably late 1947]), pp. 54-65.

[32] Kahin, *op. cit.,* p. 115; and McVey, *op. cit.,* p. 21. McVey calls Gerindo "the powerful left wing of Indonesian nationalism."

[33] Pringgodigdo, *op. cit.,* p. 128.

ative parties of the right as well as from moderate parties of the center.[34]

However important an influence may be assigned to the Communists in this period, there is no question that there were other elements in Gapi and in other parties as well that feared the threat of Japanese aggression and supported the policy of an anti-Fascist front for their own reasons. For example, Mohammad Natsir, writing in the Mohammedijah paper *Pandji Islam* in March, 1941, commented on Gapi's statement to the Visman Commission[35] as follows:

> There is only one thought in the hearts of the [Indonesian] people: the Dutch and their kingdom are in danger. In the midst of this situation, we are being badgered constantly . . . by slogans of [the] Greater East Asian Co-Prosperity Sphere, etc., . . . and hints that Japan has to fulfill its sacred mission. . . . At the time that the Japanese were sending up their trial balloon, Gapi was meeting with the Visman Commission and there emerged from that meeting a strong statement that Gapi backs the Dutch. Therefore, Indonesia's nationalist movement has shown to the outside world that its ties with Western people are stronger than those with certain other Asian peoples. . . .[36]

It was on Indonesian circles in Holland, more than in Indonesia, however, that the policy of the Seventh Comintern

[34] "Right" and "center" are here defined in terms of socio-economic, not political, programs. Parindra, for example, shortly before the invasion of Holland decided "spontaneously to cease all political actions" since "to fish in front of a net [i.e., to be opportunistic] is not a characteristic of Indonesians." (Quoted in Pluvier, *op. cit.*, p. 168, from *Suara Umum*, a Parindra paper in Surabaya.) On May 15, after the invasion of Holland, PSII and Parindra as well as other parties decided to offer their support to the government in every possible way, including financial support; Parindra actually did contribute to the War Fund.

[35] The Visman Commission, headed by Dr. F. H. Visman, a member of the *Volksraad*, was established by the Netherlands Indies Government in September, 1940, to investigate the views of the various racial and social groups in Indonesia with respect to the country's future political development. The commission's report was completed a few days after Pearl Harbor and was printed shortly before the Japanese invasion, thus negating any possible effect the report might have had on later developments.

[36] Mohammad Natsir, "Gapi-Komisi Visman," *Capita Selecta* (Bandung: W. Van Hoeve Ltd., 1954), pp. 343-46.

Congress had a marked effect. As the Communist Party of the Netherlands (CPN) developed the local variation of the People's Front line, it decided to drop its demand for Indonesian independence. As noted above, many leading nationalists, members of the Holland-based Perhimpunan Indonesia (PI), had broken with Communist front organizations such as the League Against Imperialism after the Sixth Comintern Congress. But, despite this experience, ardent nationalists in and out of Holland had for the most part retained some sense of respect for, if not identification with, the CPN. The party's forceful anti-imperialist and anticapitalist slogans and its early—and, for a decade or more, its unique—militant stance for Indonesian independence had an appeal to nationalists that no amount of disappointment or political sophistication completely destroyed. But when the CPN gave up its demand for Indonesian independence, its contention that "unity" in Holland was necessary to protect Indonesia from "Japanese imperialist Fascism" damaged their appeal among Indonesians who were neither party members nor fellow travelers but who still endorsed the demand for independence as well as the struggle against the Japanese.

Some time after Sjahrir and Hatta left Holland (1932 and 1933 respectively), fellow travelers had succeeded in gaining control of PI, which after 1935 dutifully reflected CPN policy and was used by the CPN, where possible, to recapture lost ground. In 1936, PI and Dr. Sutomo, head of the moderate Parindra, drew up a joint program, which was described in the PI periodical *Indonesia* as a step toward unity within the nationalist movement, "to be based on a limited program of constructive activity which would have the approval of all participants . . . a unity which sought to join all the people of Indonesia without differentiation between left and right." [37] The draft program, which started with cultural, social, and economic planks, had as its first political goal "dominion status [for Indonesia] with national-

[37] "Naar een Nationale Samenwerking," Indonesia (January, 1937), pp. 1 f. (Formerly *Indonesia Merdeka*.)

democratic rights for the people." [38] It also contained an appeal for the establishment of an Indonesian militia—a point that was echoed in the programs of several Indonesian organizations, including Gerindo and Gapi.[39]

Through such tactics, PI was able to hold some of its non-Communist rank-and-file membership, doubtless for many of the same reasons that induced non-Communist nationalists in Indonesia to espouse a similar program of cooperation with the Dutch. However, it is interesting to note that it was left to the Dutch Socialists, in cooperation with Gapi,[40] to carry on the fight for Indonesian independence in the Dutch Parliament and press. Meanwhile, of course, the Indonesian Communists in Holland had joined with their Dutch comrades in denouncing the war as an imperialist struggle, once again reversing their policy in accord with the Nazi-Soviet pact line.

In Indonesia, the Communists apparently did not openly renounce the Popular Front during the twenty-two months of the Nazi-Soviet pact. It is difficult to determine whether this was, as in China, a response to Comintern directives and hence an officially endorsed "deviation" or whether it offers just one more example of a failure in communication between Moscow and its agents in the "illegal PKI." At any rate, the Indonesian Communists' continued espousal of the Popular Front policy paid dividends in the long run: During and after the war, when Japanese political manipulation and brutality had thoroughly alienated the Indonesian people, the earlier anti-Fascist stand of the Communists and the left-wing nationalists seemed thoroughly justified.

38 "Het Ontwerp-Program, Samengesteld door Dr. Soetomo en de Perhimpunan Indonesia," *ibid.*, pp. 8 f.

39 Gerindo at its congress on August 1, 1939 (see Pringgodigdo, *op. cit.*, p. 128); and Gapi in 1941 (see Pluvier, *op. cit.*, p. 189).

40 See Pringgodigdo, *op. cit.*, p. 145; and Pluvier, *op cit.*, p. 145.

5

The Japanese Occupation:
The Last Phase of Colonial Rule

ALTHOUGH THE JAPANESE OCCUPATION OF INDONESIA
lasted only three and a half years, in some ways it was as significant in shaping Indonesia's postwar development as were the
centuries of contact with the Netherlands. A full treatment of
the Japanese interregnum and its meaning for Indonesia lies
beyond the scope of this study, but it is important to bear in mind
the critical effect of those three and a half years on Indonesia's
future.

Arriving at a time when nationalist pressure against the Dutch
had intensified to a climax, and the foundations of Indonesian
society, long eroded, were visibly weakening, the Japanese provided the spark that set off a chain reaction of events which ultimately led to Indonesian independence. Many of these events
would very likely have occurred, sooner or later, in one fashion
or another, without the Japanese intervention, but their course
was profoundly altered and markedly speeded up by the role of
the Japanese.[1] Some of these events were the direct results of
Japanese occupation policies; more of them were unexpected by-
products of Japanese actions undertaken to bring about entirely

[1] In the view of one historian, it is "no exaggeration to say that without
the Japanese interlude, the balance between continuity and change in contemporary Southeast Asia might conceivably still be weighted in favor of continuity, or at best of more gradual, evolutionary change." Harry J. Benda,
"The Structure of Southeast Asian History: Some Preliminary Observations,"
Journal of Southeast Asian History, III (March, 1962), 106-38.

different ends. For the Japanese occupation, like all military occupations, produced a number of inevitable, if unplanned, consequences. As one Japanese student of the period has pointed out, for the countries of Southeast Asia the Pacific War meant not only "liberation from their colonial status on the one hand, but on the other it provided them with the means of acquiring a spirit of resistance to the iron rule of the Japanese military occupation forces." [2] It was not only a spirit of resistance which Japanese policy unwittingly fostered; it was also the practical training, military and managerial, which enabled Indonesians to give tangible expression to that spirit.

Initially, the bulk of the Indonesian population received the occupation forces with considerable curiosity and good will. The Japanese were, after all, fellow Asians who had routed the armed forces of the West and as such were regarded with widespread respect and almost as widespread approval. The speed with which the Japanese armed forces crushed Dutch resistance augmented the popular impression of Japanese invincibility; more important, it discredited the Dutch in the eyes of most Indonesians and convinced many of them that the Netherlands was not nearly as formidable a military opponent as they had earlier believed.[3]

Disillusionment with the new colonial masters was not long in coming,[4] but this did not lessen the impact of the changes

2 Koichi Kishi, "Review of H. Benda, *The Crescent and the Rising Sun*," *The Developing Economies* (Tokyo), I (January-June, 1963), 126-34.

3 Dutch military prowess was further discredited in Indonesian eyes when it became known, early in the occupation, that the commander of the Dutch land forces in Java had surrendered for all Allied troops on that island, although he knew that the British commander in Java, with some 8,000 British and American troops, fully intended to continue the battle. Especially in Java, Indonesians witnessed the very limited resistance put up for only a week by the Dutch Army; they did not see, and most of them did not know of the vigorous battles waged by the Dutch Navy and Air Force. Thus, Indonesians tended to write off the Dutch militarily to a far greater extent than was anticipated by those who had a more complete picture of the entire military scene in the Pacific, and Indonesians in 1945 undertook to do battle against the Dutch with much greater optimism than Indonesian resources warranted or foreign observers expected.

4 Armed uprisings against the Japanese broke out before the end of 1942.

wrought by the occupation nor did it diminish the tremendous upsurge of Indonesian morale and nationalist fervor that followed in the wake of these changes. Occupation policy differed in various parts of the archipelago, not only because different geographical areas were placed under separate military commands but also because of divisions of opinion on occupation policy and on the postwar status of Indonesia between the Japanese Army and Navy, between both forces and the military high command, and between the high command and the Japanese Foreign Office.[5] Nevertheless, the influence of occupation policy, especially as it was carried out in Java and Sumatra, had effects which reached throughout the country.

One of the most important of these occupation policies was the encouragement that the Japanese, for their own reasons, gave to a variety of Indonesian organizations, military, political, and religious. The Japanese-sponsored mass organizations, for all that the occupation authorities tried to play them off against each other, provided nationalist leaders with a better organizational base than they had hitherto enjoyed. Another important factor was the unifying effect of Japanese policies on language, education, and communications. Dutch and other Western languages were banned; although both Indonesian and Japanese were designated the official languages, in practice this meant the widespread use of Indonesian, since Japanese was not widely known. When the schools were reopened at the end of 1942, they were established on a national basis with a standardized curriculum. More important, private schools were outlawed, which meant that children of varied economic and social backgrounds were

---

Blows to Indonesian pride, the brutal measures used to suppress opposition, and the heavy economic burdens placed on the population soon turned a majority against the Japanese regime. Several million Indonesians—some estimates run as high as 4 million—died during the occupation, some while doing forced labor, others of famine and disease, others in the series of armed rebellions that flared up increasingly, especially in the last year of the war. By 1945, most Indonesians were vigorously anti-Japanese.

[5] For details on occupation policy, see Willard H. Elsbree, *Japan's Role in Southeast Asian Nationalist Movements: 1940-1945* (Cambridge: Harvard University Press, 1953), pp. 44-49, *passim*.

educated in the same classrooms. The elimination of tuition fees also brought about an increase in literacy, and the Indonesian-language press, which moved into the vacuum created by the suppression of Dutch papers, flourished in spite of wartime shortages and censorship. The loudspeakers installed in every village square for the purpose of issuing instructions to the population from a central broadcasting system helped to bind small and remote communities to the rest of the country. Finally, there was the vitally important occupation policy that gave Indonesians a vastly increased role in the civil administration. Although genuinely responsible top-level posts were not given Indonesians until almost the very last weeks of the occupation, great numbers of Indonesians were appointed to positions formerly reserved for the now-interned Dutch and Eurasians, positions higher than Indonesians had ever held under the Dutch.

The Japanese had unlocked the door behind which Indonesians had been clamoring for greater participation in the direction of their own country and their own lives. Once liberated from the control of their long-time rulers, and then made aware of the weaknesses of the Japanese administration, the Indonesians rushed to take advantage of the new situation. The Japanese had sought to make use of the reservoir of Indonesian nationalist sentiment for their own purposes; instead, they released a torrent of forces that they could not control. The nationalist fervor spurred by the Japanese, the encouragement given to Indonesian organizations of all varieties, the opportunities provided for developing the national language and displaying the national symbols, the destruction of the myth of Dutch might, the participation of Indonesians in government, the spread of military training, the development of an anti-Japanese underground which heightened Indonesian self-confidence—all these gave the nationalist movement an impetus that carried it farther in those three and a half years than in the decades since 1908.[6]

[6] There are those who maintain that the Indonesian anti-Japanese resistance was of negligible proportions and minimal consequence. It may well be that

By 1942, when the Japanese invaded Indonesia, all nationalists, of whatever political coloration, had almost uniformly arrived
at a common outlook: either the Dutch government in exile
in England would make some commitment as to the kind of
self-determination that Indonesia was to have, or the nationalists
would forever be confirmed in their view that nothing was to be
gained from dealing with the Dutch. Few nationalists expected
the former, and only the Communists stood to benefit from the
latter, as they could fight against the Japanese while collaborat-
ing with and receiving support from the Allies—a pattern re-
sembling the role of the Communists in Burma.

For the non-Communist nationalists, there remained two al-
ternatives: to fight on two fronts, against the Dutch and the Japanese—which some nationalists elected to do—or to "welcome"
the Japanese for opportunistic reasons or because the Japanese
might become the instrument of eventual liberation. This decision with respect to the Dutch and the alternative decision with
respect to the Japanese made for three kinds of responses to the
Japanese occupation: to fight the Japanese while carrying on the
struggle against the Dutch by whatever means possible, to col-
laborate with the invader, or to use the Japanese to further nationalist ends.

The details of the nationalists' activities during the Japanese
occupation have been related elsewhere.[7] For our purposes, the

---

for the energy, time, lives, and money expended, the results were negligible,
but not unduly so by comparison with similar wartime resistance efforts in
other occupied territories. As for size, the total resistance movement was of
substantial proportions. The weaknesses lay not in numbers but in faulty
organization.

[7] See Elsbree, *op. cit.*, especially Chapter 3; Kahin, *op. cit.*, especially Chap-
ter 4; Muhammad Abdul Aziz, *Japan's Colonialism and Indonesia* (The Hague:
Martinus Nijhoff, 1955); and F. C. Jones, *Japan's New Order in East Asia:
1937-1945* (London: Oxford University Press, 1954).
For a study of Islamic political development during the occupation, see
Benda, *The Crescent and the Rising Sun.* Benedict R. O'G. Anderson, *Some
Aspects of Indonesian Politics Under the Japanese Occupation: 1944-1945,*
Interim Reports Series, Modern Indonesia Project (Ithaca: Department of Far
Eastern Studies, Cornell University, 1961), provides useful data on the final
months of the occupation and the outbreak of the revolution.

Japanese occupation had three interesting consequences: The underground movements formed during the occupation emerged as contestants for power in the postwar period; the Marxist education sponsored by the Japanese increased Indonesian susceptibility to that doctrine; and Japanese policies led to a sharpening of the race issue into a major element in Indonesian social attitudes.

Four major underground organizations were formed under the Japanese occupation. They were led by left-wing nationalists, including avowed Socialists, or by Communists of both the Stalinist and national Communist factions. As the Japanese rapidly succeeded in turning the bulk of the population against themselves, the resistance leaders gained prestige and popular support. This made them figures to be reckoned with in the postwar period, as against other leaders who had risen to the top ranks in the Japanese-run administration.[8]

Of the major underground movements, initially the largest and best-organized was the one led by Amir Sjarifuddin which had been set up by the Dutch on the eve of the Japanese invasion. Its leadership was drawn mostly from the ranks of the "illegal PKI," although the lower-level membership of most branches of the movement were probably not Communists. This group came to disaster fairly early in the occupation with the capture of several of its members, and in 1943 Sjarifuddin and some of the other leaders were arrested. The next major group in order of importance was that set up by Sjahrir. Slower to take shape and more carefully organized, it developed into a stronger organization than Sjarifuddin's, and operated in many parts of

---

I. J. Brugmans *et al.* (ed.), *Nederlandsch-Indie onder Japanse Bezetting: gegevens en documenten over de jaren 1942-1945* (Franeker: T. Wever, 1960), although a highly uneven collection of materials, does contain some interesting documentary background on facets of the occupation including the development of some of the Japanese-sponsored Indonesian political and military organizations.

8 For Sjahrir's doubts concerning such cooperation, see his *Out of Exile,* pp. 242 ff; and also H. Van Den Brink, *Een Eisch van Recht: De Koloniale Verhouding als Vraagstuk Getoetst* (Amsterdam: Kirchner, 1946), pp. 49-50, fn. 1.

Java, where it established a working-base among the peasants through the setting up of seemingly innocent peasant coopera- tives. Closely allied with the Sjahrir movement was the under- ground group set up by university students and known as the Persatoean Mahasiswa or University Students' Association. The students, who conducted a fairly daring campaign of open de- fiance of the Japanese, were drawn mostly from the medical school in Djakarta. To the extent that they had a political ori- entation, they were the products of the immediate prewar period of the Popular Front and were mostly left wing in their inclina- tions. The fourth major group, headed by Sukarni, included among its leaders Adam Malik, Chairul Saleh, and Maruto Nit- imihardjo; Sukarni and Adam Malik had been prewar leaders of the Tan Malaka-led organization, Pari. Since a large number of Sukarni's men were also employed by the Japanese propaganda service at the same time that they were claiming to be engaged in underground activities, there was some doubt among mem- bers of Sjahrir's group about the trustworthiness of the Sukarni organization, and Sjahrir attempted to keep liaison between their two groups at a minimum.

A subject that may be related to the role played throughout the occupation by these followers of Tan Malaka, and by Tan Malaka himself, is the purpose behind the establishment by the Japanese of a number of schools for training Indonesian political leaders.[9] The most important of these schools was the Asrama Indonesia Merdeka (Student Quarters for a Free Indonesia), established in Djakarta in October, 1944, under the aegis of one of the figures of the occupation period, Rear Admiral T. Maeda, Chief of Japanese Naval Intelligence in Indonesia.[10] These supposedly na- tionalist educational institutions offered courses in nationalism,

---

[9] For details on these schools, see Elsbree, *op. cit.*, pp. 103-8.

[10] There are so many conflicting accounts of Admiral Maeda's personal political persuasions and of his actual role in the final weeks of the occupation and in the steps leading up to the declaration of Indonesian independence that it is impossible at this stage to make any conclusive assessment of his true role. However, much of the available evidence supports the analyses that place Maeda somewhere in the Trotskyist camp.

politics, economics, sociology, and Marxism. The students were a select group, presumably chosen for their leadership potential. The criteria governing the selection of faculty members are somewhat more difficult to determine. Among those invited (i.e., ordered) to lecture at the Asrama schools were members of the "illegal PKI," former Comintern workers, Hatta, and Sjahrir—an odd combination indeed.[11] Whatever the original Japanese purpose, the net effect of the courses offered at the Asrama schools must have been somewhat ambiguous, given the variety of political viewpoints represented by this unusual faculty.

The purpose of the schools has yet to be satisfactorily explained. One set of clues revolves around the close relationship between Maeda and Tan Malaka during the occupation; apparently, Tan Malaka was intimately involved in the establishment of the numerous Asrama. Some light is also shed by the similarity between the courses offered at these schools and the rather loose variety of Marxist-Leninist doctrine taught in Japanese universities in the prewar decade. If the teaching in the Asrama schools was supposed to inculcate anti-Western and antiwhite feeling, as it did in Japan, this would have been reason enough for establishing the schools. But this still leaves unresolved the question of why, in that case, such men as Hatta and Sjahrir were invited to teach there, since it must have been obvious to the Japanese that Hatta and Sjahrir would give a rather different emphasis in their lectures. Any of the alternative explanations of this strange Japanese maneuver leaves the picture somewhat obscure.[12] All that is clear is that many graduates of these schools emerged in the revolutionary period as younger leaders of the PKI and of PKI affiliates.

Also significant among the many changes wrought by the Japa-

11 Brackman, *op. cit.*, p. 40, writes that the appearance of so many members of the "illegal PKI" in this heterogeneous faculty was the result of infiltration by the Communists, carried out as a counterintrigue directed against Maeda's stratagem. However, it is hard to imagine the Japanese appointing Wikana. a member of the "illegal PKI," director of the Djakarta Asrama without being aware of his Comintern affiliation.

12 Kahin, *op. cit.*, pp. 116-21, and Brackman, *op. cit.*, pp. 38-40, record various possible explanations for the founding of the schools.

nese in Indonesian social attitudes were those concerning the matter of race. At the start of their occupation, the Japanese had a definite advantage in their relationship to the general populace because of the sense of racial identity. As noted above, the bulk of the Indonesian people, like so many other Asians, took pride in the success of Japanese armed forces against the West, much as the Japanese victory over Russia at the turn of the century had served as an inspiration. Furthermore, however delicately it may have been dealt with by most nationalist leaders, the question of race had clearly been of major significance throughout the nationalist movement. Some of the most bitter experiences of Indonesians under colonialism could be traced more or less directly to this fundamental problem. Although the Dutch recognized Eurasians as Europeans for legal purposes—a relatively enlightened attitude for prewar days—the socially discriminatory policies and attitudes characteristic of any colony were prevalent throughout their reign. These policies and attitudes were supplemented by the legal and economic barriers that stood in the path of the Indonesian and were reinforced by a strong element of paternalism. Thus, when the Japanese appointed large numbers of Indonesians to posts in the civil service previously held by the Dutch, this gave a boost to Indonesian morale comparable to no other experience in their modern history.

As has been pointed out, before the Japanese occupation the problem of race, in spite of its malignant character, had been treated with considerable tact and moderation by the various nationalist groups. Since educated Indonesians were generally freely accepted in liberal Dutch circles and since students in Holland were usually treated without prejudice, there was a firm bond of friendship and understanding between the Western-educated Indonesian leaders and their Dutch friends. This mutual tolerance, however, did not usually extend beyond personal social contacts. The race issue, which was to become such an important factor in the wartime and postwar era, had manifested itself before the coming of the Japanese in less violent fashion than was the case in some other Asian colonies. Resentment was certainly present but, partially because of the skillful handling of the question by most of the nationalist leaders, the race issue as such had not been allowed to play a dominant role in the major nationalist parties.

The Japanese consciously and deliberately fostered racist feelings, especially among those who may have suffered prejudice and discrimination at the hands of the Dutch. In selecting members of the Peta, the Volunteer Army of Defenders of the Fatherland (Soekarela Tentara Pembela Tanah Air), the Japanese reportedly gave preference to those locally influential Indonesians who were victims of such experience.[13] Such devices might have served Japanese purposes better had the occupying forces not exhibited their own prejudices about the superiority of the Japanese over other Asians. Their insistence upon Japanese supremacy alienated most of their potential friends. Nevertheless, the Japanese did succeed in molding Indonesian feelings on race into a much more positive form than they had assumed before. Since the war, Indonesia has manifested elements of xenophobia, attributable in part to the experiences of the revolutionary years and in part to this experience under the Japanese.

13 Aziz, *op. cit.*, p. 228.

6

Socialism in the Revolution: Ideologies and Behavior

WITH THE COLLAPSE OF THE JAPANESE, THE RISING TIDE of Indonesian pressure for national self-determination burst the dikes that had restrained it with ever-diminishing ability, and culminated in the proclamation of Indonesian independence on August 17, 1945. Even the promulgators of the declaration of independence had little hope that this gesture would accomplish more than demonstrating to the world at large the true nature of Indonesian feelings. They were, however, favored by a constellation of events that included the complete demoralization of the Japanese forces in Indonesia and a delay of some six weeks before the victorious Allied troops could return to Indonesia. In this brief interim, the Indonesian Republic grew from a gesture of defiance to the outside world to a national state with a government that, despite its many weaknesses and inadequacies, represented the territory of the former Netherlands East Indies. The ensuing struggle for survival, which lasted until the end of 1949, drew the masses of the Indonesian people into the political arena and, to an infinitely greater extent than any previous period in the country's history, set the lines for the shape and structure of contemporary Indonesia.[1]

[1] The best single source for the history of this period is Kahin, *op. cit.*, chapters 5-13. See also Charles Wolf, Jr., *The Indonesian Story: The Birth, Growth and Structure of the Indonesian Republic* (New York: The John Day Company, 1948). For the role of the United Nations in the Indonesian dispute, see Alistair M. Taylor, *Indonesian Independence and the United Nations*

The Indonesian Revolution was fought on the basis of nationalist principles strongly flavored with socialism. Both the leadership and the major political organizations of the revolutionary period were predominantly left wing. The dominating philosophy of the times was a synthesis of three strains: nationalist-revolutionary principles in the tradition initiated by the 1927 PNI and summarized so eloquently in *Indonesia Klaagt Aan!;* the eclectic socialism propounded in the early 1930's by Hatta and Sjahrir; and the religious socialism rooted in Modernist Islamic doctrine as it had been developed over the years from Sarekat Islam to the Mohammedijah. The principal deviations from this philosophy were those of the Stalinist Communists and the Tan Malaka national Communists on the left, and that of the orthodox, conservative Moslems on the right.

Pantja Sila

The essence of the predominating political outlook is to be found in the Pantja Sila, the five principles first enunciated by Sukarno on June 1, 1945, some weeks before the declaration of independence[2] and still regarded as the cornerstone of the nation's political and social philosophy. The first principle Sukarno stated is nationalism—not, as he carefully explained, a narrow chauvinism, but a nationalism that, transcending tribal and regional ties and based on the "unity between men and place," sought to place the state of free Indonesia in a family of nations.[3] The sec-

---

(Ithaca: Cornell University Press, 1960); *Peaceful Settlement in Indonesia,* U.N. Publications No. 1951/I/6 (New York: United Nations, 1951); James Foster Collins, "The UN and Indonesia," *International Conciliation,* CDLIX (March, 1950), 115-200; and William Henderson, "The Indonesian Question, 1946-1949," *Pacific Settlement of Disputes* (New York: Woodrow Wilson Foundation, 1954). For a documentary chronology of the period from August, 1945, to the end of 1946, see Osman Raliby, *Documenta Historica: Sedjarah Documenter dari Pertimbuhan dan Perdjuangan Negara Republik Indonesia* (Djakarta: Bulan-Bintang, 1953), I.

2 The quotations given below are taken from an English translation of a stenographic record of the speech issued under the title *The Birth of Pantja Sila* (Djakarta: Republic of Indonesia, Ministry of Information, 1950).

3 *Ibid.,* pp. 7-9.

ond principle he laid down is internationalism, or, as it later came to be translated, humanitarianism. This principle is not, he said, "cosmopolitanism, which does not recognize national- ism. . . . Internationalism cannot flower if it is not rooted in the soil of nationalism. Nationalism cannot flower if it does not grow within the garden of internationalism." [4]

The third principle is representative government, the details of which Sukarno left for future discussion. In his speech, how- ever, he did seek to forestall critics among the advocates of a Moslem state by pointing out not only that representative govern- ment offered the Islamic religion the best opportunity to pros- per, but that Moslems and Christians would work best together in a nation dedicated to representative government. In describ- ing the fourth principle, the "principle of prosperity," Sukarno emphasized that the democracy Indonesia needed was not that of the West "where capitalists bear sway" but rather a political- economic democracy able to bring about social prosperity. This concept he then redefined as social justice, basing it not on a Western use of the term but on an ancient Indonesian refer- ence to Ratu Adil, the god of justice. The fifth principle, belief in one god—not any specific deity but rather the worship of god according to individual religious tenets in a spirit of mutual re- spect—summed up the traditional Indonesian attitude in the sphere of religion.[5]

[4] Sukarno notes that, despite having been influenced originally by the Dutch Socialist Baars, who condemned nationalism, there was "another man who showed me the right way and that was Dr. Sun Yat-sen," whose works "exposed cosmopolitanism as taught by A. Baars." Another Indonesian nation- alist whose socialism was rooted in vastly different origins from Sukarno's, Hadji Agus Salim, had condemned the Marxist concept of internationalism almost twenty years earlier and advocated in its stead the internationalism of Islam that "wants to unite all of mankind in a united community but, contrary to Marxism, it makes only positive demands rather than negative. Therefore it does not demand the abolition of individualism and nationalism. The rights of the independent free individual to exist, of the family, of village and other communities, of independent nations or nationalities are recognized and guaranteed by Islam." "Onwelwillend, onbillijk, onwaar, maar niet onpartijdig," *Het Licht*, No. 1, Th. 2, reprinted in *Djedjak Langkah Hadji A. Salim. Pilihan Karangan Utjapan dan Pendapat Beliau dari Dulu sampai Sekarang* (Djakarta: Tintamas, 1954), pp. 96-103.

[5] The order in which the Five Principles are customarily listed today varies

The concepts embodied in the Pantja Sila have been echoed, in one form or another, with or without reference to the basic document, in all the major statements of principle that form the core of Indonesia's political philosophy. They guided Indonesia's leaders during the years of the revolution. The essence of the five principles is contained in the preamble to the constitution drawn up in 1945 and is listed in more concise fashion in the preamble to the provisional constitution adopted in August, 1950.

The Views of Hatta and the Sjahrir Socialists

While the Pantja Sila—and especially the principle of nationalism—very likely represented the sum of the average Indonesian's revolutionary credo, there were other writings at that time which, while reaching a considerably smaller audience, nonetheless became classics of the revolution. In this category is Vice-President Hatta's brief statement entitled *Indonesian Aims and Ideals.* Writing late in 1945, and primarily for foreign consumption, Hatta declared that the Indonesian people "are opposed to all forms of autocratic or fascist rule [and] are desirous of building up a national life on a firm basis of mutual cooperation, in order that there may be full social security. What we Indonesians want to bring into existence is a 'cooperative commonwealth.' " [6]

The Political Manifesto of November 1, 1945, written by Sjahrir but representing the views of the government of the time, was also directed principally at foreign audiences. It was this reasoned and moderate document summarizing the experiences

---

somewhat from that used in the original speech. They are normally given as belief in God, humanitarianism, nationalism, democracy, and social justice.

Sukarno, in the Pantja Sila speech, indicated that the five principles could be reduced to three: God, socionationalism, and sociodemocracy; these three could be further reduced to the single guiding Indonesian concept, *gotong-rojong,* or mutual cooperation.

[6] This statement, with very minor alterations, can be found in Hatta, *Verspreide Geschriften,* pp. 311-13, where the date is given as August 23, 1945.

that had led the Indonesian people to make their stand for independence, with its offer, among other points, to restore the private holdings of foreigners as soon as formal recognition was achieved, that first evoked widespread sympathy for the Republic abroad.[7] Another classic of the period is a series of articles devoted to a much more detailed analysis of the substance of Indonesian nationalism. First appearing in the Ministry of Information magazine *Het Inzicht* in early 1946,[8] these articles acknowledged and took to task the reactionary and negative elements participating in the revolution, but also made clear that the significance of these elements was peripheral when contrasted with the spirit motivating the bulk of the Indonesian people. The *Inzicht* articles show a keen insight into the mental processes of the nationalist intellectual from the time when nationalism was "a reactionary resistance to a life in servility and submission to Western countries" through the period when Asian intellectuals were obsessed with the philosophy of positivism, while at the same time they demonstrated an "inner cultural seclusion" that led them to reject the cultural background out of which Western technical progress had emerged. This dichotomy was eased when it became evident that "the movements for freedom in India and Indonesia [had] broken the contradiction between East and West. . . ."

[7] The Political Manifesto has been reprinted in numerous editions. The introduction to the Manifesto is signed by Hatta, in his capacity as Vice-President, and the body of the document is unsigned, which has led many observers to credit its authorship to Hatta.

[8] *Het Inzicht (Insight)* was the Republican government periodical aimed at an audience of intellectuals. It was followed closely by official observers abroad for what it revealed about the views of the men in authority. Its editorial staff was headed by Sudjatmoko and Sudarpo Sastrosatomo, two former leaders of the students' wartime underground resistance movement that had been closely linked with Sjahrir's underground, and the magazine generally reflected the stand of the groups close to Sjahrir and Hatta.

This particular series of articles was signed only with the initial "S"; often attributed to Sjahrir, they are actually the product, in part if not in full, of the leading economist of the Republic in that era, Sumitro Djojohadikusumo. The excerpts given here are taken from an English translation of the articles that appeared under the title "Our Nationalism and its Substance: Freedom, Social Justice and Human Dignity" in *The Voice of Free Indonesia*, Vol. I, April 27, May 4, and May 18, 1946.

The essential task for the modern man today, whether he may come from the West or the East, is . . . to fix again his own position, the re-establishment of his absolute presence, his destination in the cosmos. . . . [He must be] led by the ethical standards of truth, beauty and kindness, which form together the components of human dignity. . . . This universal value is today no monopoly of the East, neither that of the West; it is the task for the fundamental man.

The second article in the series dealt with the economic problems of the country and specifically with what it defined as the fundamental problem of colonial economies—distribution. Beginning with the statement "Freedom doesn't mean anything if we fail to give it a social content," the writer analyzed the development of the Indonesian economy under Dutch rule and drew the following conclusions:

It is evident that mere absolute increase of production and welfare is not of sole importance. It is also paramount that as many groups as possible of the community involved should have their share in the increase of production. . . . [T]he political liquidation of the colonial system should be accompanied by a change in social economic conditions. The distribution of the social product should no longer be left to the forces of a free market. A planned economy, led by the socialistic idea, is the organization of economic life which we bear in mind. Because only in the atmosphere of socialism is a just distribution of the social product conceivable, which would fulfill the demands of human dignity.

While the *Inzicht* articles included a somewhat more academic analysis of Indonesia's economic prospects than did the usual run of statements by political leaders on that subject, their approach reflected quite accurately the general views of the majority of nationalist leaders on the future economic organization of the state.

The most complete exposition of the socialist content of Indonesian nationalism in the days following the declaration of independence is to be found, however, in a pamphlet written by Sjahrir at the end of October, 1945, called *Perdjoeangan Kita*

(*Our Struggle*). It is a searching analysis of the mental and emotional climate of the country in the first weeks of independence. With his characteristic realism, the author frankly outlines the shortcomings as well as the strengths of the infant nation while he presents the tasks ahead with no attempt at minimizing them. Sjahrir characterized the revolution as one that "outwardly . . . resembles a national revolution; when seen from within, it resembles a revolution of the people." [9] He also carefully developed the many domestic and international reasons why this particular revolution must necessarily have a social orientation. He castigated not only those guilty of excesses against foreigners and other minority groups and those who had blindly followed the Japanese, but also those who would place nationalism above the social goals of a democratic revolution. The new Indonesia, he wrote, must be built by men free of any taint of collaboration with Dutch or Japanese Fascism—a statement that was not designed to win him many friends among the recent collaborationists then seeking high office in the Republican government. Many of those whose sole object in politics was nationalism, he reminded his readers, had not been deterred from seeking this goal along Fascist roads. Indonesia's revolution, he proclaimed, was "a democratic revolution, of which the national revolution is only an offshoot. Not nationalism but democracy is the number one aim."

The pamphlet also examined the meaning of the struggle for independence as it affected specific groups of the population: labor, farmers, the youth, and the army. The passages devoted to labor exhorted the workers to remember that their present fight, in defense of an independent Indonesia, was but a part of the total battle that must be waged by labor internationally against imperialism; the farmers must emerge from the revolution free of the feudal structure that had kept them in poverty and bondage; the youth, who were playing such a vital role in the struggle,

---

[9] The quotations given here are from the Dutch edition of the pamphlet, published under the auspices of PI: *Onze Strijd* (Amsterdam: Vrij Nederland, 1946), pp. 20, 22.

must keep in mind the social foundations of the revolution and avoid the misconception that this was a military struggle to be waged by military leaders; and the army, despite its importance, should not supersede the organs of the state in the democratic revolution. The two evils to be avoided at all costs were those of militarism and Fascism.

This document, while never as widely circulated as the Pantja Sila speech, became in its way a kind of bible in the intellectual and student circles it did reach. Unlike most of his colleagues in government, Sjahrir did not seek to compromise sharp differences of opinion for the sake of unity when those differences touched at the heart of the principles of the revolution.

The Religious Socialists

The third dominant strain in the political thought of the Indonesian Revolution was expressed by a group called the Religious Socialists, who drew upon the teachings of Modernist Islamic doctrine for their principles. This group was inspired by such Moslem leaders as Hadji Agus Salim, who had been a proponent of a philosophy combining a liberal or progressive view of Koranic doctrine in religion with related attitudes toward socioeconomic and political issues. Within the Masjumi (Madjelis Sjuro Muslimin Indonesia, or Council of Indonesian Moslem Associations), these leaders provided a base for contemporary Moslem political thought akin to the foundations provided by Sukarno, Hatta, and Sjahrir in other parties. The most vigorous exposition of their views is found in such works as Sjafruddin Prawiranegara's *Politiek dan Revolusi Kita* (*Politics and Our Revolution*) and in the formulation of the party's political program.

The Religious Socialists defined their concept of "social justice" or "socialism" as one that "has no spiritual connection with Marxian socialism," which they associated with force or imposition; for them, Religious Socialism "does not abolish individualism, individual initiative and individual responsibility." It is opposed to "the elimination of a certain class or groups." It guarantees the freedom of the individual and the nation "without closing the door for possible nationalization or socialization of vital enterprises." The latter coexists with "private initiative." Both are necessary.

Such views were incorporated in the Masjumi party statement of principles and program. These were designed "to bring about greater political consciousness among the followers of Islam in Indonesia, to organize and strengthen the unity of Islam, to guide the people towards humanity, socialism, brotherhood and equality in accordance with the teachings of Islam [in a republican state] based on Moslem teachings [and] a guided economy." [10]

The ideas cited in the foregoing political spectrum represented in varying degrees the philosophy of the majority of the Indonesian people and their leaders in the years from 1945 to 1950. These formulations either preceded or emerged from the platforms on which the political parties were organized. Sukarno's general statement of nationalist-revolutionary sentiments was largely adopted by the newly created PNI.[11] Two Socialist groups, led by Sjahrir and Sjarifuddin respectively, combined to form the Partai Sosialis, or Socialist Party, but later, in the months immediately following the organization of the Cominform, split once again. The latter joined the Communist forces, and the former reorganized this group as the Partai Sosialis In-

[10] *Kepartaian dan Parlementaria di Indonesia* (Djakarta: Republic of Indonesia, Ministry of Information, 1954), pp. 441 ff. This wing of the party is careful to avoid any confusion between its stand and the concept of a theocratic state. As explained by Mohammad Natsir, "Islam cannot conceive of a separation of religion and community, or society, or nation, or state, or for that matter of mankind. But this is a far cry from what is understood as theocracy." (Natsir, *Some Obeservations Concerning the Role of Islam in National and International Affairs*, Data Paper No. 16, Modern Indonesia Project [Ithaca: Department of Far Eastern Studies, Cornell University, 1954], p. 4.)

[11] The postwar PNI was not a reconstruction of the prewar PNI founded by Sukarno. However, the similarity in name did help it to win popular support, especially since many of its leaders had been active in the 1927 PNI, its successor Partindo, and the PI of the 1920's.

donesia (PSI). The Masjumi, long regarded as the majority party, reflected the views not only of the Religious Socialists but also of the Nahdatul Ulama, the conservative Moslem group that formed one of its original component organizations. These three were the major parties, in terms of popular support, prestige, and the power of their leaders, during the early years of the revolution. After the rupture in the Partai Sosialis, the PNI and the Masjumi continued to dominate the scene. In addition, there were a number of smaller parties, most of which traveled in the orbit of one of the three major parties or of those now about to be discussed.

There were other points of view that motivated certain leadership groups and led them into political behavior that jeopardized the existence of the young republic. As noted above, the most important of these dissident elements during the revolution were the Stalinist Communists and the national Communists; they are perhaps better understood in terms of their behavior than in terms of their professed programs.

The Role of the PKI in the Revolution

The Stalinist Communists entered the revolutionary period with certain decided advantages. From the days of the "illegal PKI" in 1935, they had played an able political game: They had cooperated with the nationalists in an anti-Fascist, anti-imperialist front; they had refrained from publicly espousing the Stalinist line during the era of the Nazi-Soviet pact; their leaders in Indonesia had, with Dutch support, been active in a reputable underground movement; and their leaders in Holland had been widely praised for their very active role in the anti-Nazi underground. The dissolution of the Comintern in 1943 and the "right" united-front line pursued by the Kremlin during the war and the first postwar year enabled the Communists in Indonesia to command a role in the revolution despite some preliminary confusion.

This initial confusion arose on two counts. In Indonesia the PKI was first re-established in October, 1945, under the leadership of an individual of questionable political background and dubious ability, Mohammed Jussuf. Meanwhile, the Indonesian Communists in Holland and elsewhere outside of Indonesia had followed in the footsteps of the CPN, denouncing the revolution as a "Japanese time-bomb," and labeling Sukarno and Hatta as "Fascist collaborationists." Encouraged by this attitude, the Netherlands Government flew a number of PKI leaders back to Indonesia, in the full expectation that, once there, these men would present the Dutch case. However, within a very short time, the returned Communists had grasped the scope and significance of the revolution and switched to support of the Republic.[12] From that point on, the confusion disappeared, the party line straightened out, and both sets of old-time Communists—those who had been abroad and those who had remained in Indonesia —showed no further hesitation about re-embracing the wartime strategy of united front from above, this time in the presumed interests of independence. In pursuit of this goal, some joined the Partai Sosialis or one of the minor left-wing parties in the same orbit; others, notably Sardjono and Alimin, took control of the PKI and reorganized its central command.

The political haze created by the united-front policy enabled Communists and crypto-Communists to reach positions of high power within the Republican government, extending up to the post of Premier, held by Amir Sjarifuddin. It also made possible their participation in a left-wing coalition of Socialists, Stalinists, and national Communists, the Sajap Kiri (Left Wing). This coalition gradually developed into a new front, which was to become a mass instrument for the PKI in the prelude to the Madiun uprising of 1948.

Almost from its establishment this awkward alliance was rocked by disputes, which increased in vehemence after the

[12] In evaluating the Dutch premises concerning this famous flight, it should be remembered that a number of Indonesian Communists had become national Dutch heroes during the war as a result of their activities in branches of the Dutch underground.

"Zhdanov line" was laid down in September, 1947, and Cominform policy hardened into its new mold. The Communists' decision to oppose the Indonesian revolutionary government did not, however, take place until February, 1948. At that point the Partai Sosialis split, the Sjahrir Socialists forming the Partai Sosialis Indonesia (PSI), while Sjarifuddin's group took the lead in transforming the Sajap Kiri into the Front Demokrasi Rakjat (FDR), or People's Democratic Front. The FDR made little attempt to cloak its true political color; purged of the Sjahrir group, the FDR denounced the Renville agreement (which had been negotiated under Sjarifuddin's leadership), and, when its parliamentary maneuvers to join Hatta's new cabinet were rebuffed, used that treaty as a convenient excuse for opposing his new administration. Through the spring and summer of 1948 there was growing evidence that the FDR was preparing for a showdown of some kind with the government.

In August, Musso, Communist leader from Moscow, arrived on the scene, unheralded and incognito, in the company of Suripno, the Republican envoy to Eastern Europe.[13] Armed with what he termed his "Gottwald Plan"—a reference not without pertinence in the rapidly developing situation—Musso threw off his disguise, assumed command of the PKI, and briskly set about whipping that organization into shape for the challenge it was to give to the central government.

In the Communist plans, it was the FDR that was expected to

[13] At the time that Suripno was dispatched to Eastern Europe, it was not generally known that he was a Communist. The non-Communist government officials who approved his selection for that post accepted him in the guise he had adopted while fighting in the Dutch resistance in Holland during World War II: that of a socialist, affiliated with the Dutch Social Democrats. Suripno's increasingly open pro-Soviet stand during the spring of 1948 caused considerable confusion at the time in the offices of other Republican diplomatic missions abroad. The confusion was climaxed by the Soviet announcement of May, 1948, of the treaty negotiated with Suripno for the exchange of consular representatives between the Soviet Union and Indonesia. For details on that treaty and its repercussions in Indonesia, see Brackman, *op. cit.*, pp. 75-77; and Ruth T. McVey, *The Soviet View of the Indonesian Revolution: A Study in the Russian Attitude Towards Asian Nationalism*, Interim Reports Series, Modern Indonesia Project (Ithaca: Department of Far Eastern Studies, Cornell University, 1957), pp. 47-57.

provide the mass organization and backing that the PKI counted on in its bid for power. The strength of the FDR came principally from two sources: the loyalty of certain army officers to Sjarifuddin—a loyalty nurtured in the days when he had been Minister of Defense; and the support of the Sentral Organisasi Buruh Seluruh Indonesia (SOBSI), or All-Indonesia Central Labor Organization, the largest labor federation in the country. When the conflict finally did break out, at Madiun in September, 1948, neither of these sources of support proved to be as strong or as dedicated as the PKI leaders had anticipated, and the Communists suffered a disastrous defeat.[14]

There can be no doubt about the origins of the Madiun coup. Although the popular discontent and the deteriorating position within the Republic might have encouraged such an adventure, there is sufficient evidence to show that the coup followed upon decisions reached in top Soviet circles abroad.[15] It can be cited as

[14] For details of the Madiun rebellion, see Brackman, op. cit., chapters 7 and 8; and Kahin, op. cit., pp. 290-300. Extensive excerpts from Musso's program as adopted by the PKI just before Madiun are given in McVey, The Soviet View of the Indonesian Revolution, pp. 60 ff.

[15] There has, nevertheless, been a good deal of speculation by some scholars about whether the Communist insurrections of 1948 in Burma, Malaya, and Indonesia can be attributed to Soviet directives. For a comprehensive analysis of the evidence indicating the Soviet origins of the Madiun coup and of the other Southeast Asian uprisings of 1948, see Frank N. Trager (ed.), Marxism in Southeast Asia: A Study of Four Countries (Stanford: Stanford University Press, 1959), pp. 263-73. For an illuminating discussion of the coordination of Communist strategy in Southeast Asia on this and other occasions, see Milton Sacks, "The Strategy of Communism in Southeast Asia," Pacific Affairs, XXIII (September, 1950), 227-47. See also Brackman, op. cit., p. 67.

The possibility for speculation on this point arises because there is no documentary evidence of actual Soviet instructions to the Southeast Asian parties, nor is it likely that such evidence will ever be found. As Trager notes, "the assumption that a written directive from Moscow ever existed is, to begin with, gratuitous; even if it did exist, it is reasonable to assume that, in much the same way as the Soviet encyclopedia is periodically rewritten to conform to policy changes, Communist government files are subject to occasional cleaning out or doctoring" (p. 264). In the absence of conclusive documentary proof, one must sift both the negative and the positive evidence available in order to determine which provides a more coherent picture. On this, the present writer finds the arguments advanced by Trager particularly cogent. He traces the series of steps leading up to the announcement of the new, Zhdanov line at the September, 1947, Cominform meeting; the communication of the new line to the Indian Communist Party in December of that year, and to the other

one more example either of the Kremlin's failure to assess properly the political and military realities of the situation in Indonesia or of its willingness to engage in expendable actions for "larger" purposes.

It has been suggested by some observers that the outbreak at Madiun may in a sense have forced the hand of the PKI leadership before it was ready to go into action, and that the uprising came when it did because local Communists were feeling the

---

Asian parties in February, 1948, at the Calcutta Conference sponsored by the World Federation of Democratic Youth and the International Union of Students; the subsequent Communist strike movement in India, followed by the beginning of the Communist insurrections in Burma in March, the opening of the Malayan rebellion in June, and the Madiun revolt in September. Each of these events followed upon the appearance on the scene of one or more leading Communist officials who had attended the Calcutta Conference and the simultaneous Second Congress of the Communist Party of India (Than Tun in Burma; Lawrence Sharkey, the Australian Communist leader who stopped off in Singapore for two weeks on his way home from Calcutta for conferences with the Malayan Communist Party leadership), or of Communist officials who had come directly from Moscow (Musso in Indonesia). In the absence of evidence to the contrary, and in light of the public statements emanating from Moscow throughout this period, it would seem reasonable to infer that the series of rebellions followed upon orders from Moscow.

A good deal of attention has also been paid to the question of when and where the word was passed from Moscow to the Southeast Asian parties, assuming that it was passed at all. See, e.g., Joseph Frankel, "Soviet Policy in South East Asia," in Max Beloff, *Soviet Policy in the Far East 1944-1951* (London: Oxford University Press, 1953), pp. 208-10; John H. Kautsky, *Moscow and the Communist Party of India: A Study in the Postwar Evolution of International Communist Strategy* (New York: John Wiley & Sons, Inc., 1956), pp. 33-34; and Ruth T. McVey, *The Calcutta Conference and the Southeast Asian Uprisings,* Interim Reports Series, Modern Indonesia Project (Ithaca: Department of Far Eastern Studies, Cornell University, 1958). While Miss McVey questions the role of the two-camp doctrine in instigating the Communist outbreaks in Southeast Asia and concludes that the Calcutta Conference does not seem to have been the place at which the two-camp doctrine first became known to the Southeast Asian Communists, her study provides ample evidence to suggest that in the case of the Indonesian Party, at least, the Conference was of major significance. Among other pertinent information, she notes that it provided the Indonesian Communists with their first opportunity to learn the details of the new policy, and that it was shortly after the Conference that the PKI shifted from its former moderate stance to one of opposition to all compromise with the Netherlands and thus of stiffer opposition to the Hatta government. Here again it is the contention of the present writer that the positive evidence of policy and program statements, the behavior of groups and individuals, and the movements of persons outweighs the negative evidence of the absence of documentary proof.

pressure of the government's campaign to disarm them and remove from crucial areas military figures whose loyalties it had
reason to suspect.[16] However plausible this interpretation may
be, there are a number of other considerations which lend support to a view that, while the revolt may have been off schedule
by a matter of days, it had been planned for a time very closely
approximate to September 18, 1948, the actual date it began. For
one thing, Indonesian Intelligence had acquired Dutch documents detailing plans for a new attack on the Republic scheduled
for the fall of 1948. This information also became known to the
PKI. While the captured plans came as no surprise to many Indonesians since tangible evidence of the Dutch military build-up
was on hand in many quarters, these documents presumably indicated, among other things, the relative imminence of the date
set for the attack. It is reasonable to suppose that under the circumstances the PKI might have felt that its bid for power would
either have to be executed before the Dutch action or else postponed, perhaps for an inordinate length of time. Second, there
was the Indonesian reaction to the so-called Cochran proposals,
submitted privately to Indonesian and Dutch representatives in
early September.[17] The Cochran proposals were regarded in Indonesian quarters as favoring the Dutch at the expense of the Indonesians and thereby served to weaken the Hatta government.[18]
In addition, economic conditions in Java had deteriorated sharply
as a result of the Dutch blockade. The defeat of Indonesian attempts at the United Nations to force the lifting of the blockade
made it clear that conditions would continue to grow worse. The
reaction both to the Cochran proposals and to the blockade situation intensified sources of disaffection among the Indonesian peo-

16 See, e.g., Kahin, *op. cit.*, pp. 284, 287; and McVey, *The Development of
the Indonesian Communist Party*, pp. 63 f. Kahin, however, clearly indicates
that the PKI leaders had made plans for a coup and did not hesitate to put
themselves at the head of the Madiun uprising; he writes that the PKI bid
for power could not have been readied until November.

17 Ambassador Merle Cochran was the American representative on the
United Nations Commission for Indonesia.

18 The Indonesian view of the Cochran proposals as favoring the Dutch was
shared in other circles (see, e.g., Collins).

ple. Fourth, there was the significant timing of the return of Musso with his "Gottwald Plan." Finally, there was the sudden and dramatic shift in the attitude of the Soviet delegation to the United Nations toward the Indonesians. After having championed the Indonesian cause at the U.N. with a degree of vigor that was sometimes embarrassing to the Indonesian representatives, the Soviet delegate to the Security Council on September 1, 1948, abruptly "dropped" the Indonesians and their cause.[19]

The defeat at Madiun, the execution of many of the rebellion's leaders, and the storm of popular reaction against this attack on the central government drove the PKI from the scene— but only for a short time.

The second dissident movement that ran counter to the gen-

---

[19] Although the Soviet-bloc delegates at the United Nations had begun applying the new, two-camp doctrine to the Indonesian case in February, 1948, beginning with a rigorous denunciation of the U.N.-sponsored Renville Agreement, their behavior that spring toward the Indonesian Republic had included such apparently friendly gestures as the announcement of the treaty for exchange of consular representatives, and they had continued to treat the Indonesian delegates at the U.N. as the helpless victims of imperialist fraud. The Indonesian delegates, therefore, were all the more surprised when, en route to Paris for the General Assembly sessions of 1948, they discovered that they had suddenly become "invisible" to Soviet and other bloc delegates on the same liner. This about-face was carried out so blatantly that not only the Indonesians but other interested delegates aboard began haunting the ship's radio room, seeking news of what they anticipated would be a violent new tack in Communist policy toward the Indonesian Government. Somewhat to the astonishment of the newsboys on the pier when the ship reached Cherbourg on September 5, debarking Asian and Western delegates snatched up all available copies of French Communist papers. There they read, some two weeks before the outbreak at Madiun, that the Indonesian Government had indeed become "running dogs of the imperialists."

The value that one attributes to this kind of evidence depends on one's feel for Soviet methods of operation, especially as they existed at that time. But there are a sufficient number of parallel instances, where behavior of this type has been related to Communist decisions, to alert the observer. In assessing the events just cited, the Indonesian delegates at the U.N. reviewed them in conjunction with such related matters as the extremely poor state of communications at that time between the Republican-held areas of Java and the outside world, which made it unlikely that the PKI was able to send abroad in late August, 1948, information about decisions reached inside Java. In the light of this fact and given the Soviet behavior just described, when the Madiun revolt began the Indonesian delegates at the U.N. concluded that not only had the Russians participated in the planning of the uprising but that the attack had been scheduled for a date very close to September 1.

eral ideological temper and behavior during the revolution was that of the followers of Tan Malaka, who, for want of a more precise term, are called here the national Communists. As will be remembered, Tan Malaka had himself been called a Trotskyist by Bukharin during the Sixth Comintern Congress. It is certainly questionable, however, if Tan Malaka was ever any kind of Trotskyist; his views and conduct throughout three decades of political activity show a kind of internal consistency even when he was serving as an official Comintern agent before and after the 1928 Comintern Congress. Tan Malaka was a Communist; he was at home in the Marxist-Leninist tradition; he was obviously a man who attracted a dedicated following. But perhaps the single most important element in his consistency and thereby in his ability to attract a following was the fact that he was almost always—if not always—a nationalist first, an Asian regionalist second, and a defender of tactical Pan-Islamism third, as well as a Communist. As Indonesians would say, and often have said, he was first of all an Indonesian.

There is some obscurity about Tan Malaka's role during World War II, but, as indicated, his followers remained in Indonesia and were active in an underground apparatus of sorts. Many of them made their first postwar appearance in a mass organization led by Subardjo.[20] Subardjo's party had originally been organized during the Japanese occupation, supposedly as an underground force, but its members included, besides many graduates of the Asrama schools, a number of Indonesians who were working in

[20] It is difficult to identify Subardjo's political affiliations in this era. He had been a leader of PI in Holland in the early 1920's. Thereafter he spent at least a year in Moscow (see Kahin, *op. cit.*, p. 115, fn. 2) and was apparently active in the League Against Imperialism in Berlin in the late 1920's (see Blumberger, *De Communistische Beweging in Nederlandsch-Indie*, p. 140). Despite numerous conversations with Mr. Subardjo in 1950, the author has not been able to form a clear-cut picture of his basic political views. This blurred impression was not dispelled when, in 1951, Subardjo as Foreign Minister signed the Japanese Peace Treaty and in 1952 reached an agreement with the American Ambassador to Indonesia, Merle Cochran, for U.S. aid with the military security provisions (Sec. 511A) of the Mutual Security Act. This forced Subardjo's resignation and ultimately helped to bring down the cabinet in which he sat.

the Japanese-run civil service. Within a few weeks after the declaration of independence, his party had grown to massive proportions because other political leaders were at first unwilling to organize parties. When this problem was resolved by the Republican government in favor of a multiparty system, Subardjo's organization faded out of existence and a majority of his following joined one or another of the various organizations led by the followers of Tan Malaka.

Tan Malaka, strongly opposed to the Republican government's policy of negotiations with the Dutch, tried to establish himself and his lieutenants in controlling positions in the government and in the numerous parapolitical, paramilitary popular organizations that sprang up throughout the country in the first months of the revolution. He even attempted, through a rather elaborate scheme, to supplant Sukarno as leader of the state. In January, 1946, frustrated in his series of attempts to wrest power from the Republic's central leadership, Tan Malaka established a coalition known as the Persatuan Perdjuangan (PP), or Fighting Front, which initially encompassed members of all parties and organizations. The PP's program demanded not only the dissolution of all political parties but the abandonment of any negotiations with the Dutch until all foreign troops had left Indonesian soil. The first point in this program alienated much of Malaka's support from the major parties in the government, and his uncompromising stand on negotiations ultimately led the authorities to arrest him along with several other leaders of the P.P. Nevertheless, his organization continued to grow in strength, possibly because its extreme position on negotiations appealed to certain elements in the population. Encouraged by this support, the PP leaders, upon their release from prison, attempted a *coup d'état* in June, 1946, which included the much-publicized incident of the kidnaping of Sjahrir. The leaders involved in the coup, Tan Malaka included, were reimprisoned, and the PP, after a few uneasy days when it appeared that a civil war might well break out, ceased to be a factor in domestic politics. In a way, the PP was a classic example of the curious amalgamations that arise on the

Indonesian political scene. Besides Tan Malaka and several of the key figures from his prewar organization, Pari, its leadership included Abikusno Tjokrosujono, leader of a faction in the Masjumi; Suprapto, of the PKI; Subardjo, whose wavering political orientation has already been discussed; Iwa Kusumasumantri, whose previous activities included a year of teaching in Moscow; and Mohammad Yamin, who was consistently listed as an independent nonparty man and had a voting record in the parliament that, while generally leaning to the far left, was sufficiently confusing to support that designation.[21]

Despite the disappearance of this strange coalition, Tan Malaka's adherents continued to be active in a variety of smaller Marxist-oriented parties and especially in the leadership of small armed units. In June, 1948, a number of these groups banded together in a new federation, the Gerakan Revolusi Rakjat (GRR), or People's Revolutionary Movement. While following in the footsteps of the defunct PP in opposing any negotiations with the Dutch, the GRR was nevertheless able to reconcile this position with support for the current Republican government, in contrast with the FDR. Indeed, its opposition to the Stalinist-oriented FDR seems to have been one of the GRR's principal reasons for existence. The GRR, like its postrevolution successor, the Partai Murba, espoused essentially the same program as the Stalinist Communists but renounced any tie whatsoever with the Soviet Union.[22]

The GRR fought bitterly against the PKI-led troops at Madiun—as did Tan Malaka and the other PP leaders released from prison shortly before that event—and hence emerged from the

[21] It is of some interest that later official summaries of the attempted coup by the PP list as the prime movers only Tan Malaka, Major General Sudarsono, and Mohammad Yamin. See, for example, *Lembaran Sedjarah* (Jogjakarta: Republic of Indonesia, Ministry of Information, 1950), p. 9.

[22] Murba has been claimed by the Trotskyist Fourth International, though the claim is open to some question. See *Kepartaian dan Parlementaria di Indonesia*, pp. 547, 551. It is pertinent that the trade-union confederation of this group, known as SOBRI (Sentral Organisasi Buruh Republik Indonesia), joined the Communist World Federation of Trade Unions after the death of Stalin and the execution of Beria, and announced in late 1953 that it would cooperate with the Communist-controlled SOBSI.

revolution with a reputation considerably better than that of the PKI. However, this record of loyalty to the Republic in its darkest days was not enough to place the Murba forces in the front rank of Indonesian parties, as the 1955 general election results showed.

These two groups—one led by the PKI, which followed conventional international Communist policies, and one led by Tan Malaka, whose consistency is clear but whose rationale of political conduct is yet to be discovered—were the principal forces on the left that, in political behavior and program, ran counter to the major themes of the revolutionary era. Despite the very grave threats posed at different times and places by both these forces, the Republic fought its war with the Dutch to a successful conclusion, and the Sukarno-Hatta government was duly recognized in the transfer of sovereignty on December 27, 1949.

7

From the Transfer of Sovereignty to Guided Democracy: Background to the Political Struggle

THE POLITICAL ATMOSPHERE IN INDONESIA AT THE TIME of the transfer of sovereignty was far from healthy. While most of the Republic's leaders regarded the actual transfer of sovereignty at the end of December, 1949, as a victory, despite the shortcomings of the Hague agreement and the general dissatisfaction with the federalist form of government it imposed, the popular reaction was quite different. For one thing, however much Indonesia's leaders maintained that the Hague agreement represented the final treaty in the war for independence, it appeared to large masses of the population to be no different from the two previous agreements that were to have brought peace and independence, Linggadjati and Renville. Twice burned, the Indonesian people were a good deal more skeptical of the finality of the new agreement than was generally realized abroad. For another thing, within days after the formal transfer of sovereignty, the first of a series of armed attacks in which Dutch units were involved broke out in Bandung, followed not long after by similar eruptions in Makassar and Ambon. To many Indonesians it began to look like a repetition of the previous pattern of truce, negotiations, and political agreement only to be followed by further military attacks. Finally, the continued presence of Dutch troops increased the general sense of uneasiness and contributed to the feeling that a new explosion was impending.

To the leaders in Djakarta it was clear that the Republic would not be openly challenged again by Dutch arms, but the understanding of the international situation and of the role of the United Nations on which this optimism was based was, of course, not shared by the masses. The tension inherent in such a situation was but one aspect of the general confusion and chaos that prevailed throughout the country after eight years of military occupation and warfare. In a far worse position than the European nations at the end of World War II, the Indonesians had not only to rebuild the most basic economic facilities, restore their transportation and communications systems, secure adequate food supplies, textiles, medicines, and other necessities; but they had also to create a civil administration that would function on a permanent footing in place of the makeshift wartime services that had operated on an emergency basis. Here, the drastic shortage of trained personnel was a problem of the first order. Added to these difficulties were the other special problems that characterized the postwar scene in Indonesia: the social upheaval that, in the course of eight years, had wrenched loose from their traditional moorings all but a small part of the country's population; the widespread disappointment and discontent with the seemingly blurred outcome of the revolution; and the rancor that embittered relations between the majority of the people and the minority who had collaborated with the Dutch.

The entire fabric of Indonesian life had been torn apart by the experiences of the revolutionary years, and with it had gone many of the old traditions, patterns of authority, and ties of family life. Guerrilla bands roamed the countryside, as they had since 1945. In some instances, their refusal to lay down their arms and settle back into civilian life arose from disgust with the final result of the revolution; in others, it was motivated by disbelief in the finality of the Hague agreement. Certainly, the continued presence of Dutch troops and the series of major armed clashes in 1950 in which the Dutch were involved encouraged this belief. Finally, the lure of sheer banditry should not be overlooked. Encouraging many Indonesian youths in their drift away from society was the dimly sensed feeling that the caliber of their individual contributions and sacrifices should have culminated in something more than the dubious advantages of settling down into a village life that many of these youngsters scarcely remembered. These young people still form the core of the numerous armed gangs operating today in various parts of the country, sometimes under the name of Darul Islam (DI), sometimes under another banner chosen to indicate some local grievance with the central government.

This sense of disappointment and resentment was not confined to the youth, or to any one section of the population; within a few weeks after the transfer of sovereignty, there was a general miasma of disillusionment, as the revolutionary *élan* faded and no single equally inspiring force came to take its place. From the masses of the Indonesian people, who had played an active role in achieving their independence, there came a rather inarticulate but nonetheless real demand that independence bring in its wake something positive and tangible, some visible differences from the poverty and hardship of their daily lives. As some of their leaders had anticipated, the Indonesian people soon made the discovery that independence is not enough. At the same time, these masses were now receding from the political arena, and their leaders, isolated in the halls of power, began the seemingly interminable political poker game that would ultimately decide which factions would survive and hence what the content of this new freedom would be.

Reactions to the International Scene

The elements of Indonesian life noted earlier—the traditional social values, the role of religion, the *desa* system—had been undermined, and in some cases destroyed, by occupation and war. This left a largely disoriented society open to the changing winds of doctrine. In many ways, the cards seemed to be stacked in the

Communists' favor from the outset, despite the fact that the domestic Communist Party was still in disrepute as a result of the events at Madiun. A number of factors were involved. The residue of ill feeling for the Dutch naturally affected Indonesian attitudes toward the entire Western bloc. Furthermore, the feeling that Indonesia's fight for freedom was part of a general postwar struggle against colonialism was more widespread than foreign observers might have anticipated,[1] and helped to exacerbate the sense of hostility toward Holland's allies. Spilling over from this reservoir of bitterness into the economic sphere was a strong reaction against Western holdings in the country; this reaction in turn fitted into the pattern of the nationalists' historical stand against Western capitalism. The depth and range of this antipathy toward foreign capital can be judged from the fact that no Indonesian party has really dared to challenge this attitude in any consistent fashion. It is true that on occasion a few leading political figures have publicly proclaimed their view that this inclination toward xenophobia should not be allowed to stand in the way of reaping the advantages to be gained by Western, especially American, capital investment, but these moderate and measured statements have been all but lost on the domestic scene in the deluge of denunciations of foreign capital and nonspecific demands that Indonesia's economy be freed from any taint of colonialism.

This generalized anti-Western reaction of the Indonesian people at the end of the revolution continued to be nourished by a variety of incidents. The Indonesian farmer may be remote from world affairs and often only vaguely aware of the real issues at

[1] At the height of the revolution, when newsprint was painfully scarce and shortages of personnel crippling, both the newspapers and the Ministry of Information's publications devoted a significant amount of space to international affairs and especially to the war in Indochina. See, for example, "Outburst in Vietnam," *Voice of Free Indonesia*, II (December 28, 1946), 124-26, which gives a rather cynical but highly perceptive analysis of the attitudes of the big powers on the fighting that had just broken out in Vietnam. While this publication was meant for foreign consumption, it is typical of articles then appearing in the Indonesian-language press. See also *Rakjat* (otherwise unidentified), quoted in *Sari Pers* (Djakarta: Republic of Indonesia, Ministry of Information), January 11, 1947.

stake in the national political scene, but a considerable number of generalizations about world affairs have nevertheless trickled down to the village level and helped to form fairly widespread attitudes. Among the issues on which popular opinion was thus formulated were the struggle in Vietnam, the war in Malaya, and the Korean War. Many Indonesians seemed to have an undifferentiated picture of these situations, seeing them in terms of their own revolution—a fight of Asians against Western imperialists. There was no lack of sympathy for the Vietnamese in their fight against the French, however noncommittal the Indonesian Government's stand may have been on that question.[2] Although knowledge of the Malayan situation was less widespread, the impressions formed about it seemed to be much the same; the fact that the Malay insurgents were labeled Communists did not impress the average Indonesian, since it was assumed that this was just one more Western attempt to justify an attack against an Asian people in revolt. As for the fact that the insurgents in Malaya were almost exclusively Chinese rather than Malays, curiously enough this point just did not seem to register, or, if and

---

[2] The author was surprised to find the extent to which villagers in fairly remote parts of Java were aware of the war in Vietnam in 1950. The name of Ho Chi Minh was recognized in a number of places far from Djakarta or any other major city. This might have been the result of a rather successful propaganda tour conducted in the area some months before by an emissary of the Ho government. Among his campaign materials was a film that included a number of battle scenes; the first time this movie was shown, in a small theater in Glodok, in Djakarta, the audience, many of whom apparently mistook these battle scenes for pictures of their own revolution, became so overwrought that they charged down the aisles and ripped the screen apart.

The Indonesian Government in 1950 had not yet decided which side to recognize in Vietnam. (This problem was resolved some years later, following the partition of the country, by the simple expedient of entering into relations with both North and South Vietnam.) The Ho emissary referred to above entered Indonesia without a visa. He was met at the airport by an official of the Ministry of Information who placed a jeep and an interpreter at his disposal for the three or four months that he remained in Indonesia, and presumably provided him with the necessary papers for extensive travel within the country. The Ministry of Foreign Affairs, meanwhile, maintained the fiction that the Ho emissary was not in Indonesia, if indeed he existed at all—although many Foreign Ministry officials frequently dined with the young man in question whenever he was in Djakarta.

where it did, did not appear to alter the popular view that the Communist insurrection in Malaya was the war of a colonial people fighting for independence.

Finally, the prestige of the United Nations and the United States, which had been damaged in Indonesian eyes during the revolution, received a telling blow from the Korean War. In the first place, the original news of the attack, as it came through to Djakarta and spread out from there, did not make clear the fact that the attacking force had undeniably been North Korean. It was some time before the entire story was accurately recounted, even in the capital. In any case, the basic reaction in many quarters was resentment at the contrast between the prompt response to the violation of the Korean agreement and what most Indonesians regarded as the halfhearted, ambiguous reaction of the United Nations to the second Dutch attack in 1948. Many Indonesians in government circles, who were in a position to know that the United Nations was in a stronger situation with respect to Korea than had been the case in regard to Indonesia in 1948, still persisted in their claim that this was simply proof that the United States and Britain would never take strong action against a nation that they regarded as "wearing the same school tie" (i.e., the Netherlands) but would only react with such vigor to the contravention of a United Nations truce by the other side in the Cold War.

It was also obvious, both at the outbreak of the Korean War, when the badly outnumbered American forces were being pushed back, and later, when the war finally reached its dusty conclusion, that many Indonesians took a certain pride in what they regarded as the apparent success of Asian troops pitted against the West. In Indonesia, the popular view of the Korean hostilities was that of a well-equipped, highly trained, well-fed American force being held at bay by the sheer determination of North Korean and, later, Chinese peasants mobilized to fight with little more than their bare hands. All the resentment toward, and disillusionment with the United States that had started to snowball after the breakdown of the Renville agreement was expressed in this reaction. It pervaded many circles not in sympathy with the Communists on political grounds.

The natural inclination of much of the population to accept this picture of current world tensions was fortified by the heavy inflow of propaganda designed to capitalize on this general outlook. With the arrival of the first ambassador from Peking, in August, 1950, the quantity and distribution of this material expanded tremendously.[3] The traditional dislike of the local Chinese in Indonesia—which had been vastly increased during the revolution, when a substantial portion of the Chinese population sided with the Dutch—made many Indonesians wary of this representative of the new China, but this suspicion did not carry over to the new supply of reading material in Indonesian, which was seized upon eagerly, especially by the younger students.

This world view, which was to a large extent a projection of Indonesia's recent experiences onto the global scene, was enhanced by the continuing tangible evidence of the blurred outcome of the revolution: the continued presence of Dutch troops for more than a year after the transfer of sovereignty; the employment of Dutch civil servants in the administration for two years after the war, as arranged by the Hague agreement; and finally the thorny question of Irian, which, left unsettled in 1949, remained, until August, 1962, the one issue on which all parties and political leaders agreed—at least in public.[4]

---

[3] The Ambassador arrived without his family but with some sixty-seven trunks of personal luggage. Twenty-four hours later, a tour of the bookshops in the Chinese section of Djakarta revealed a newly acquired supply of books and pamphlets, in Indonesian or Chinese, which included works of Mao Tse-tung, Lenin, and some simplified summaries of Marx. Rather well printed, these books sold for the equivalent in purchasing power of a nickel, in contrast with the very few and prohibitively expensive books then available elsewhere in the Indonesian language.

The shortage of reading matter for the younger generation was a serious problem, since English-language books were extremely expensive even for those whose knowledge of English was sufficient to read them; furthermore, unlike their older brothers and sisters, the postwar crop of students did not know enough Dutch to read the many books available in that language.

[4] Those political leaders who originally took the view that there was no point in focusing public resentment on Irian when so much of a positive na-

Thus the attitudes formed during the revolution, coupled with these other factors, continued to give Indonesian politics all across the political spectrum an anti-imperialist, anticapitalist, anti-Western—indeed, a Marxist—tinge.

Domestic Party Politics: The Background

These were the underlying attitudes that conditioned the political scene at the time of the transfer of sovereignty and that have largely persisted ever since. Against this political background moved a variety of individuals and groups engaged in an increasingly bitter struggle for power. Some of the contestants, mindful of this background, consciously took it into account; others ignored or misread it, to their detriment.

With the transfer of sovereignty, the ties that had bound together men and groups of vastly disparate beliefs disintegrated. Many of the same leaders remained in the foreground and continued to manipulate the strings of authority, but much of their maneuvering was irrelevant. While their energies were engaged in partisan politics, control of the country beyond the capital was slipping, unnoticed, from their grasp. New and significant factors had come to the fore and power was crystallizing around new centers. New figures competed with the old leadership in the domestic political infighting that now monopolized the scene.

The fight seesawed back and forth for almost a decade. It culminated in the eclipse of most of the political parties and the centralization of power in new sets of hands: primarily the President's; to a lesser extent the Army's and the PKI's. Before examining some of the features of political party behavior during this period of strife, it would be helpful to consider very briefly two

---

ture remained to be done soon learned that this was one question that would not permit any deviation: Irian must be restored to Indonesia as rapidly as possible. Too much political capital had been made of the question by various individuals and parties to let any political group seeking popular support sidestep the issue. Thus, each and every Indonesian party included the return of Irian to Indonesia as part of its political program.

factors important to the functioning of the political party system: the role played by trade unions and the structure and character of the political parties themselves.

THE LABOR UNIONS

Indonesia's labor unions, several of which are among the largest mass organizations in the country, have always been primarily political organizations.[5] They function as arms of political parties, although they do give some attention to purely trade-union issues. The result, as stated by a former Minister of Labor, has been "that unionism of a nonpolitical nature is unknown to the Indonesian workers." [6] This political orientation has been as marked in the postwar years, with its proliferation of trade unions and federations of unions, as it was in the 1920's when the SI and the PKI battled to win control of the first labor-union federation. All union activity was suppressed during the Japanese occupation, but within a few weeks of the founding of the Republic in 1945, new unions were formed and soon became a potent force in the internal politics of the nation.

Under the provisional constitution in force from August, 1950, to July, 1959, trade unions were recognized and received government subsidies for educational activities. During this same period, there were about 180 national or regional federations of workers organized in a half-dozen confederations, each of which paralleled a major political party or group of parties. The first such

[5] The first "pure and simple" Indonesian trade union, the Staatspoorweg Bond, an organization of employees of the government railway system, founded in 1905, predated the first nationalist organization. However, it was not only the first but also the last of its kind, disbanding in 1912 after having lost much of its membership to the Vereeniging van Spooren Tramweg Personeel, VSTP, established in 1908 under the aegis of Dutch socialists. The VSTP rapidly developed a political character, especially under the leadership of Sneevliet and Semaun. See *Vakbeweging*, p. 1.

For a detailed analysis of the political role of Indonesian trade unions, see Iskandar Tedjasukmana, *The Political Character of the Indonesian Trade Union Movement*, Monograph Series, Modern Indonesia Project (Ithaca: Department of Far Eastern Studies, Cornell University, 1958).

[6] Tedjasukmana, *op. cit.*, p. vii.

confederation to develop after the war was the Barisan Buruh Indonesia (Indonesian Labor Front), organized by Iwa Kusumasumantri in September, 1945. The major labor confederation in Indonesia, the Sentral Organisasi Buruh Seluruh Indonesia (All-Indonesian Central Labor Organization), generally known as SOBSI, was founded on November 29, 1946. From its founding congress, it was led and controlled largely by known and crypto-Communists. SOBSI's president, Sardjono, who was chairman of the PKI, and its general secretary, Harjono, a prewar leader of the Railway Workers' Union, VSTP, had both been active in the Australian wartime Communist movement; its vice-president, Setiadjit, was a crypto-Communist while serving as the chairman of the Indonesian Labor Party and as a minister in the Sjahrir cabinet of 1946. All three participated in the Madiun rebellion.

From its founding in 1946 to 1948, SOBSI represented a high-water mark of united frontism. In this sense, it reflected the success of the PKI in executing its rightist line during the early post-war nationalist-socialist-Communist honeymoon. Scarcely six months after its founding, SOBSI, at its May, 1947, congress at Malang, voted to affiliate with the World Federation of Trade Unions (WFTU) and dispatched its newly elected president, Setiadjit, and a commissioner, Oei Gee Hwat, to attend the WFTU's Prague conference in June. SOBSI also played a significant role in the revolutionary parliament, in which it held 40 seats out of 400 and in which it could usually count on the support of 35 delegates of the Indonesian Labor Party (headed by Setiadjit) and the 40 delegates of the BTI (Barisan Tani Indonesia or Indonesian Peasant Front). SOBSI operated first as part of the Sajap Kiri and later as part of the FDR.

In May, 1948, SOBSI lost a small part of its following to a rival trade-union confederation set up by Tan Malaka and the national Communists.[7] Right after the outbreak of the Madiun

7 This was Gabungan Serikat Buruh Revolusioner Indonesia (Federation of Revolutionary Trade Unions of Indonesia) or GASBRI. GASBRI was short-lived, but many of its members found their way into the Murba-backed federation, SOBRI, founded in February, 1951.

rebellion, SOBSI lost a substantial part of its following: 16 affiliated trade unions representing almost 50 per cent of SOBSI's total membership repudiated the top leadership's support of the rebellion and broke away. Despite these defections, despite internal splits, and despite the loss of several of its key leaders killed during the Madiun revolt or executed soon thereafter,[8] SOBSI managed to emerge from the revolution with its national reputation as a genuine workers' organization virtually intact. There were several reasons for this. For one thing, SOBSI was the largest, best-known, and best-organized standard-bearer for labor. Another reason was that its leadership's militancy during the revolutionary years stood the organization in good stead in the wave of disillusionment that swept over the Indonesian masses soon after the transfer of sovereignty. Finally, SOBSI's leaders have never ceased developing and refining their remarkably effective techniques of winning and holding members.[9] Although other political parties, including PNI, Masjumi, Murba, and PSI, invested considerable effort in establishing rival unions and confederations to combat SOBSI's domination of the labor sphere, none of these organizations ever came near challenging SOBSI's pre-eminent position.

[8] Harjono, then president of SOBSI, and Oei Gee Hwat, another top leader of the organization, were executed for their part in the rebellion. Most SOBSI leaders were imprisoned or went underground.

[9] SOBSI's techniques and the basis of their appeal to the masses are worth a little study. Utilizing whatever the local employees' grievances may be, willing to counsel tactics of violence without regard to the effects on the economy or stability of the country, running a kind of claims bureau in each locality in which the personal problems and needs of its members are met, SOBSI probably reaches more individual Indonesians than any other organization in the country. SOBSI makes full use of the value of recognizing and rewarding individual merit and achievement. Awards and decorations are handed out in impressive public ceremonies to which are invited not only union members but the whole population of the vicinity; speeches by well-known leaders are followed by dramatically staged presentations in which the recipients of the awards are called forward individually over the microphone from the platform and treated to enthusiastic ovations. The look on the face of an Indonesian oil-field worker as he marches back to his seat from the platform where he has been decorated—a formerly obscure man now raised to the heights of prestige and fame among his fellow villagers—is sufficient explanation for the kind of loyalty that SOBSI can depend upon from so many of its followers.

Today, as one of the largest and the most efficiently run of the Communist fronts, SOBSI is virtually indispensable to the PKI. It is difficult to determine accurately what SOBSI's actual membership is, as opposed to its claim of having close to 3 million members; the best-informed recent estimates agree on a figure somewhere in the area of 1.5 million. SOBSI is thus considerably smaller than the Communist peasant front, BTI, which probably has some 4 million members. But SOBSI has the advantage of an unusually large number of full-time officials who maintain close liaison between SOBSI's central headquarters and its many local affiliates. It is SOBSI that supplies the bulk of the participants and the carefully worded banners for the "spontaneous" mass demonstrations that mark each phase of PKI activity. It is SOBSI that lays a smokescreen of labor unrest behind which the PKI can mount an indirect campaign to pressure the President into more favorable treatment for the Party. It was SOBSI, for example, that raised the political temperature in the spring of 1960 by demanding a 25 per cent increase in wages and a 50 per cent cut in prices, as a prelude to PKI charges of Army mismanagement of the nationalized Dutch enterprises. SOBSI's freedom of action has been somewhat curtailed since the August, 1957, ban on strikes in all "vital enterprises" went into effect, and more recently by the extension of the strike ban to almost all branches of industry. Nevertheless, SOBSI continues to be an eloquent and versatile front for the PKI.

THE POLITICAL PARTY SYSTEM

Much as Indonesia's trade unions are inclined to concern themselves with other than purely trade-union issues, so do Indonesia's political parties, with certain notable exceptions, tend to be preoccupied with matters other than policy and program. The political party system, especially as it functioned in the 1950's, reflects the highly personalized character of Indonesian politics, a phenomenon often encountered in, though by no means limited to, societies in an early stage of political development. The plethora of political parties,[10] the weakness of party structure (with the exception of the PKI), and the lack of party discipline (again excepting the PKI and, to a lesser extent, the PSI) are all symptomatic of the extent to which personalities tend to supersede programs. This is a very real, if intangible factor;[11] it can be observed in the ability of various parties and politicians to work together, however unlikely such cooperation might appear in the light of the professed stands of the parties and people involved. It can also be seen in the bitter strife that divides parties and figures who would seem, logically, to be ideal political bedfellows.

It was not until the last months of the election campaign of 1955 that the lines of division separating the major parties began to be expressed in terms that indicated basic divergencies among their respective programs. Before that time, there was a good deal of truth in the jokes circulating in Djakarta to the effect that one had to read the masthead in order to tell whose

[10] The years of contact with the Netherlands, with its multi-party system, no doubt had something to do with the proliferation of political parties in Indonesia.

[11] The extent to which Indonesian political alignments are determined by incredibly complicated histories of personal relationships has been the subject of comment by several observers of the Indonesian scene. The classic description of the situation was provided by Robert C. Bone, Jr., who wrote that "Indonesian political life is a kind of poker game played by a few thousand people all of whom have known each other much too long and too well." ("The Future of Indonesian Political Parties," *Far Eastern Survey*, XXIII [February, 1954], 17.) Bone's comment has been quoted, ruefully, over the years by many Indonesians, especially members of the younger generation.

Another analyst, noting that the divisions among parties include "a history of twenty or more years of intense personal conflicts among the members of the country's political elite" adds: "Thus, the Indonesian parties, in spite of the confusing emphasis they give to arguments about the nature of Utopia, do in fact provide a fairly realistic breakdown on the fundamental question of who among the Indonesian elite gets along well enough with whom to be able to share power effectively." Lucian Pye, "The Politics of Southeast Asia," in Gabriel A. Almond and James S. Coleman (eds.), *The Politics of the Developing Areas* (Princeton: Princeton University Press, 1960), p. 111.

The effect of this internecine warfare among party leaders is heightened by the structure of Indonesian political parties. Indonesian parties, as Kahin has noted, are built from the top down, the leader organizing the mass following, rather than a mass movement thrusting up its own leader. George McTurnan Kahin (ed.), *Major Governments of Asia* (Ithaca: Cornell University Press, 1958), p. 549.

campaign platform or speech was printed below. For the bulk of the population in any case, the debate over national issues, which became explicit in the closing period of the election campaign, was largely irrelevant. Votes at the mass level, particularly in the villages, were garnered on the basis of loyalty to local leaders, who in turn generally gave their support to a particular party on the basis of allegiance to individuals rather than on matters of substance.[12]

More than in the finale of the election campaign, it was during the last stages of the Constituent Assembly debates that some parties finally presented their positions in clear, unambiguous fashion. Then, pushed to the wall, certain party leaders at last came to grips with the issues that confronted them and formulated their responses—too late. Their swan songs caused barely a ripple beyond the inner circles of party contenders. The speeches in which they set forth their views on the basis of the state hold little more than academic interest.

Personalities rather than programs motivated and continue to motivate not only the electorate at large but in many cases the leading political figures themselves. It was a matter of personalities, for example, that to a large extent divided the Wilopo wing of the PNI from the Natsir wing of the Masjumi or from the PSI. Indeed, a significant part of Wilopo's following in the period before the elections was made up of former PSI members who decamped from Sjahrir's party either because of personal dislike of Sjahrir or, as time went on, because of a growing suspicion that the political future of the PSI might not, after all, be too rosy.[13] In the same way, men whose political views are

12 Palmier notes that "the cement that binds the parties is loyalty to a leader, and a party is not chosen because of its political attitude. The elections of 1955 simply showed the allegiance given to either the village headman or the religious teacher or both. Political issues such as corruption, high prices, or economic development meant little to the villagers." Leslie H. Palmier, *Indonesia and the Dutch* (London: Oxford University Press, 1962), p. 151.

It has been suggested that along with these local personal ties went some broader meaning, indicating some commitment to certain ideological principles. See Herbert Feith, *The Decline of Constitutional Democracy in Indonesia* (Ithaca: Cornell University Press, 1962), p. 434.

13 Perhaps because of the preoccupation with personal rivalries, perhaps for

in outright opposition often have a sympathy for each other that derives from their joint struggle as comrades-in-arms during the prewar and revolutionary years. This complicated web of historically conditioned personal relationships adds to the haze enveloping the leadership group. The picture is additionally blurred by the tendency in circles beyond the inner clique of party leaders to equate social and family relationships with political affiliations.

Because of the predominance of personalities over programs, a final point to be kept in mind when considering the role of the different parties after 1950 is the outlook of many of the older nationalist leaders, most of them veterans of the movement during the 1930's. By the time undisputed independence was achieved, these men had spent the better part of their lives fighting against colonialism—a battle against an identifiable foe. Suddenly they found themselves catapulted into a world they could not fathom, where the negative politics of opposition were useless and where the need was rather for a positive approach. Yet few of them in the years of struggle had had the opportunity to develop in more than a hazy fashion any concept of the independent state they were fighting for or to consider in detail the many problems this hard-won freedom would bring. For many

---

other reasons, virtually no one in Indonesia from the President down, was able to estimate with any degree of accuracy the probable outcome of the 1955 elections. The results held surprises for everyone. Even the Communists did not anticipate the excellent showing made by the PKI. It was obvious that the success of the NU was as astonishing to the inner circle of nationalist leaders as it was to foreign observers. But the real surprise lay in the small vote—2 per cent of the total votes cast—won by the PSI.

Not only the Socialist leaders but many of their bitterest foes were apparently misled by the vast audiences who turned out to hear Sjahrir and his colleagues speak at PSI rallies. A few weeks before the election, high-ranking members of the PNI were operating on the assumption that the PSI would take anywhere from 35 to 50 per cent of the vote. On the basis of that misguided guess, key PNI leaders, including one former cabinet minister slated for a major post if the PNI were victorious, were eagerly searching out supporters and presumed supporters of the PSI to explain that after all there were no real differences to divide the PNI and the PSI and that they, the PNI leaders, still had a lingering affection for and fundamental agreement with the principles and programs of the PSI.

of these men, the experience of being uprooted from the familiar role of opposition came too late in life; their mental and psychological processes were too rigid to make the abrupt transition that the new situation required. As a result, many political leaders, perhaps dazed by the dimensions of the task before them, turned their backs on these seemingly insurmountable problems and devoted their energies to grappling for the tangible and familiar elements in the scene: the trappings of personal power and prestige within the limited arena of party politics. Many of these leaders were astute enough to sense the hollow character of the foundation on which their authority rested, but they were slow to formulate a response to the problems that confronted them. As a result, the political atmosphere in Djakarta, from the time of the transfer of sovereignty until the results of the first general election were available, had a curious air of unreality. This translated itself into a generalized uneasiness and a continuing expectation of an impending showdown.

The Haze Lifts Briefly:
The 1955 Election Results

At first glance, the September, 1955, elections seemed to have cleared the air somewhat. But they did not prove to be the hoped-for turning point in the country's fortunes. It was soon evident that the fundamental instability plaguing the nation and its leaders had scarcely been diminished. The old problems were still there; indeed, to them had been added some new ones, not the least of which was the massive strength of the PKI as demonstrated by its impressive showing at the polls.[14] But in spite of some reshuffling of political alignments in the upper strata, relatively little meaningful change took place. Real change came not with the elections but some eighteen months later, when the

14 For a detailed analysis of the results of the September and December, 1955, elections, see Herbert Feith, *The Indonesian Elections of 1955*, Interim Reports Series, Modern Indonesia Project (Ithaca: Department of Far Eastern Studies, Cornell University, 1957).

collapse of the second Ali cabinet precipitated the abandonment of parliamentary democracy and its gradual replacement with President Sukarno's guided democracy.[15]

The election did, of course, provide answers to some highly pertinent questions. Which groups would prove to be little more than a body of doctrine with no real power? Which groups, lacking any coherent doctrine, would emerge with strong popular support? Which groups would be strengthened in the election and develop their doctrine as they advanced? Which groups would prove to have successfully adapted their professions of ideology to meet the situation? To these questions the elections supplied reasonably accurate answers. The victors were obvious: Four parties emerged as the strongest in the Republic, several parties that had been presumed to be second-rank contenders achieved a foothold in Parliament, and a number of small splinter parties were eliminated from the political arena. The question that the elections could not answer was where power lay in the country outside the sphere of party alignments. In a newly emerging country, this is a question of crucial importance.

While it is impossible to ignore the importance of an election in which some 95 per cent of the registered voters participated, it is easy to overestimate the meaning of that event as a guide to relationships in the total power structure of the country. Developments since 1955 have increasingly suggested that the seat of power both before and after the elections lay elsewhere than in the Parliament or the cabinet. Of the 4 parties that together received some 80 per cent of the votes, 2 are of little significance today. The Masjumi and its leaders no longer wield any authority; the party has been banned and its leaders, despite pockets of supporters principally outside Java, are virtually powerless. The NU, at the national level never much more than a hastily constructed framework glued together to fill the vacuum

---

[15] The definitive study thus far of the period from the transfer of sovereignty to the collapse of the Ali cabinet, is Feith, *The Decline of Constitutional Democracy in Indonesia.*

provided by voters who rejected the other parties, has come unstuck. Its local following has been plucked by other more cohesive and more energetic parties and groups; its leaders meander in and out of shifting coalitions of power in the capital. The PNI no longer commands the same importance it had when parliamentary government gave meaning to party politics, although many important personalities in the PNI remain close to the center of power today. Only the PKI has grown in strength and importance since 1955, but its power stems not so much from its electoral majorities in 1955 or the even greater victories it won in the provincial elections of 1957 as it does from other facets of the party's organization and deployment of its forces. On the other hand, the fortunes of Murba, which received only 0.5 per cent of the total vote in 1955, have flourished, its leaders, always prominent in the palace coterie, figuring heavily in the highest councils of government today. Rather than providing a definitive guide to the power structure, what the elections did bring about was a sharpening of the issues. Although the election results did not resolve the question of the basic political direction of the vast electorate, the lines of demarcation separating the major party alliances became more distinct.

Despite much reluctance to admit it, the overriding issue in domestic politics following the elections has been the attitude taken by political leaders and parties to the strength and role of the PKI. This is not surprising. Yet during the years in which the PKI was rebuilding its strength, political leaders of all parties with a few notable exceptions in PSI and Murba continued to deny stoutly that the issue of Communism versus anti-Communism played a significant role in Indonesian political life. The fundamental problems the Republic faced, these leaders said, were "Indonesian" problems: problems of reconstruction and rehabilitation of a devastated country and a weary populace; problems of economic development to sustain a nation then numbering 80 million;[16] problems of education, health, and all the

---

[16] The Indonesian population, generally estimated at 80 to 90 million in the 1950's, as of 1964 was assumed to be about 103 million.

other fundamentals necessary for a life of freedom and dignity. These problems, they claimed, would exist whatever the international situation, and would continue to call for solution if the Kremlin and Peking were to vanish from the globe tomorrow.

There is no question that a good deal of truth underlies these assertions. Indonesia's basic economic and social problems are largely independent of the Cold War; many of its political difficulties, rooted in the peculiarities of Indonesian social organization and institutions, would doubtless be the same whatever the situation beyond its shores. Nevertheless, this refusal to admit that Communism posed a problem of genuine relevance to Indonesia's development was, in the face of the facts, a surprisingly strong and widespread viewpoint. To some extent, it may have been a projection of vain hopes that this would indeed prove to be the case and that Indonesia would be allowed to pursue its efforts at development unhindered by subversion or counterrevolution. To a certain degree, it may have been a reaction against Western warnings that were regarded either as ill founded or as special pleading. Whatever the origins of this attitude—and they were many and extremely varied—it is significant that the rapid comeback of the PKI after its defeat at Madiun was only belatedly recognized in many quarters as a development—and a threat —of major proportions.

Economics and Party Politics

Before turning to an examination of the individual political parties and their roles in the period between the revolution and guided democracy, it is important to note briefly one element common to all the parties or, more precisely, an element lacking in all of them. The missing factor is a clear exposition of party views on principles of economic policy.

Although it might be expected that political parties which place such great emphasis on their commitment to some form of socialism would display a strong preoccupation with economic matters, this is not the case in Indonesia. One of the many anomalies of

socialist politics there has been the prevailing indifference to economic doctrines, socialist or otherwise. Disagreement over economic policy has never been really central to the internal political struggle, although specific economic questions have figured
in the wrangling among political parties both within and outside Parliament.[17] This does not mean that genuine differences
on fundamentals of economic policy have not split the national
leadership. On the contrary: Economics lay at the root of the
disaffection that led to civil war in 1958, and it is widely recognized that economic difficulties foment much of the unrest and
instability that have haunted the country since its birth. But the
cleavage between political parties does not occur along the folds
of economic doctrine. Economic issues, like trade unionism, education, and most other aspects of modern life, are rarely dealt
with in their own terms but rather as an extension of party politics.

In large measure, the general lack of interest in economic doctrine reflects the fairly widespread agreement among all Indonesian parties about the kind of economy they want. Colonial and
postcolonial nationalism has been, as we have noted, historically
anti-imperialist and anticapitalist. Indonesia is no exception to
the rule. Those groups and individuals harboring more precise
ideas about the total pattern of the economy have, for reasons of
practical politics, refrained on the whole from publicly spelling
out their plans in detail.[18] All Indonesians are vociferously for a

17 One of the most highly charged of these economic issues, and one which
succeeded in dealing the final blow to the Wilopo cabinet and forcing its
resignation in 1953, is that of the peasant squatters on lands leased to foreign
estates. Like Indonesia's other economic problems, this one remains essentially
unresolved. Incidents involving squatters continue to erupt across the country
like a chain of restless volcanoes, and are a constant source of friction between
the peasants and the Army. Other economic issues that have contributed fuel
to the political fires have revolved around the role of foreign private capital,
and the allocation of revenues between densely populated Java, the main con-
sumer, and the other islands that include the major producers.

18 The reception accorded those who have been less reticent about the spe-
cifics of economic doctrine and program has not been one that would encourage other contestants in the political power struggle to be equally frank. The
prime example of what happens to a man who expresses home truths about
the realities of the Indonesian economy is Dr. Sumitro Djojohadikusumo, a

"national" as opposed to a "colonial" economy; all Indonesians are vigilant in guarding against any program or policy that might be said to smack of foreign control; all Indonesians favor some degree of government planning and control of the economy; all Indonesians agree that cooperatives have a valid place in the national economy. Beyond these generalizations and a few stock positions taken by party leaders—positions drawn from these broadly stated goals—remarkably little has been said by any party about the details of the national economy and the many economic problems the country faces. The resolution of these problems awaits the settlement of the political power struggle absorbing the national leadership.

Not only the inherently anticapitalist bias of colonial nationalism but the economic pattern peculiar to Indonesian society have militated in favor of this vague but genuine commitment to a socialist economy. Indonesia did not have any indigenous capitalists before the war. Both large- and small-scale enterprises were in the hands of foreigners: the Dutch, other Westerners, the Chinese, the Arabs, and the Indians. The new class of Indonesian capitalists that has emerged in the past decade is not only tiny in size, but its members, whatever riches they may personally derive from their current dabbling in business, are almost without exception men who for many reasons continue to express an outlook paralleling the socialism of the political parties that made them what they are today. The rising group of new entrepreneurs did not achieve their present status by virtue of their business acumen or hard effort; they have been the beneficiaries of the privileges and largesse dispensed by the political parties in power.[19] A majority of the new businessmen are little more than

leading economist and several times a cabinet member, who was one of the most thoroughly disliked men in Indonesian politics long before he cast his lot with the rebels in 1958.

[19] There are, of course, exceptions to this generalization. Curiously, the exceptions are almost all some bright young men of the PSI. Their Western training and perhaps even more important their Western contacts have enabled several of these young men to establish and maintain substantial business concerns that rank among the most prosperous in the country. This is so

front men who supply the names and hold the necessary licenses for what are popularly known as Ali-Baba firms: Ali for the Indonesian license-holder, Baba for the Chinese who conducts the actual business operations of the firm and, more often than not, has put up the capital for it as well.[20] A new group of entrepreneurs came into existence with the takeover of Dutch properties in December, 1957, following the United Nations rejection of a pro-Indonesian resolution on West Irian. The takeovers, which began after the government had declared a one-day general strike against all Dutch firms, were initiated by a PNI-affiliated union, followed in rapid succession by a series of SOBSI-directed takeovers. By mid-December, with almost all Dutch property in Indonesian hands, the Army placed the seized establishments under military control and Army officers have been at the head of these enterprises, which include mines, plantations, shipping companies, banks and trading firms, ever since.[21] Thus it is not only possible but entirely logical for the directors of Indonesia's major business enterprises to espouse, in varying degrees, the principle of government ownership and control of the economy, for their own role in the economy is the extension of their position in government.

These factors account for the universal satisfaction with the content of Article 33 of the Indonesian Constitution of 1945, the

---

in spite of the disabilities these men operate under because of their isolation from the parties in power.

[20] On the operation of these Ali-Baba firms, see Willard A. Hanna, "The Chinese Take a Second Look," *Bung Karno's Indonesia,* Part XXII (December 3, 1959).

[21] Still more government officials became embroiled in the day-to-day operation of the economy after the Presidential decree prohibiting aliens in rural areas from engaging in retail trade after January 1, 1960. The Chinese stores in every hamlet, at which this regulation was aimed, were replaced in part by government-operated retail trading centers, government-organized local cooperatives, and a variety of other official and semiofficial substitutes, none of them very successful. The effect on the economy has been almost as disastrous as the seizure of the Dutch properties proved to be. Thus, the PKI, which opposed the expulsion of the Chinese from the villages, in this instance did not forfeit too much popularity by its defense of the local Chinese because the villagers themselves were soon aware of the damage done by the removal of the Chinese.

Constitution in force during the revolution and again since 1959.[22] Article 33 in a very real sense embodies all the principles and values that Indonesians deem vital on the subject of the organization of the economy. Its very lack of precise detail also reflects the vague quality characteristic of the commitment most Indonesians feel to a socialist economy. Indonesian socialist economics, for most political parties and spokesmen, is much more definite about what it opposes than it is about what it stands for. In this, it is part and parcel of the larger picture of Indonesian socialism, a doctrine deeply cherished but not spelled out to any appreciable extent.

The Constitution of 1945 was a hastily prepared document that covered, as briefly as possible and often in somewhat ambiguous language, those vital areas of national life that the founding fathers felt it essential to include in such a fundamental charter. Significantly, Article 33 dealing with the economy, is part of that chapter of the Constitution headed Social Welfare. Article 33 reads:

Section 1: The economy is organized cooperatively, based on the principles of a Family State.

Section 2: Branches of production, which are important for the State, and which dominate the life of most people, are regulated by the State.

Section 3: Land and water and natural riches therein are regulated by the State and shall be used for the greatest possible prosperity of the people.[23]

---

[22] The Constitution was drawn up by the Independence Preparatory Commission in July and early August, 1945, and hastily adopted a few days after the August 17 declaration of independence. Much of its content reflects the familiarity of its authors with the American Constitution.

[23] P. 5 of typed copy of the Constitution, source not indicated but known to be a copy of an English translation issued by the Ministry of Information in late 1946.

The other article of Chapter XIV, Social Welfare, provides that: "The State takes care of the poor and the uncared-for children." This represents both a translation to the national level of the traditional social organization of the Indonesian village and, at the same time, something of a break with Indone-

The history of the effort to put Article 33 into practice is a dismal record of official promises never backed up by the needed legislation and still less by performance, of efforts to appease the growing demands of an increasingly dissatisfied population and to placate an increasingly uneasy community of foreign investors, and succeeding in neither. It is a tale of half-measures: a beginning made at introducing small-scale industrialization (1950-53, approximately) followed by a sudden shift in emphasis to large-scale industry; of a five-year plan, intended to be carried out from 1956 through 1960, with a major role given to foreign capital, but making no provision of the necessary economic climate for attracting new foreign capital or even for holding on to that already operating in the country.

The magnitude of the economic problems besetting postrevolutionary Indonesia has been dealt with elsewhere.[24] The aspect with which we are concerned here, the economic policies enunciated by the major parties, sheds very little light on the differences among those parties. Rather, what it reveals is the continual subordination of economic questions to those that were more purely or more recognizably political. The almost interminable

---

sian custom. The welfare of the individual has always been the responsibility of the family and the strong family system in the old days provided most of what care was needed for orphans, the handicapped, the destitute, and those otherwise unable to care for themselves. But the community too has also felt the responsibility to look after its less fortunate members. Since in village society the community generally consists of a number of closely related families, there was little need for any clear-cut distinction between family responsibility and the broader community responsibility for social welfare. By introducing this article into the Constitution, the national leadership in effect acknowledged the transition to a new social pattern, the explicit introduction of government into the family-based community system.

The other relevant section of the Constitution indicating the extent of the commitment to the principles of a welfare state is the second section of Article 27, dealing with citizenship, which reads: "Every citizen is entitled to work and to a reasonable standard of life."

24 For a useful analysis of the structure of the Indonesian economy and the principal economic problems its leaders currently face, see Douglas S. Paauw, "From Colonial to Guided Economy," in Ruth T. McVey (ed.), *Indonesia* (New Haven: Human Relations Area Files, 1964). A short but comprehensive study of the economy from the transfer of sovereignty through 1956 is contained in Benjamin Higgins, *Indonesia's Economic Stabilization and Development* (New York: Institute of Pacific Relations, 1957).

debate over the role to be assigned foreign private capital high-
lights both the essential agreement among parties and the absence
of any widely held understanding of the role of foreign capital in an economy such as Indonesia's. At the outset, no party
really questioned the continued need for foreign private investment in the foreseeable future.[25] At the same time, any specific
measure that would have facilitated the entry of new private capital became a political football. The problems of squatters on
foreign-owned estate lands, the takeover of Dutch oil holdings in
North Sumatra, and the economically unreasonable demands of
the SOBSI-controlled unions operating in foreign-owned enterprises were all left to be resolved by default. As the national economic situation deteriorated, the response of the political parties
in turn became more frantic and less realistic,[26] and slogans increasingly took the place of policy formulation.

The two parties of this period that did have a sophisticated
approach to economic issues, the PSI and the PKI, were in the
one case unable, in the other case unwilling, to advance their policies to fill the vacuum left by the failure of the parties in power
to provide any coherent approach to the economic problems of
the times. The PSI was at all times a minority party both within
parliament and out; therefore, while its counsels were influential far beyond the lists of party members, it could never rally
the kind of support needed to put through such politically
unattractive measures as the economic dilemmas of the moment called for. The PKI, on the other hand, had little to
gain from any genuine improvement in the economic situation
and in any case had far greater interests invested in supporting

[25] In the early stages of this debate, even those sections of the press generally hostile to the moderate Wilopo cabinet of the time (April, 1952, to June,
1953), approved the Prime Minister's statement that Indonesia wanted—and
would shortly provide the legislation necessary to attract—foreign private investment. See *Pikiran Rakjat* (Bandung), September 2, 1952.

[26] An exception to this generalization was the policy of the short-lived and
otherwise largely ineffective Burhanuddin Harahap cabinet, August, 1955, to
March, 1956. During this interim regime between the first and second Ali cabinets, the energetic Minister of Finance, Sumitro, aided by competent colleagues
in other ministries, put through a number of economic reforms that made
their effect plain even in the limited lifetime of that cabinet.

the politically popular if ineffectual programs of the parties in power through most of this time. Operating much of the time through its front organizations, the PKI participated vociferously in demanding higher wages, lower prices, increased *Lebaran* bonuses, expulsion of foreign capitalists and nationalization of their holdings, measures against the "compradores" of the imperialists (PKI parlance for leaders of the Masjumi and the PSI), free land to the peasants, and lower rents for tenant farmers. But the character of the mass demonstrations staged and the manifestoes proclaimed in support of these measures indicated that these activities were intended to be limited to agitation and propaganda and were not aimed at achieving any of the professed goals.

Thus, as will be seen in the following chapter, neither the doctrines nor the programs of Indonesia's socialist parties are concerned more than peripherally with economic policies.

8

From the Transfer of Sovereignty to Guided Democracy: The Socialist Parties

IN SPITE OF THE DWINDLING IMPORTANCE OF ALL POLITICAL parties except the PKI in the years since the elections, it will be relevant to glance briefly at those that emerged from the 1955 elections in strong positions, and at some of the minor ones as well. Of the four major parties, all but one, the NU, represented or claimed to represent a variety of socialist doctrine. We shall first examine the principal winner and the professed standard-bearer for marhaenism, the PNI. Next we will look at the Religious Socialists of the Masjumi. Then we will turn to the three Marxist parties: the two which were all but wiped out in the election, PSI and Murba, and the one which survived and waxed ever stronger and more prosperous, the PKI.

PNI

The impressive showing of the PNI (Partai Nasional Indonesia, or Indonesian Nationalist Party) in the 1955 elections demonstrated the effectiveness of its steady campaign to broaden support and reach beyond the ranks of civil servants which had been its initial source of strength. It continued to draw heavily on the reservoir of government officials, who, by virtue of the status traditionally associated with rank in Indonesia, commanded considerable support among the peasants. The party also increased its village support by the judicious handling of the appointment of new headmen from 1953 to 1955, the period when Ali Sastroamidjojo first headed the government. The party's prestige in the pre-election period was further enhanced when President Sukarno, finding his path blocked in other directions and especially after his break with Vice-President Hatta which dates from 1950, began to work more and more closely with PNI leaders. The popular impression that this PNI was truly the successor to the prewar PNI was once again affirmed when it took over as the foundation of its party principles and program the philosophy of marhaenism, so eloquently expounded by the President. Virtually all Indonesians today are marhaenists, or at least willing to endorse marhaenism, much as they are for church and the family. But it is the PNI that attempted and to a large extent succeeded in capturing marhaenism for itself. By identifying themselves at every opportunity with this philosophy so closely associated with the President, they rode to victory in the elections clutching the President's coattails.

The PNI program shows no striking differences from those of the other nationalist parties, nor, for that matter, does it differ radically from the programs of such religious parties as the Masjumi or of several of the Marxist parties. The PNI defines its basic guiding principle, marhaenism, as social-national-democracy, which it explains in the following terms:

> Indonesian society is still a poor and feudal society. The majority of the Indonesian people are small peasants. Marhaenism wants to achieve a society with equality and happiness for all. Thus, marhaenism is the principle which fights for the achievement of such a society, a socialistic society brought into accordance with the principles of *gotong rojong*.
>
> The ideals of marhaenism can only be realized in an independent democratic nation. Therefore, the marhaen's struggle is based on social-democracy, and it rejects all forms of dictatorship.
>
> An individual's actions are always determined by his needs and these needs are to some extent determined by society. Thus the individual

and society are inter-dependent. All events in history are manifestations of man's and society's needs, economic needs as well as ideological needs. Sometimes economic needs are more strongly felt, but sometimes ideological needs take precedence. The principles of historical
materialism contain much truth but are not entirely true.[1]

The party's election program was a mixture of recommendations for helping labor, aiding farmers, fostering economic development, nationalizing vital industries, and organizing youth
"as the new pioneers of society"; its foreign policy planks called
for an independent and active (neutralist) foreign policy and
opposition to imperialism and racial discrimination.

While the party's fortunes fluctuated erratically after the 1955
elections,[2] falling when the President in effect abandoned the Ali
cabinet to the attacks of its many opponents, rising when it became clear that his *konsepsi* as originally stated did not for the
moment mean a decisive shift in the distribution of power, its
doctrinal base remained unchanged. Doctrine had never, in any
case, been the party's strong point, nor did doctrine in any way
hamper the party's close cooperation with the PKI or, for that
matter, with the NU, either before or after the elections. Meanwhile, as it became increasingly clear that the center of power
was shifting to the palace, the party's program more and more became a chorus of "me too" sung to whatever tune the President
piped. Within the party, the cleavage grew between those leaders
who supported the President at the expense of the party and
those who were reluctant to put the party at the mercy of the
President's whim. Some party notables, the outstanding example
being Ruslan Abdulgani,[3] in effect moved into the palace and
became extensions of the President's policy; those who for one
reason or another had not seized the opportunity to identify

[1] *Kepartaian dan Parlementaria di Indonesia,* p. 27.
[2] For a detailed examination of the second Ali cabinet and the position of
the PNI during that period, see Feith, *Decline of Constitutional Democracy,*
Chapter 10.
[3] Because of Ruslan Abdulgani's identification with the President rather
than with the party whence he came, his many writings of recent years on
political ideology cannot be imputed to the PNI.

themselves with the growing centralization of power in the palace found themselves shunted off to a siding, away from the main road of events. By the time the President was well launched along the path of guided democracy, it was clear that the PNI as a party, for all its impressive showing in the 1955 elections, was no longer a major factor in the power struggle. It had lost whatever initiative it had once held; by the close of the 1950's it was not a maker of policy but a follower.

Masjumi

The Masjumi, once assumed to be the largest party in the Republic, still the second party after the elections, today banned from existence and tainted with alleged support of the 1958 rebellion, was always one of the more unwieldy and indeterminate organizations in a country notable for amorphous political groupings. The Masjumi was originally formed in November, 1954,[4] out of a merger of a number of Islamic organizations that included groups as far apart in principle as the welfare-oriented Mohammedijah and the conservative Nahdatul Ulama (NU). With the withdrawal of the latter group from the Masjumi in 1952, the Religious Socialists within Masjumi, led by Natsir, Rum, and Sjafruddin, together with Sukiman, the leader of a more politically conservative wing of the party, were confirmed in the leadership of what was still the largest single religious party in the country.

The Masjumi enrolled both individual and group members. Its curious and highly variegated assortment of supporters was reflected in the factionalism and fundamental disagreement among its top leadership. The presence of the NU[5] until 1952

---

[4] This Masjumi (Madjelis Sjuro Muslimin Indonesia, or Council of Indonesian Moslem Associations) was a new organization, and distinct from the wartime Masjumi founded under the auspices of the Japanese occupation forces. However, neither the similarity in name nor the existence of units left over from the earlier group was a handicap to the new political party.

[5] Another fairly amorphous body, the NU represents a large body of conservative Moslems who adhere to a much Hinduized, traditional Javanese interpretation of Islamic theology. Their watering of pure Islamic doctrine with

was only one source of friction; there were cleavages as well between the Religious Socialists and the long-time party chairman,
Sukiman, and between both these factions and that represented
by the West Javanese leader, Isa Anshary, a dogmatic proponent
of pure Islamic doctrine and an uncompromising foe of a secular
state. Isa Anshary, despite a meteoric rise early in the 1950's, was
never too much more than an embarrassment and a nuisance to
the rest of the party's leadership, although he clearly cost the
party many votes in Java. Much more serious was the bitter feeling between Sukiman, the man who could deliver the vote in
Central Java, and the Religious Socialists, headed by Natsir, who
wanted those votes but vigorously opposed Sukiman's conservative nationalist politics. Forced to remain together in an increasingly unhappy alliance, the Religious Socialists increased their
efforts to acquire more congenial mass support, which they found
for the most part in the Moslem communities outside Java.
Sukiman, meanwhile, whose approach to religion was more akin
to that of the Natsir clique than to the mystical heterodoxy of
NU, but whose politics more nearly resembled the extreme nationalist faction in PNI, gradually faded in importance, even in
his role of vote-getter.

Given this highly complex variety of supporters and the loose,
not to say disjointed, structure of the party, Masjumi's leaders
were always concerned to avoid alienating any more of its potential support than it had already lost. Thus, although the Masjumi alone sought to isolate the PKI from the other contesting
parties in the election campaign, its program in other respects
was not markedly distinct from those of the other leading parties. But the Masjumi suffered in the elections not merely from

---

ancient Javanese customs and beliefs makes them, of course, anathema to such
fundamentalist elements in Masjumi as that led by Isa Anshary. Lacking a
leadership of national reputation or sufficient experience to conduct the necessary parliamentary maneuvering, NU vacillated weakly among the more
dynamic forces in the political constellation. Its popular following and its
weak central organization made it a tempting base for any politically sophisticated group. The PKI and, to a lesser extent, the PNI have taken advantage
of the opportunity offered.

the defection of the NU and the voters alienated by the dogmatism of Kiaji Isa Anshary. It suffered as well from the fairly successful attempts of the PNI and the PKI to link the Masjumi leadership with the armed bands of fanatic Moslems known as Darul Islam.[6] At the same time, NU, and a smaller religious party, PSII, as well as the PNI and PKI siphoned off votes from the Masjumi in Java by claiming that a victorious Masjumi would impose restrictions on the customary Hindu-Javanese religious practices of the Moslem majority.

In spite of the participation of five of its ministers in the second Ali cabinet, the Masjumi had little influence on that government's policies. Almost invariably the other parties represented in the cabinet teamed up with the PNI against Masjumi. The greatest impact that the Masjumi had at the central government level during that period was to bring about the downfall of that cabinet by withdrawing its ministers in January, 1957. But even that was not only a negative but a fairly negligible accomplishment, since the days of the Ali cabinet were clearly numbered in any case.

The fate of the Masjumi was sealed when its two principal leaders, Mohammad Natsir and Sjafruddin, cast their lot with the rebels and defied the central government in the civil war that broke out in early 1958.[7] However stanchly other Masjumi

[6] Not all groups calling themselves Darul Islam endorsed the views of the leader of that group, Abikusno, who called for an Islamic state. Indeed, many armed bands with no link to Darul Islam or any other central organization usurped that name because it sufficed to terrorize the villagers in the areas they plundered. In the early 1950's, uprisings in such widely separated areas as Atjeh in North Sumatra and Menado in Sulawesi were attributed to Darul Islam when it was clear that neither group had any possible link of communication or of ideology with the original Darul Islam.

[7] Both Natsir and Sjafruddin had left for Sumatra some weeks before the rebels proclaimed their state in defiance of Djakarta. There is much evidence to indicate that both leaders had fled the capital, not with the intention of setting up a rival government, but because of the threats and harassment to which they had been subjected for some time. Their decision that the only path open to them was civil war reportedly came at a later stage.

However that may be, it is interesting to note that only a very few months before the establishment of the rebel government, which among other things charged Djakarta with selling out to the Communists, Sjafruddin, who was

leaders declared their loyalty to Djakarta and their refusal to seek the path of rebellion, the actions of those two leaders as well as the defection of numerous local Masjumi leaders in Sumatra to the rebel side were more than enough to condemn the party as a whole long before the President banned it from existence in August, 1960. Inflamed public opinion opposing the Masjumi was hardly appeased by the refusal of those party leaders who did not join the rebellion to condemn outright the ones who had. Leaders of rival parties faced no difficulty in labeling the Masjumi a party of traitors.[8]

Before its demise, however, the party made one more stand. In a last eloquent outpouring, the Masjumi leaders proclaimed their beliefs and principles in a series of brilliant speeches during the Constituent Assembly debates on the nature of the state. The most complete of these statements, and the one that generated most interest in political circles, was that of the party chairman, Natsir. Abandoning his usually cautious efforts to avoid alienating diverse groups, he argued passionately and determinedly for a state based on Islam. Never an advocate of a theocratic state, Natsir now declared that only Islam and not the Pantja Sila could serve as the basis for the state and the foundation of its constitution. The constitution, he said, must have its roots "in the character, way of thinking, aspirations and religious beliefs of the

---

to head the rebel group, still clung to the widely prevailing Indonesian thesis that Communism was not the essential issue involved and that in any case Indonesian Communism would be more Indonesian than Communist. See his speech to the Far East-America Council of Commerce and Industry, New York, October, 1957.

[8] Visible aid to the rebels from the Chinese Nationalists and from the Australians (who carelessly neglected to remove the identifying marks from some of their planes dropping supplies to a rebel outpost) and unproved but nonetheless widely alleged aid to the rebels from the United States, made the task of Masjumi's rivals still easier. The PNI and the PKI had for years been accusing the Masjumi of accepting aid from the West, and principally from the United States. As early as 1951, the PNI launched a vigorous campaign of charges, claiming among other things that the funds and the actual newsprint for the Masjumi-backed paper, *Abadi,* came from the American Embassy in Djakarta. With this background, it was not difficult to hurl accusations at the rebels and at the Masjumi of being in league with Western imperialism.

people living in the state. The Moslem religion will meet all these requirements." [9]

The basic principles of democracy, said Natsir, are twofold: Those who have the authority derive it from the majority, and the minority who differ from the majority have room to live in the society. The advocates of Pantja Sila, by rejecting Islam, the religion of the majority, as the basis of the state were thereby violating the first of these principles, he said, because their state would not reflect the philosophy or way of life of the majority. Pantja Sila, he continued, is only a common denominator, a boiling point of all different opinions; it is neutral, not active. On the other hand, Islam contains the principles that have been put forth as the basis of Pantja Sila, but in Islam these principles are not just sterile concepts but living values that have real substance and are clearly defined.

Any state based on religion is superior to states with no religious foundation, Natsir said. If the basis of a secular state is said to be humanity, one must define the basis of humanity:

> Communism, for example, has a concept of humanity which differs from ours. In the state they strive for, they consider the existence of property rights to be contrary to the principles of humanity while for us the existence of property rights constitutes an absolute requisite for humanity. . . . Religion gives a guideline for living one's life. . . . Such is not the case in a state without religion. A Marxist or a Darwinist has no place in his philosophy where a person can himself solve the struggle of life. All is looked at from the point of view of a process in nature; what is considered to be of importance for a human being is only his role in the group.

Pantja Sila, because it is secular, cannot be accepted as a religion; furthermore, its supporters do not necessarily support religion, he went on. "Communist ideology does not, for example, acknowledge God even though they (the Communists) accept Pantja Sila as the foundation of the state."

[9] Speech of November 12, 1957. Reprinted in *Abadi* (Djakarta), November 14, 15, 16, 18, 19, 1957.

Natsir's forthright call for a state based on religion and a constitution derived from Islam, and his rejection of any compromise with Marxist principles might have had more impact at an
earlier stage. Coming as it did when the Masjumi retained only
the shell of its earlier importance as the leader of a significant political faction, his speech caused no more than a ripple of interest outside Masjumi centers and was quickly lost in the flood of
declarations in support of Pantja Sila-*cum*-marhaenism advocated by the PNI, the PKI, and their numerous satellites.

PSI

The PSI (Partai Sosialis Indonesia, or Indonesian Socialist
Party), always small in size, all but wiped out at the polls in 1955,
abolished by Presidential decree in 1960, continues nevertheless to
exercise a disproportionately large influence on Indonesian political life. This capacity to affect the views and sway the decisions
of men far beyond the circle of its own membership has been
true of the party from its origins in the early days of the revolution.[10] Long after its leader, Sjahrir, had been forced out of office
as prime minister in 1947, his views and those of his principal
lieutenants were eagerly, if clandestinely, sought by an astonishing array of national figures from all points along the political
spectrum, including some of the party's most militant and out-
spoken rivals. Thus, in spite of the fact that the PSI received only
2 per cent of the total vote in the September, 1955, election and
thereby was reduced from the 14 seats it held in the provisional
parliament to only 5 seats in the elected parliament, the program
of this party merits some attention.

In large measure, the wide-ranging influence of the PSI can be
attributed to the personalities of its leader, Sjahrir, and some of

[10] The original Partai Rakjat Sosialis, formed in November, 1945, merged
the following month with the party led by Amir Sjarifuddin, to form the
Partai Sosialis, which, with its affiliates, formed the Sajap Kiri referred to in
Chapter 6. Following the split within the Sajap Kiri, the anti-Amir group
resigned from the Partai Sosialis and founded the present PSI on February
12, 1948.

his chief aides. But, whatever the extent and depth of their influence, the party's limited capacity to enlist loyal supporters in intellectual circles, let alone among the masses, was evident from the outset. Much of the failure to broaden the party's base was the result of the leadership's own decision to keep it a cadre party for the first two years after the revolution.[11] Later, when it was decided to seek a broader membership, many local leaders still clung to the earlier habits of carefully controlling entrance into the party and, as Sjahrir ruefully remarks, many candidates remained candidates for years, awaiting acceptance into the party. The party's energies were directed, in the early postrevolutionary years, not to attracting new members but to strengthening and clarifying its doctrinal base. The first PSI Congress, held in February, 1952, was devoted to a lengthy debate over ideology, a debate in which the question of whether or not to retain certain references to Marx and Engels in the party's statement of principles figured heavily. The references were retained but, as Sjahrir points out, those who argued for their retention were far from orthodox Marxists. Marxist doctrines were to be considered not as "a political credo or panacea, but as one of the tools for the solution of the many problems which the party faced within the framework of the realities of Indonesian society," and the retention of these references constituted "a confession of the party's faith and a declaration of its appreciation of the historical significance of Marx and Engels in the struggle for Socialism and for workers' emancipation." [12] The statement of principles and policy adopted at this first party congress therefore read: "The Indonesian Socialist Party . . . will endeavour to bring about social progress and change. . . . For this purpose it employs the methods of analysis and the conceptions used by modern socialism with

11 Decision taken at the first executive council meeting of the PSI, held in February, 1950. The PSI at that time had a few thousand members scattered around the country; by 1952, the membership had grown to 14,000 organized into 147 branches. By June, 1955, when the party held its second congress, it still had only 50,000 members at a time when the PKI had 500,000 and the PNI several million.

12 Sjahrir, *Indonesian Socialism*, p. 48.

regard to the capitalist world. It also employs the analysis used by Marx-Engels with regard to the development and the organization of capitalist society." [13]

The preamble to this statement of party principles contains an exposition of the special character of socialism in the newly liberated countries of Asia. For, as Sjahrir noted on a later occasion, socialists in the underdeveloped countries of Asia have had to face problems unknown to socialists living under different conditions; this has led some Asian socialists to feel like "underdogs" even among the socialists of the world.[14]

Principles and Policy goes on to state that the ills of capitalism, "i.e., the evil of liberalism and disproportionate unlimited individualism," the main targets of Western socialist criticism today, are not the problems of the Asian socialists. "Socialism in Asia, especially in our country, is faced with the task of increasing the means of production through mutual effort. This is in Asia more important than the transfer of property-rights of the existing means of production from the hands of an individual or a small group to the control by the communty. Socialism in Asia is faced with a lack in means of production." And, in extension of this point, the party statement declares that "Socialist planning does not exclusively mean nationalisation or socialisation. . . . There are means of production which are collective property, and there is also private and individual property. The organization of these three types of production is the object of socialist planning. In Indonesia, the main objective of socialist planning is to increase the level of production" and to abolish inefficient and outdated methods of production.

Like several European socialist parties, the PSI set about redefining Marxism in humanistic terms. Distinguishing itself carefully from the national socialism of Hitler and the socialism "taught by Moscow or the Cominform," the party, in its statement

---

[13] *Principles and Policy of the Indonesian Socialist Party, Adopted by the First National Congress of the Party at Bandung, from February 12 to 17, 1952* (Djakarta: Sekretariat Dewan Partai, Partai Sosialis Indonesia, 1952), p. 4.

[14] Speech at Asian Socialist Conference, 1953. *Asian Socialist Conference Daily News Bulletin* (Rangoon), January 6, 1953.

of principles, affirms its dedication to a democratic socialism that is "the consummation of all democratic ideals. . . . Socialism will succeed to create those conditions in which material economic conditions will not any longer constitute an obstacle for progress and development of all the potentialities of each human being towards goodness and beauty." And socialism as an international movement is defined to include those who support socialism on the basis of its humanism, those who do so on the strength of their religious feelings, and "the greater part (who) base themselves in this respect on the verity of the analysis and theories of Marx and Engels."

While the party membership was able to reach agreement on this statement of principles, no similar consensus was achieved on the strategy or tactics of party organization. As late as June, 1955, at the second PSI Congress, many party leaders still questioned the value of participating in the coming elections, preferring to concentrate their efforts on the development of thoroughly trained cadres. Despite the reluctance of these leaders, the party finally decided to engage actively in the campaign, with the poor results already noted.[15] Undaunted by its defeat at the polls, the party leadership drew the conclusion that its energies must be redirected to popularizing its aims, and set about organizing at the village level. While its parliamentary leaders were increasingly being forced on the defensive by the combined attacks of the PKI and PNI, other members of the party apparatus, working with unflagging if ill-founded optimism, were methodically setting up youth groups, women's organizations, and labor associations.

15 Sjahrir and other party leaders maintained that their electoral defeat was not the result of a program or an election platform that was too Western, too rational and therefore alien to the Indonesian people, as some foreign observers had suggested. The conclusion reached by these same critics—that for a country at Indonesia's stage of political and social development the only answer is dictatorship—is vigorously denied by the PSI's leaders. The triumph of essentially democratic parties and the fact that the PKI with full freedom of movement gained only some 16 per cent of the vote are cited by Sjahrir as evidence that Indonesia's masses are firmly oriented toward democracy. It remained for the PSI, he felt, to translate its program into the language of the masses. See *Indonesian Socialism*, p. 64.

For the PSI as for the Masjumi, the civil war that broke out in 1958 was a personal tragedy and a party disaster. While there was much sympathy in PSI circles for the rebels' point of view, PSI leaders were quick to condemn the resort to rebellion. Nevertheless, in spite of this vigorous disavowal of the rebels, in many quarters the PSI was charged with complicity in the civil war. These charges were not lessened by the defection to the rebels of the party's chief economist, Sumitro Djojohadikusumo,[16] and of a prominent military figure, Colonel Alex Kawilarang, popularly associated with PSI circles, as well as some lesser lights. Many foreign observers who sympathized with the rebels concluded that the PSI had lost its soul in the uprising and that, whether or not its leaders approved of the attempt, it was still the PSI's uprising in a sense, even if PSI leaders did not recognize it as such. Despite its attempts to dissociate itself from the rebels, in spite of the very genuine opposition in PSI circles to the rebellion, the party, like the Masjumi, was tarred with the brush of armed defiance of the central government.

There is no doubt that the PSI's leaders, like so many other Indonesians, knew essentially what plans were afoot in Sumatra. But, like former Vice-President Hatta, the PSI had tried to dissuade the incipient rebels from taking the irrevocable step of civil war. The political sophisticates of the PSI, perhaps more than other Indonesian leaders, had always dreaded the possibility of their country degenerating into a banana republic. Solving Indonesia's crisis by extraparliamentary means, they argued, would open the door to continued solutions of the same character. But this time, as in the October 17 affair, the facts of the case were immediately swamped in a torrent of accusations from rival groups eager to use the weapon so conveniently at hand.

---

[16] Sumitro's abrupt and secret departure from Djakarta came about in the first place because he was under indictment on charges of corruption and feared that in the temper of the times he could not expect a fair trial. Conferring with Sjahrir before his departure, Sumitro agreed that he would not go to rebel territory, nor would he under any circumstances join the rebels. As soon as he reached Sumatra, however, he reneged on both pledges, causing his erstwhile party considerable discomfort.

Once more, the PSI was branded guilty of something it might have done but in reality had had no part in.

Curiously, although the PSI's fortunes declined at an accelerating pace after the outbreak of the civil war, its counsels were still sought by some of its bitterest enemies. The palace itself was not immune from the habit of soliciting Sjahrir's views on a given subject, although this was always carefully done via third parties. While his advice more often than not was either neglected or deliberately flouted, Sjahrir remained one of the most frequently consulted political figures in Djakarta.[17] With its outlawing in several regions after the outbreak of the civil war, followed by the Presidential decree of August, 1960, ordering it to disband, the PSI as such came to an end. While it is unlikely that the party will be revived in the foreseeable future, it is less clear that its leaders will remain in the political limbo to which they were consigned with the consolidation of guided democracy.

Murba

Partai Murba (the Party of the Common People), like the PSI, has consistently exerted an influence far beyond the limits of its enrolled membership. Its leaders, too, are mostly younger men many of whom played an active military role in the revolution. And, also like the PSI, Murba's presumed popular support melted away before it reached the polling booths in September, 1955: With 0.5 per cent of the total vote, Murba's seats in Parliament were cut from four to two. But there the parallel with PSI ends. Murba, despite its smashing defeat in the elections, has steadily gained in importance since 1955 and has moved from the position of a militant but minor and somehow peripheral party to that of a major factor exerting significant leverage at the core of the present power structure.

This disparity between Murba's narrow mass base and its

17 To some extent, this is true even today, when Sjahrir is a prisoner confined to a military hospital in Djakarta. Together with a number of his aides and some of the key figures in Masjumi, he was placed in "protective custody" in early 1962.

influence at high levels of government is one of the many apparent paradoxes of contemporary Indonesian politics. But, unlike some of these paradoxes, the puzzling features of Murba's climb to the top can be unraveled. The evidence of Murba's current status in top government circles is obvious: Murba men (some of them not officially party members but so closely identified with Murba that for all practical purposes they can be referred to as such) hold some of the leading posts in the present government. Their position apparently derives from two sources. One is that Murba's leaders have always enjoyed a close personal relationship with the President. The other is that, unlike many parties that after 1950 deliberately or involuntarily cut their ties to their wartime armed auxiliaries, Murba reportedly has at its disposal, or at least retains close links with, several illegal military organizations of substantial size and strength.[18]

Given Murba's present pivotal position in Indonesian politics, it is logical to examine the party's origins and ideological base. Murba's origins in the Tan Malaka-led Gerakan Revolusi Rakjat and that organization's predecessors have been mentioned above.[19] Reference has also been made to the party's declared doctrinal base that would locate it along the political spectrum among the national Communists. Events since 1950, however, suggest that doctrine is not as crucial to the party's high command as one might expect from a vociferously Marxist-Leninist party, or

[18] Understandably, there is much speculation about the real strength of Murba's alleged military support and about the source of its firepower. Some highly placed PNI sources who are extremely antagonistic to Murba claim that Chairul Saleh, one of the nominally nonparty figures widely identified with Murba, "has his guns stashed away. He didn't get them from the Army, nor from the same sources as the PKI, but he definitely has them."

It is also possible that Murba's reputed military support comes from those units within the Army that are led by men close to Murba's leadership. Some observers find support for this possibility in such facts as that *Soemba*, a newspaper that had always had a tinge of Murba politics, died out at just about the time that *Nusantara*, a paper generally believed to represent Army views, came into existence and took over *Soemba*'s plant.

[19] See Chapter 6. Partai Murba was founded in October, 1948, immediately after the Madiun revolt, out of a merger of three of the chief component parties in the GRR. Symbolically, the actual date set for the party to come into being was November 7, the anniversary of the Russian revolution. See Kahin, *Nationalism and Revolution in Indonesia*, p. 313.

at least that its leadership demonstrates a well-developed capacity for flexibility when faced with a choice between ideology and expediency. As Feith has remarked: "The instructions which the party's leaders gave to their cadres, however, reflected much less of Marxism and Leninism than of an inchoate messianic radicalism." [20]

Until the advent of guided democracy, Murba's leaders had not suffered the disadvantages or burdens of high government office. It had been able to remain, and indeed had fed on the opportunity to be the clamorous opposition, no matter what the government in office. Thus it did not suffer for the failures of the successive cabinets of the 1950's; at the same time, it was able to contribute its mite to destroying or at least immobilizing those governments. Meanwhile, the Party's loudly professed opposition to Moscow- or Peking-dictated Communism did not hamper it from allying itself on occasion with its presumed enemy, the PKI. It also wound its way in and out of a series of alliances, sometimes tacit, sometimes proclaimed, with the radical nationalists of PNI, PSII, and numerous like-minded minor parties and splinter groups within parties.

Murba's party structure and organization is, by Indonesian standards, generally considered to be fairly cohesive and tightly knit. However that may be, Murba's leaders apparently do not feel that their path to power necessarily depends upon the party itself. They were not only the first group to declare themselves in favor of the President's proposal to bury the parties, but the only group to support his proposal without reservations. Again, in the Constituent Assembly debates over the President's proposal to return to the Constitution of 1945, Murba's spokesmen were among his most vociferous supporters. Some indication of Murba's views can be gleaned from the speech of one of its members, Sudijono Djojoprajitno, during that debate. His attack was leveled principally at "liberalism," which had to be rooted out by returning to the 1945 Constitution. Adopting the original Constitution, he said, would provide "a legal basis for finishing the revolution

[20] *Decline of Constitutional Democracy*, p. 132.

٠ . . a tactic which conforms with the logic of the Indonesian
revolution," and would negate the effect of the Political Manifesto of November 1, 1945, which had as its purpose "setting the
economic bases of liberalism."[21] Sudijono also placed great stress
on the fact that his party viewed the return to the original
Constitution as providing for the adaptation of guided democracy to the Constitution of 1945 and not the reverse. His arguments, as we shall presently see, were among the most complete
paraphrases and elaborations of the original proposal as presented by the President. On this occasion, as on many others, the
spokesman for Murba seemed to out-Sukarno Sukarno.

Is this willingness to accept and further the president's ideas
without question or qualification the source of Murba's favored
position in the palace? Doubtless it is part of the reason. But
there would seem to be other, more essential factors involved.
One of them might well be Murba's very lack of a strong, mass-
party base. A group of men whose chief claim to power is its relationship to the man who dispenses all privileges and power is
not likely to constitute much of a threat to its patron, and
Murba's reputed armed support is not of a size or character to
represent a threat to the palace. On the other hand, President
Sukarno, increasingly squeezed from below by a restless populace
and surrounded by an Army that has become a formidable power
in its own right and a Communist Party whose strength makes it
the other major contender for power, understandably would seek
to surround himself with a group of supporters whose primary
loyalty would be to him.

Murba and the PSI were two of the three Marxist parties of
significance in early postrevolutionary Indonesia. Whatever questions there may be about the future role, if any, of these two
parties, or about the parts their leaders may play in the days to

21 Speech of May 26, 1959, in *Inti Sari Pidato-Pidato Para Anggauta Kon-
stituante Berkenaan dengan Amanat Presiden Tanggal 22 April 1959, "Res
Publica! Sekali Lagi Res Publica!" dalam Pemandangan Umum Babak Ke-II
Sidang Pleno Pertama Konstituante Tahun 1959, pada tanggal 25-26 Mei 1959*
(Djakarta: Republic of Indonesia, Ministry of Information, 1959).

come, there can be no question about the continued importance of the third of these parties, the PKI.

PKI

The PKI (Partai Komunis Indonesia, or Indonesian Communist Party) has not only retrieved the position of influence it had before Madiun but has advanced so far that it has made its presence in Indonesia today the single most important issue in the country's political life.

At the beginning of 1950, the PKI had a long way to go to re-establish itself as a political party and to wipe out the opprobrium that still clung to its name as a result of the Madiun revolt. By 1951, it was clearly to be counted among the stronger parties in the country; by 1954, it claimed a membership of 150,000; and, in September, 1955, the election results revealed not only that the PKI was the fourth largest party in Indonesia but also that, with its trade-union affiliate and the splinter parties in its orbit, it had attained an unpredicted high level of political strength and maneuverability.[22]

The Communists restored themselves to this position by a variety of techniques: by extending their control and influence first in the trade-union movement, then in the peasant and youth organizations and in several minor parties that represented special local or racial (i.e., Chinese) issues; by careful wooing of and playing on the factions in the PNI's leadership; by campaigning ceaselessly to isolate the Masjumi while attempting to blacken

[22] Alimin, who had been the scapegoat for the Communist rebellion in 1926-27, had the responsibility for rebuilding the PKI after Madiun. He worked with a group of Indonesian Chinese Party members, including Tan Ling Djie, Siauw Giok Tjhan, founder of the PKI newspaper *Harian Rakjat,* and Tjoa Sik Ien, Indonesian delegate to and presidium member of the Warsaw World Peace Conference. By 1951 they had been replaced in the top posts by the present leadership of the PKI: Aidit, Lukman, etc. Both Alimin and Aidit had had their time in China, the latter particularly in 1949. In 1953 Aidit was responsible for eliminating the Indonesian Chinese from leading positions in the PKI.

the name of the PSI; by exploiting the numerous crises and divisions that beset the national leadership, including the upheavals in the armed forces; by nurturing a relationship with President Sukarno until he could no longer afford not to weigh the advantages and disadvantages of their support; and by pursuing for general public consumption a propaganda line that, subsequent to the 1952-53 Cominform shift to the right, adjusted itself neatly to the prevailing sentiment on major domestic and foreign issues, especially anti-imperialism and world peace.

The PKI's first postwar victories were achieved in SOBSI, where Communist leadership largely continued to dominate, despite the Madiun disaster, and there the PKI was able rapidly to resume control of those portions that had temporarily slipped from its grasp because of the uprising. The general unrest in the first months of official peace following the transfer of sovereignty manifested itself in the defiant attitudes, wildcat strikes, and disorder prevailing in many of the labor unions. It took little effort on the part of SOBSI's leadership to consolidate this situation into one of more carefully planned and organized strikes. By the summer of 1950, labor disorders had reached a point where the Natsir government felt obliged to arrest a number of union leaders. Nevertheless, the SOBSI unions continued their pattern of strikes until, in February, 1951, the government placed a temporary ban on strikes in vital industries. At this point the PKI-SOBSI strategy turned to sporadic strikes, sabotage of plantation crops and cargoes at the ports, and similar incidents to maintain and feed the unrest in the country and to dislocate the economy, especially in remote areas to which the government had difficulty in dispatching troops. The unions, meanwhile, increased their wage demands and pressed for shorter working hours and larger bonuses for Lebaran (the most important Moslem holiday in Indonesia) as well as for other benefits that, in the light of the decrease in production in most industries, placed unreasonable demands on the economy. Resentful of decisions by the official arbitration units established by the government, the union members' loyalty to SOBSI increased and the union leadership's hold on labor was tightened.

Guaranteed a good-sized mass following through its manipulation of SOBSI, the PKI next turned its attention to the various peasant groups and the rump youth organizations still clinging to their wartime associations. In both instances, the party was able to gain effective control of the central command of the most important of these groups, among them the BTI (Indonesian Peasant Front) and the Pemuda Rakjat (People's Youth), the successor to the wartime Pesindo, the socialist youth group.[23]

It is not difficult to account for the success of the PKI's appeal to youth groups. Dissatisfied, restless, uprooted, Indonesia's postrevolutionary youth responded eagerly to any leadership that played upon their discontent and offered them a rallying point for expressing their opposition to the *status quo*. The Communists' early success with important segments of the peasantry derived from much the same circumstances: widespread dissatisfaction and the restlessness attendant upon the dislocation of village life, especially in those areas that had suffered heavily in the course of the fighting. In spite of the PKI's relative neglect of land policy and peasant problems for some years (the party held the first National Peasants' Conference in its history in April, 1959), it won widespread support through its vociferous championship of such appealing, if vague, slogans as "land for the peasants." With the mass backing thus gained and with its long-standing close ties with key figures in the BTI's leadership, it was comparatively simple for the PKI to complete and solidify its takeover of this leading peasant organization.

Meanwhile, the PKI's representatives in Parliament had been active almost from the start in utilizing the disagreements between the Masjumi and the PNI to initiate cooperation with the PNI at the Parliamentary level. The first such instance was the

23 Pesindo, led by Wikana and with many graduates of the Japanese-sponsored Asrama schools in key positions, was closely affiliated with the PKI by the time of Madiun.

Communists' support of the PNI motion in October, 1950, demanding that the Natsir cabinet be replaced by a broader coalition; although the PNI maneuver was a failure, the support it received from the PKI helped to improve relations between some of the PNI leaders and the PKI. This was a strategy that the PKI continued to use profitably on various occasions.

In addition, although still denouncing the major nationalist and religious parties as members of the imperialist camp, the PKI in mid-1951 attempted to achieve a consolidation of forces by advocating the adoption of a National Unity Program in co-operation with PSII, Partai Buruh, and Partai Rakjat Indonesia. This attempt at establishing a limited united front collapsed rather quickly.[24] Thwarted in some measure by the governmental ban in February, 1951, on strikes in vital enterprises such as plantations and shipping, and hampered by the Sukiman government's arrest of large numbers of Communists and their associates in the summer of 1951, the PKI began to set the stage for its next gambit: the public defense of the PKI role at Madiun, undertaken in order to erase this issue from future politics. This the party attempted to achieve by issuing a "White Paper" on Madiun.

This document is an interesting exercise in the rewriting of history. The rebellion became the Madiun "provocation," a provocation described as the "climax of imperialist attempts to destroy the Indonesian Democratic Republic. . . . It also gave courage and solidarity to an oppressed people in their fight against the white terror." [25] The background of Madiun was related to the establishment of the Republic by "revolutionary groups which, due to their weakness and lack of understanding, were infiltrated from the start by pro-Dutch and pro-Japanese elements." Hatta, whose cabinet replaced that of the "democratic cabinet of

---

[24] In 1955, however, the PKI negotiated a "treaty" with the PSII, in which both parties agreed not to attack each other in the election campaign.

[25] The document appeared as an article by Miradsi in *Bintang Merah* (Red Star), VII, No. 12/13, 1951. All quotations are from a translation in the possession of this writer. The use of the old Comintern term "white terror" has a rather special anti-Dutch meaning of which, no doubt, the authors of the document were fully aware.

Amir Sjarifuddin," was accused of carrying on secret negotiations with van Mook by which "the reactionaries gained in their attempt to stem the tide toward a People's Democracy and the influence of the Communists." Mass demonstrations at various centers against their government's policy—which "violated democratic rights," illegally introduced "censorship" and other repressive measures, and removed "revolutionary and progressive elements from the military," turning the army "into a loyal instrument for the suppression of the people's movement"—were "ignored." The Republican leadership was also called to task for permitting foreigners to participate in the politics of the Indonesian Republic.[26]

The Paper further claimed that the incidents leading up to Madiun included attacks on PKI men and kidnapings and executions by the Siliwangi Division. The readiness to attack the Siliwangi Division, at the time the most revered and respected force in the Army, suggested considerable confidence on the part of the PKI, as did the attack on President Sukarno that followed. The document alleged that the final straw had been supplied by Sukarno himself, who "precipitated" the battle that began on September 19: "The people and soldiers who had been consistently anti-imperialist were finally forced to defend themselves as a result of President Sukarno's speech on the night of September 19, 1948. In his speech the President ordered a general armed attack, and the arrest and brutal slaughter of those branded troublemakers." This passage was an open challenge to Sukarno,

[26] Although this was not the only target at which the charge about foreign participation in government politics was leveled, the Republican leadership was open to attack on this issue to the extent that it related to the handful of foreigners working in its offices in Jogjakarta and abroad during the revolution. Any foreign assistants in the PKI were, naturally, not publicly visible. By the time the White Paper on Madiun appeared there were a number of foreigners working for the government in Indonesia, most of them technical experts assigned under the terms of Indonesia's Technical Assistance agreement with the United Nations. Although in government circles attitudes toward these foreign experts vary depending upon the individual expert's competence and personality, it has never been too difficult, in the current atmosphere of dissatisfaction and injured national pride, to create mass resentment against their presence.

who was apparently expected to recognize that in this era when his prestige was still virtually unchallenged, the Communists felt powerful enough to criticize him. At the same time they withdrew from an earlier propaganda line that had called him a "collaborator" with the Japanese Fascists.

Despite the fact that the White Paper appeared not long after the PKI had attempted to establish a *modus vivendi* with Murba, it is Tan Malaka and his followers who are accused therein of having spread false information about the program and plans of the FDR, information that is supposed to have instigated Sukarno's speech. Finally, the "Madiun incident," it is flatly stated, "absolutely was not an attempted *coup d'état,* as was falsely alleged by domestic and foreign reactionaries." Then, contradicting the official Soviet line used in 1948, the document stated: "To have made Sukarno's action legal, it would have been necessary to have definite proof [that] at the specific time of these accusations, the night of 19 September 1948, a Soviet Government had been set up in Madiun."

In this rewriting of history, a eulogy of Musso contains indications that not only the Madiun incident but some earlier Communist errors needed rectification. Thus, it stated: "From the first, Musso and the Soviet people did not believe Dutch accusations that the Republic was Japanese inspired. This was due to the fact that the revolution was then clearly anti-imperialistic," and "Comrade Musso patriotically published the independence proclamation in the USSR capital." [27]

The document ended with a plea that the anniversary of Madiun be marked by continuing the spirit of the united national front and quoted a statement adopted by the PKI Central Committee on February 6, 1951:

The success of the provocation plan of the Sukarno-Hatta government resulted in the division of the national anti-imperialist union, which

[27] Musso is reported to have carried out negotiations for the Soviet Union's recognition of the Republic since "Musso's conviction was that recognition by the USSR would be beneficial because, as a land of workers, the USSR was necessarily anti-imperialistic."

was being built up by the PKI, based on a national program which had been approved by all parties and people's organizations. The destruction of the anti-imperialist national revolutionary strength was brought about, among other things, by the killing and arrest of 36,000 people who were the backbone of the revolution. These incidents aided the Dutch attacks during the second police action, and the Sukarno-Hatta government's policy of capitulation to the Dutch.

In spite of the fury that the document aroused in many better-informed quarters, the Communists were fairly successful in using it to repair their damaged name. Except for those who had fought in the Madiun area against the Communists, and those who were consistently well informed about the internal situation, the exact details of the Madiun revolt had doubtless been blurred in the memories of most Indonesians who had been remote from the scene and who were soon thereafter fully occupied with the Dutch onslaught of December, 1948.

Having launched its campaign to clear its name and to refabricate the history of the Madiun revolt, the PKI kept forging ahead both in its efforts to gain mass support and in its Parliamentary activities, garnering strength in the latter sphere from the general dissatisfaction with the Sukiman cabinet's handling of the Japanese Peace Treaty in the fall of 1951 and reaping a harvest of unearned profit from Subardjo's clumsy handling of the Mutual Security Act incident in February, 1952. Soon after that event, which brought down the Sukiman cabinet, the PKI made its bid for a broad national front, which was in effect a bid to the dissatisfied elements in the PNI leadership who had lost out to the Wilopo wing of that party in the reshuffling of the government. The new plans were introduced in May, 1952, on the grounds that "the national bourgeoisie who had fled the democratic camp in 1948 were now sufficiently disabused of their imperialist allies that the restoration of four-class cooperation was again possible." [28]

This was an opportune time for the PKI. Though the Masjumi and the PNI were both represented in the cabinet, the

[28] McVey, *Development of the Indonesian Communist Party,* p. 78.

former found itself increasingly at odds with a wing of the PNI that felt deprived of Cabinet position. The latter group, led by Sidik, was willing to work with the PKI Parliamentary faction even to the disadvantage of its own party. Later in 1952 there occurred the "October 17 Affair," [29] which had adversely affected the fortunes of the PSI. The badly weakened PNI cabinet led by the Wilopo-Mukarto wing, which favored cooperation with both Masjumi and the PSI, managed to limp along until June, 1953. At that time, it was brought down by the Kertapati motion on the eviction of squatters from the oil lands in Sumatra, an issue manufactured by local leaders of the PNI and blown up to national dimensions by the PKI. It was at this point that the PKI's strategy of cooperating with willing leaders in the PNI moved into high gear. The first Ali Sastroamidjojo cabinet was formed in July, 1953, with the blessing of the President and the support of the PKI. In some respects the key to the cabinet was the new Minister of Defense, Iwa Kusumasumantri,[30] then a member of the Progressive Party, one of the splinter groups under the wing of the PKI. His handling of the Defense Ministry in this cabinet suggests either that he did not recognize the true strength of the PKI and hoped to utilize the Communist-oriented officers he placed in key spots for his own purposes, or else that he had revised the views he held in 1946 and also, presumably, at the time of Madiun and later, and was now ready to work with the PKI.

The PKI announced that, while not participating in the government, it would support the Ali cabinet. Still somewhat vulnerable as a result of Madiun, the party needed a close tie with a nationalist organization led by respected public figures whose loyalty to the Republic had never been doubted. Furthermore, the PNI, with its carefully nurtured following in the villages, especially in the outlying areas where the Communists had never

[29] An abortive and somewhat halfhearted coup generally ascribed to the PSI, in fact largely the brainchild of Nasution.

[30] Iwa Kusumasumantri appears to be one of those Indonesian Marxists whose views were sufficiently eclectic throughout that period to permit them to vacillate between the Stalinist and non-Stalinist camps.

gained a foothold, and with its first line of supporters, the civil servants, offered a new potential base to the organizing and propaganda skills of the PKI. At the same time the PKI provided the PNI with a source of support through its well-organized unions (SOBSI) and through its purveying of a right line always closer to the nationalists than the reverse.

The members of the Ali cabinet had barely taken their seats when the PKI put its first card on the table. Sakirman, leader of the PKI in Parliament, cited the new cabinet as "the outgrowth of a violent struggle between the forces of democracy and the reactionaries" and called for an active program to eliminate Darul Islam (DI) and other terrorist gangs. In his speech, he made the first demand for supplying arms to enable volunteer battalions and village self-protection units to fight DI; he also suggested that the apparatus used to fight DI be cleansed of any possible pro-DI elements by transfer and dismissals from its ranks—a clear recommendation to the Minister of Defense to start reorganizing the armed forces along lines more amenable to the new government.

There were two other ways in which PKI-PNI cooperation fitted into mutually agreeable patterns. One was the violent antipathy of the PNI wing represented in the Ali cabinet for the PSI; the other was the close tie between many of these PNI leaders and that essential figure in Indonesian politics, the President. On the first point, the PNI group then in power had until that time been the most aggressive in its attacks on the PSI. The PKI now joined in the fray in Parliament, expanding its attacks on the PSI as the "compradores of the capitalists," knowing that these attacks would be fully supported by the government's spokesmen. Apparently, there was never any doubt in the minds of the PKI leadership about which group constituted their most serious ideological rival; not long after the transfer of sovereignty, Sjahrir remarked on several occasions that the only thing that had kept a number of the disillusioned younger students and army officers from joining the PKI was the existence of his party as an alternate rallying point for those opposed to the old-line nationalist leaders and parties. While the election results in 1955 demonstrated that the PSI had grossly overestimated its popular following and shown little ability in the realm of political campaigning, the PKI, like other perceptive observers, realized that the PSI's central leadership still had an influence far beyond the boundaries of its own small membership or election-time supporters.

The other feature of this new and open PNI-PKI cooperation was the attempt to capture the President's ear and at the same time to utilize his overwhelming prestige. Many of the Ali cabinet members were associates and friends of the President from prewar days. Although there is little doubt that the PKI's leadership could have carried on its own public-relations job of wooing the President singlehanded, it was unquestionably faster and easier to use the numerous doors into the Presidential Palace opened with so little effort by the PNI ministers. Thus, the PKI used its new role of government supporter to build a closer relationship with the President through a friendly approach, while at the same time brandishing its growing power rather ostentatiously in the background to remind the President that, back door or front door, the PKI intended to move into the Palace courtyard.

Throughout this period of PKI-PNI cooperation, there were several basic issues in behalf of which the Communists utilized their position to heighten the alignment with the PNI and to extend their influence in the country. Their treatment of foreign policy is an example of the first, and their handling of the "Chinese question" illustrates the second.

The PKI started with the advantage that Indonesian foreign policy, no matter the party in power, is committed to a neutralist formulation. On most questions of the day it agrees with the predominating temper of the African-Asian bloc within the United Nations. International Communist policy in the 1950's was prepared to accommodate itself to this view to the greatest extent possible. The PKI in Indonesia found little or no fault with this policy as it was carried out by the first and second Ali Sastroamidjojo PNI cabinets. The PKI was also able to make po-

litical capital out of such events as the travels of Khrushchev
and Bulganin to India and Burma, widely reported throughout
the Asian press, and President Sukarno's trip to the U.S.S.R. In
Indonesia, the Communists were able to utilize the opportunities offered by the Bandung Conference of 1955 for their own
ends and made it in part a triumphal tour for the Peking delegates. Although there was hostility evident at Bandung between
anti-Communist delegates and the Chinese Foreign Minister's
entourage, the net effect of the conference on many Indonesian
first- and second-rank figures was an impressive picture of Chinese
strength and Chinese "friendship."

The complex of problems surrounding the Chinese in Indonesia and the rise of Red China has been dealt with by the PKI
in a highly opportunistic fashion. On the one hand, the party
has not hesitated, especially in areas where there have been particularly strong local grievances against the Chinese, to jump on
the prevailing anti-Chinese bandwagon. On the other hand,
the PKI has rather deftly spread the word not only of Peking's
might and relative proximity but of Peking's answers to the
rapid industrialization of a primitive economy. Peking in turn
has done its part with a continual parade of grand tours through
its territory by visiting Indonesians, at first mostly Indonesians
of Chinese descent, later any willing Indonesian, then top-ranking
political leaders, including Sukarno and Hatta. Scholarships for
study in China have been handed out in generous proportions,
and the numerous visiting cultural, trade, technical, and other
missions to China have been lavishly treated, notwithstanding
Peking's periodic attacks on Djakarta for its treatment of local
Chinese.

In the first phase of their upward climb the PKI defied local
antagonism toward the Chinese by having Indonesian Chinese
play prominent roles in the party's central leadership. This was
partially the result of the leadership's respect for the obvious
vigor of the new Chinese People's Republic, a respect that was
shared by a large part of the Indonesian political elite and that
led the Indonesian Government to recognize Red China quite

early.[31] It was also in part the result of the pro-Mao leanings of Alimin and other figures in the PKI who were beginning their rise to the top. Once the Chinese Embassy was established in Djakarta it became a valuable source of support for the PKI. At a peak it maintained a staff of more than 300 in the capital embassy, plus a string of well-staffed consular offices that were ostensibly concerned with the interests of the overseas Chinese.[32]

Meanwhile, in the fall of 1953 the PKI had reversed its earlier position by removing from conspicuous posts the Chinese members of its leading cadre. While playing down its partnership with the local Chinese Communists, the party did, however, for some time rely on a variety of Indonesian Chinese organizations as well as on less open but equally effective liaisons with "bourgeois" Chinese, who were more and more coming to the conclusion that the wind was blowing in the direction of Peking. Thus the Communists, while reaping the benefits of their "Peking" stance, have rarely risked forfeiting popular Indonesian support because of relying too openly on local Chinese.

More recently, the PKI has been able to profit by an ironic combination of these two factors: Indonesia's foreign policy predilection for being neutral on the Communist side and Indonesian antipathy toward overseas Chinese. The opportunity arose in connection with the establishment of the state of Malaysia.

[31] The ease with which recognition of Red China was achieved was no doubt to some extent the result of the ambivalent attitude the Nationalist Chinese Government had displayed toward the Indonesian Revolution. It might be noted that this official attitude was softened somewhat at the United Nations by the fashion in which the Chinese delegate interpreted his government's instructions. As for attitudes toward the local Chinese, the fact that a sizable proportion of Indonesia's Chinese population had sided with the Dutch, passively if not actively, coupled with the traditional resentment of this minority, left anti-Chinese feeling running strong at the time of the transfer of sovereignty.

[32] Associated Press dispatch by William L. Ryan, *Washington Post*, August 13, 1954. Reference has already been made to the large supply of low-priced reading matter made available by Peking and, after the opening of the U.S.S.R. embassy in Djakarta in the summer of 1954, by Moscow. Several Indonesians have commented on the very high proportion of these books that deal with military tactics, especially guerrilla strategy.

Not only has the PKI been the President's most enthusiastic and vociferous supporter in denouncing the establishment of Malaysia as an attempt at encirclement by neocolonialists; it has also backed up its views in material fashion. The best available evidence indicates that the PKI was the source of the initial bands of raiders that periodically surged across Indonesia's borders with the British-held areas of North Borneo, Brunei, and Sarawak in hit-and-run attacks designed to create havoc within those territories. At the same time, the PKI has not overlooked traditional Indonesian anxieties about the dangers inherent in a strong neighboring state in which the Chinese merchants of Singapore and Sarawak would play a major role.

Any number of circumstances have combined to play into the PKI's hands over the past decade. Perhaps the most convenient of these was the long-drawn-out dispute with the Netherlands over Irian. Until the settlement of that thorny question in August, 1962, it provided the PKI as well as the President with their most valuable political weapon: the ideal target for attacking the West, the perfect rallying point for extremist nationalism, and the never-failing smoke bomb ready at hand to becloud the scene whenever other, less desirable issues had reached the nuisance stage. Throughout that period, the statements issued from Moscow and Peking, as well as the myriad resolutions adopted by the endless bloc-sponsored congresses and conferences of Asians and Africans, never failed to include support for Indonesia's claim to Irian, support always couched in highly aggressive language.

The demand for West Irian had, of course, the perfect note of patriotic appeal to qualify it for inclusion in the PKI program of this period. That program increasingly embraced the slogans of nationalism, religion, and Communism, the threefold rallying cry into which the President gradually transformed his concept of guided democracy. Initially somewhat reluctant to adopt the President's *konsepsi,* the PKI soon realized the potentialities of this substitute for parliamentary government and today the leader of the PKI declares unequivocally that "Nasakom must form the core of the national cooperation." [33]

As Aidit has said in assessing the PKI's achievements over the past decade, the outstanding characteristic of Indonesia's Communists has been "their adherence to principle and flexibility in practice." [34] Shaken somewhat from its pro-Peking stance by the risks inherent in a split within the bloc, the PKI has been eager above all to overcome its own internal organizational problems and expand its role in domestic politics. Any concessions that this has required, from modifications of the party's position on the intrabloc dispute to alliances at home with religious ultraconservatives or bourgeois nationalists has not been too great a sacrifice. Indubitably, as Chairman Aidit has said, flexibility has been the hallmark of the postrevolutionary PKI.

[33] Aidit in an address to a mass rally at Bandung, December 16, 1962, *New China News Agency*, Peking (hereafter referred to as *NCNA*), December 18, 1962. See also the statement of the party's Second Vice-Chairman, Njoto, on February 6, 1963, in *NCNA*, February 8, 1963.

[34] "The Pressing Tasks of the Indonesian Communists and People," December 24, 1962. Excerpts from this statement by Aidit, as published by the PKI Central Secretariat, can be found in *NCNA*, January 1, 1963.

9

The March to Guided Democracy

ON OCTOBER 28, 1956, PRESIDENT SUKARNO TOOK THE first major step toward launching his own solution for Indonesia's problems: the adoption of a new structure of government to be known as guided democracy. In a speech marking the twenty-sixth anniversary of National Youth Day, he said that the 1945 decision to form political parties was "a big mistake" which resulted in too many political parties and in "political sickness. . . . This sickness is very dangerous when added to the sickness of regional and tribal feelings which now divide us." [1] Two days later he made a much more emphatic attack on the parties, declaring in another speech: "I propose that the leaders of the people confer and decide to bury all parties." [2]

Almost four years elapsed between this call for the dissolution of political parties and the order suspending overt public activities by all parties not yet banned.[3] During those four years, the Republic of Indonesia was transformed from an attempt at parliamentary democracy, however diluted in content and distorted in

[1] *Antara Daily News Bulletin* (hereafter referred to as *Antara*), November 8, 1956. *Antara* is the official Indonesian news agency; unless otherwise specified, the edition cited here is the one published in New York.

[2] Speech to the Eighth Congress of the Indonesian Republic Teachers Association, Bandung, October 30, 1956. (Broadcast over Radio Indonesia Home Service, Bandung.)

[3] Overt public activities by all parties were banned by decree on September 30, 1960. The Masjumi and the PSI had been ordered to disband on August 17. The other parties were subsequently permitted to resume limited activities for a time, but in April, 1961, all but 8 parties were dissolved by executive decree. Two additional parties were granted official recognition in July, 1961. The parties permitted to remain in existence were those that satisfied the re-

structure, to its present system of personalized rule. The steps by which this transformation was accomplished were paced far apart and followed frequent detours. They were carried out against a background of civil war, accelerating economic deterioration, and near hostilities with the Netherlands over the return of West Irian. Nevertheless, the final outcome was surprisingly close to the President's original concept as formally presented in early 1957.

The President's remarkable success in carrying out the major parts of his plan can be attributed in large measure to his consummate skill in the arts of politics. He kept the initiative at all times, appealing to the people over the heads of the parties, splitting the leadership within parties; at one point, when he despaired of cajoling or coercing the PNI leadership into line, he even covertly sponsored the establishment of a new party designed to support his plan.[4] He divided and confused his opposition, played his rivals off against each other, and bargained off-stage with the leaders of the only substantial sources of potential opposition, the Army and the PKI. Throughout this period, Sukarno held the center of the stage, campaigning for his plan in a barrage of speeches that did not appear to lose any of their effectiveness because of continual exposure of the same ideas and slogans.

Some of the President's success can also be attributed to the failure of his opponents to seize and maintain the initiative for any significant period of time, to formulate any viable coun-

---

quirements laid down by the President in a July, 1960, decree aimed at the simplification of the party system. The regulations stipulated that the parties must agree to uphold Manipol/Usdek (see below, this chapter) and various other ideological tenets, and that each party had to submit complete lists of its members to the government. In order to qualify for continued existence, a party was required to have a minimum of 150,000 members in at least 65 regencies.

[4] This was the new Partai Indonesia or Partindo, founded in August, 1958, by a splinter group from the PNI leadership that was instigated, though never formally acknowledged, by the President. Its principal leaders are Winarno, Asmara Hadi, and Asmoro Danuwinoto. It, too, proved a disappointment, failing to attract the necessary popular following to give substance to its claim to be a significant factor on the political scene.

terplan of their own, or even to unite in opposition to him.[5] The civil war which broke out in 1958 was an obvious case of the exercise of initiative by dissident leaders. However, it also demonstrated that these same leaders lacked sufficient capacity for sustained military operations or effective political organization. The civil war as such is beyond the scope of this paper,[6] except insofar as it affected the timetable of the transition to guided democracy and altered relationships within the power structure in Djakarta. It should be noted, however, that the rebellion apparently did not have the support of a majority of the population outside Java and, despite considerable covert sympathy for the rebels' point of view in many circles in Djakarta, a majority of Sukarno's critics clearly deplored the resort to rebellion even more than they deplored the actions of the President.

This is not to say that there was no significant opposition to the President besides that offered by the rebels. Sukarno himself frequently calls attention to the modifications he was forced to

[5] The National Youth Day speech provoked some opposition from the party leaders who could no longer ignore the President's challenge to them. Until then, despite their uneasiness over Sukarno's attacks on party politicking, most party leaders had felt that the threat was not sufficient to warrant the risk of defying the President. Indeed, many of them had found Sukarno's references to irresponsible political infighting convenient springboards from which to attack their own foes. They parroted the President's charges and laid the blame for the divisive behavior paralyzing government at their respective opponents' doorsteps. But the Youth Day speech forced them to take a stand. Their response was characteristically ambiguous.

After a brief flurry of protests, all but a handful of political leaders vied with each other in publicly declaring their support of the President while privately seeking backdoor deals with the palace that would ensure their own —and in some cases, their parties'—continued role in whatever new power structure was to emerge. Except for those party leaders who threw in their lot with the rebels, what opposition remained was extremely timid and hesitant and became more so in the face of the President's obvious determination to pursue his chosen course. The opposition also retreated before the mob violence to which it was increasingly subjected and which the authorities not only did little to curb but indeed may sometimes have initiated.

[6] A comprehensive study of the civil war remains to be written. Useful, detailed dispatches on the early months of the rebellion can be found in *The New York Times* for February and March, 1958. For a British journalist's firsthand account of the first year of the rebellion and the central government's counterattack, see James Mossman, *Rebels in Paradise: Indonesia's Civil War* (London: Jonathan Cape, 1961).

make in his plan because of opposition from various groups. But his ultimate goal was to replace a parliamentary system of government based on principles of majority rule with a system based on a form of consensus. This he accomplished. When the political parties refused to dissolve themselves, he dropped his frontal attack on them and set about reaching his goal by other means. In the process, however, he was able to neutralize the parties, stripping all but one of them, the PKI, of any effective power. Today, ten political parties are legally authorized to exist.[7] However, again with the exception of the PKI, they have ceased to figure in any realistic calculations of the country's power structure. Individuals identified with the top command of these parties are found among the present national leadership but, always excepting the Communists, they derive their current status from the President's personal backing and not from their positions within their respective parties.

The sequence of steps by which the President installed his own system of government falls roughly into three stages. The first stage began with his attempt to eliminate the parties, followed by the formal announcement of his plan or *konsepsi*. The plan was presented in a nationwide broadcast on February 21, 1957, just as the second Ali cabinet was grinding to a halt.[8] In this speech, the President called for a guided democracy and outlined the mechanism for achieving it: the appointment of a *gotong-rojong* cabinet giving representation on a proportional basis to all parties represented in Parliament, and of a National Advisory Council

[7] The first eight parties to receive official recognition were PNI, NU, PKI, Partai Murba, Partai Katholik (Catholic Party), PSII (Partai Sjarikat Islam Indonesia or Islamic Association Party of Indonesia, a conservative Moslem group that had split off from the Masjumi in April, 1947), Partindo and IPKI (League of Upholders of Indonesian Independence, a small party closely connected with the Army). The two additional parties officially recognized in July, 1961, were Parkindo (Partai Kristen Indonesia or Indonesian Christian Party, a Protestant group), and Perti (Persatuan Tarbiah Islamijah or Islamic Education Party, a minor Moslem party largely Sumatran in membership).

[8] See *Abadi*, February 22, 1957. It is noteworthy that in the many volumes of the President's speeches that have been published and widely distributed over the past six years by the Ministry of Information, this original presentation of the plan for guided democracy is never included.

of representatives of "functional groups" which would "reflect society as the Cabinet would reflect Parliament." Although the widely advertised speech proved something of an anticlimax, it did provoke a series of coups by military leaders in Sumatra and Sulawesi and considerable, if less militant protests from some factions in Djakarta.[9] Undeterred, the President seized the opportunity provided when the Ali cabinet finally resigned on March 14, 1957, to declare a state of war and emergency for the entire country. He thus concentrated extraordinary powers in his own hands, although by this move he also strengthened the position of the military. Acting as his own cabinet formateur, the President then proceeded to install an extra-parliamentary cabinet of experts. While this was not the *gotong-rojong* cabinet he had demanded in his *konsepsi,* it reflected his determination to give actual if not explicit representation to the Communists.[10]

Despite growing evidence of dissension, Sukarno pushed ahead with the installation of a personally appointed National Advisory Council on July 11, 1957.[11] He also stepped up his campaign for the return of West Irian. In September, there was a final attempt to harmonize the conflicting views of the dissident leaders in the outer islands with those of the central government through a huge *Musjawarah Nasional* (National Consultative Conference), but the conference solved nothing. In December, after the U.N.'s

[9] Masjumi and the Catholic Party were the only parties to reject the plan outright. Of the other important parties, NU, PSI, IPKI, Parkindo, and PSII responded with ambiguities that reflected both their displeasure with the plan and also their fear of defying the President. PKI, which had initially attacked the President's attempt to dissolve the parties, became one of the most vigorous supporters of *konsepsi.*

Although some factions in the PNI leadership were known to oppose the plan, PNI also gave it enthusiastic public support. PKI and PNI vied with each other in organizing mass demonstrations approving the plan. Murba's leaders, having little status because their party lacked a large following, backed the President from the start.

[10] The new cabinet, headed by the nonparty figure, Djuanda, had four members each from PNI and NU, one each from Parkindo, PSII, and Masjumi, two followers of Murba, and two crypto-Communists popularly associated with PKI. For the names and backgrounds of the members of this Cabinet, see *Antara,* April 9, 1957.

[11] See *Antara,* July 12, 1957, for details on the members of the Council and the "functional groups" which they represented.

failure to adopt an Indonesian-supported motion on West Irian, the expulsion of the Dutch from Indonesia precipitated economic disaster. By February, 1958, the long-smoldering rebellion in Sulawesi and Sumatra had been fanned into a full-fledged civil war, with a rebel government established in defiance of Djakarta.

The prestige of the central government was greatly enhanced by the dispatch with which its armed forces crushed the rebellion. At the same time, much of the President's opposition in Djakarta was eliminated because those parties and groups suspected of sympathy with the rebels were badly weakened. Nevertheless, this first stage drew to a close with Sukarno unable to speed up the tempo of the transition to guided democracy.

In February, 1959, Sukarno launched the second stage of his campaign: a drive to legitimize further changes in government by a return to the Constitution of 1945, which gave broad powers to the President. Balked by the Constituent Assembly, which failed to endorse the 1945 Constitution by the necessary two-thirds majority, Sukarno dissolved the Assembly and reinstituted the 1945 Constitution by decree on July 5, 1959. The President justified this move and presented an elaborate elucidation of his *konsepsi* the following month in his Independence Day address, which, in edited form, was officially designated the country's Political Manifesto or Manipol. The five key points of that speech were summarized in an acronym, Usdek,[12] and Manipol/Usdek became the symbol of the new campaign. Manipol/ Usdek was approved as the Broad Lines of Policy of the State by the Supreme Advisory Council,[13] the installation of which on

[12] Usdek stands for the initial letters of the five phrases making up the plan: *Undang-undang dasar 1945* (the Constitution of 1945); *Socialisme à la Indonesia* (Indonesian Socialism); *Demokrasi Terpimpin* (Guided Democracy); *Ekonomi Terpimpin* (Guided Economy); and *Kepribadian Indonesia* (Indonesian Identity).

[13] Manipol, together with the President's Independence Day Address of 1960 and his speech to the U.N. General Assembly on September 30, 1960, were also approved as the Broad Lines of Policy of the State in the sense of Article 3 of the Constitution by the MPR or People's Assembly for Deliberations shortly after its installation in November, 1960. See *Keputusan Dewan Pertimbangan Agung Tentang Perintjaan Pedoman Pelaksanaan Manifesto Politik Republic*

August 26, 1959, completed the second stage of the march toward guided democracy.

The final steps in the transformation were made in 1960. In March, Sukarno suspended the elected Parliament after it refused to approve the budget he had submitted. He replaced it in June with a Parliament whose members he appointed.[14] The mechanism of guided democracy had been installed; Sukarno had achieved what he set out to do in the fall of 1956.

Each stage in the process had been symbolized for popular consumption by heavy emphasis on slogans. First came *konsepsi,* which was replaced by Manipol/Usdek. Manipol/Usdek gave way to Nasakom[15] (Nationalism, Religion, Communism); and Nasakom in time was exchanged for Resopim[16] (Revolution, Indonesian Socialism, National Guidance). These slogans were augmented by such theses as the Message of the Suffering of the People and the Djakarta Charter.[17] But the President's basic themes

---

Indonesia, No. 1/Kpts/Sd./1/61 (Djakarta: Republic of Indonesia, Dewan Pertimbangan Agung Republik Indonesia, n.d., [presumably February, 1961]).

14 The official obituary of the elected Parliament reads: "The Dewan Perwakilan Rakjat . . . proved unable to fulfill its task under the new conditions created by the 5 July Decree, although given a certain period of time . . . to adjust itself to the atmosphere of Guided Democracy. Therefore, on 5 March, 1960, by Presidential Edict No. 3/1960, the members of this Council, which still labored in an atmosphere of liberalism, were relieved of their functions." *Indonesia, 1961* (Djakarta: Republic of Indonesia, Department of Foreign Affairs, April, 1961), p. 48.

15 The Indonesian words from which Nasakom is formed are *Nasionalisme, Agama, Komunisme.*

16 Resopim is derived from *Revolusi, Sosialisme Indonesia, Pimpinan Nasional* (National Guidance). For the text of the speech in which it was introduced, see Sukarno, *Dari Proklamasi sampai Resopim: Terbitan berisi Pidato Proklamasi Diutjapkan oleh P.J.M. Presiden Republik Indonesia pada tiap tanggal 17 Agustus sedjak tahun 1945 sampai 1961* (Djakarta: Republic of Indonesia, Department of Information, n.d. [probably 1962]), pp. 481-524.

17 The Message of the Suffering of the People as described by President Sukarno, consists of three parts: (1) to establish a just and prosperous society; (2) to erect a unitary state based on the principles of unitarianism; and (3) to follow the system of *musjawarah* in a unicameral body or system. See Sukarno, *Res Publica! Once More Res Publica!* address to the Constituent Assembly on April 22, 1959 (New York: Republic of Indonesia, Permanent Mission to the United Nations, 1959), p. 9.

The Djakarta Charter is a document signed on June 22, 1945, by nine

remained the same, just as the basic problems his speeches and slogans were designed to answer remained essentially unchanged. As the officially proclaimed ideology for the present system of government, the ideas he propounded merit some detailed consideration. For the sake of convenience, these ideas can be examined under the headings provided by official Indonesian terminology: guided democracy, the 1945 Constitution, guided economy, Indonesian identity, and Indonesian socialism.

---

prominent leaders, endorsing essentially the same points as the Message of the Suffering of the People. The signers were Sukarno, Hatta, A. A. Maramis, Abikusno Tjokrosujono; Abdulkahar Muzakir; Agus Salim; Achmad Subardjo; Wachid Hasjim, and Mohammad Yamin.

10

Guided Democracy in Theory

The Basic Doctrine Expounded

ALTHOUGH CURRENT OFFICIAL HISTORIES[1] DATE THE BIRTH of guided democracy from the National Youth Day speech, there was ample evidence at a much earlier stage of the President's dissatisfaction with parliamentary democracy and its relevance for Indonesia. He set forth his views, for example, in May, 1953, in a speech to the Islamic students at the University of Indonesia:

I have never met the word democracy in Islamic terminology. I have only met *"musjawarah."* Moreover, I never met the term "votings" in the Islamic vocabulary. What is suggested by Islam is *"musjawarah,"* discussion, negotiations. It does not suggest votings, so that one can say: My party has the biggest number, I should win. No!

Democracy is *musjawarah.* . . . We do not want autocracy. . . . Not the half plus one is always in the right, not the half plus one is always winning, no, not at all! Democracy is not an aim. Democracy is merely an instrument of wisdom, a method to achieve any object in wise manner in social and state affairs. One manner, a manner we all agree with: our democracy is, as I often say, a democracy with leadership. A democracy with wisdom and not mere voting. . . . Democracy does not mean majorocracy, or more clearly *our* democracy does not mean

1 See, for example, H. Roeslan [Ruslan] Abdulgani, *Pendjelasan Manipol dan Usdek* (Djakarta: Departemen Penerangan R. I., 1960); and *Manipol/Usdek in Question and Answer* (New York: Permanent Mission of the Republic of Indonesia to the United Nations, n.d. [probably Summer, 1961]). Although no author is given for the latter document, it is generally understood that Ruslan Abdulgani supplied the material for it.

majorocracy, because we are obliged to hold *musjawarah* and not mere voting. . . .[2]

Sukarno returned again and again to the theme that a form of government that determines its course on the basis of a majority of votes is unsuitable for Indonesia and must be replaced by some form of consensus with guidance. His words had the comforting ring of familiarity for many Indonesians. Seeking guidance in public affairs from the elders of the community is by no means an alien concept in Indonesia. Traditional village society throughout the country has relied heavily on just such exercise of leadership by the elders. Nor is this approach out of line with Islamic tradition, as the President took pains to point out. Furthermore, the core of the Javanese approach to the world is to seek harmony in all relationships; and the Javanese tradition is the cultural tradition of a majority of the Indonesian people. In practice this generally means that instead of trying to alter a situation to meet his own desires, the Indonesian tries to bring himself into harmony with the prevailing situation by adjusting his behavior and attitudes.[3] Even the terms Sukarno chose to use in introducing his plan were not new and therefore not particularly strange to Indonesian ears. A call for guided democracy could hardly be expected to arouse widespread alarm in a country accustomed to hearing proposals for a guided economy from its more conservative parties.[4] In short, Sukarno once again was crystallizing and expressing feelings profoundly held by a majority of his countrymen.

Sukarno's impatience with parliamentary democracy was ap-

[2] Major portions of the speech are contained in translation in *Indonesian Affairs*, III (June–July, 1953), 36-57; other extensive excerpts are to be found in *Abadi* for May 8, 1953.

[3] In Javanese tradition there is much underlying reliance on magic to achieve this harmony. The appropriate incantation, the sudden tap of the magic wand will abruptly bring harmony out of chaos. The slogans that the President has invoked so assiduously at each stage in his drive for guided democracy apparently have for many Indonesians, if not for the President himself, a quasi-magical significance.

[4] The term guided democracy appears, for example, in the Masjumi Party platform in 1954. See *Kepartaian dan Parlementaria di Indonesia*, p. 441.

parently strengthened by his observations when he began travel-
ing abroad, shortly before he launched his campaign for guided
democracy. Although his travels began with visits to the West, it
was his guided tours through Soviet bloc countries that clearly
impressed him most. "If you were to ask me to make a comparison between what I learned and experienced during my first
wave of visits to the United States, Canada, Italy, West Germany
and Switzerland," he said in a speech shortly after his return in
1956, "and what I learned and experienced during my second
wave of visits to these socialist countries, I say firmly, once again
firmly, that I gained more experience and knowledge during
my second wave of visits." He referred especially to what he had
seen in Communist China, particularly the progress in economic
construction and the hard work, the "antlike" activity of the people there. It was this "intensive training and intensive use of
cadres without mutual strife among the people" that he cited as
partial inspiration for his demand for the dissolution of Indonesia's political parties.[5]

Although Sukarno's trips abroad strengthened his inclination
to do away with parliamentary democracy, he has always argued
that Indonesia should seek a system of government that is primarily Indonesian and not patterned on alien systems. Indonesia,
he has said, possesses an original type of democracy, a living
democracy that is rooted in thousands of years of communal life.
It is not based on formal voting procedures but is, rather, a way
of life for the Indonesian people. There is no need for Indonesians to copy foreign conceptions of democracy; they have
their own.[6]

In an effort to make clear the distinction between the guided
democracy he proposed and the forms of government flourishing
in Soviet countries, he emphasized that, in Communist states, freedom from want was given priority over freedom of speech. He

[5] In addressing the Indonesian Teachers Congress, Bandung, October 30,
1956.
[6] See his speech to police officials in Surabaya, November 25, 1956, in *Antara*,
November 27, 1956.

referred on several occasions to his exchange on this subject with
Madame Soong Ching Ling:

> I asked Madame Soong Ching Ling: "Why do you give priority to
> freedom from want?" Her reply was most striking. She replied in Eng-
> lish: "Yes, my brother, because the stomach does not wait . . . an
> empty stomach cannot be ordered to wait. One can say to others: next
> year is time enough for you to express your opinions, you will get your
> freedom of speech next year, or five years later, or ten years later, only
> then may you express your opinions, at present you just have to obey,
> just to follow, just to keep quiet. One can say such a thing. But one
> cannot say to a poor man: Wait, wait, wait—don't ask for food now—
> next year will do. . . ." Therefore, what is given precedence in their
> efforts is freedom from want. Later on—if need be, freedom of speech.

For Indonesia, the President stated, "Nothing is given priority
and nothing is postponed until later: this comes first and this
comes later. No! But, concurrently, freedom of speech and freedom from want, together." [7]

While claiming to eschew the priorities which govern the Soviet system, the President has always been much more vigorous
in attacking the Western system of parliamentary democracy,
which he consistently identifies with "free-fight liberalism." Typical of his views on this is his statement: "Let us not stand on the
idea of liberalism. According to this idea of liberalism every human being has the right to express his opinions loosely. What do
we see from the practice of liberalism? . . . We see our fatherland in a fighting arena of 46 parties." [8]

In the "Marhaen and Proletarian" speech, which Sukarno re-
gards as one of the most important expressions of his political
philosophy, he explains that it is impossible for Indonesia to seek
its socialist society through parliamentary democracy:

[7] *Marhaen and Proletarian: Speech before the Indonesian Nationalist Party
at the Party's Thirtieth Anniversary at Bandung, July 3rd, 1957,* Translation
Series, Modern Indonesia Project (Ithaca: Department of Far Eastern Studies,
Cornell University, 1960), p. 20.

[8] Speech at Gadjah Mada University, May 28, 1958, p. 18.

because parliamentary democracy grew out of the philosophy of political liberalism and liberalism is the enemy of socialism. . . . Socio-democracy . . . is in fact the challenge to parliamentary democracy. . . . Therefore, and for just that reason, we are instituting a democracy that differs from that parliamentary democracy, namely a socio-democracy. . . .

We cannot create a just and prosperous society by parliamentary democracy alone. . . . [L]et us aim not only at parliamentary democracy; we must also create economic democracy; not only equality in the political field but also equality in the economic field. Political-economic democracy, political democracy and economic democracy side by side. This is what the Indonesian Nationalist Party calls socio-democracy.

The attack on liberalism sharpened as the drive toward guided democracy gained momentum. Parliamentary democracy, branded as the liberal, capitalist system that gave rise to imperialism and colonialism, was no longer acceptable as even part of the new system. A popular official guide to Manipol/Usdek explained that "precisely because our National Revolution is opposed to imperialism, it is impossible for us to follow the Western system of democracy." Liberalism, the document charged, was responsible for the exploitation, black-marketeering, and other ills plaguing the country. Liberalism was also held responsible for corrupting the votes of the majority of the people because "the people were used for the selfish purposes of political leaders, each seeking to gain more votes for his party, so that a complicated multi-party system grew up in this liberal atmosphere." Because liberalism does not set proper bounds upon people's activities, it was charged, "individuals and groups try to win their own advantage and do as they like. Through this situation, the social consciousness became poisoned with provincialism, group-ism, multi-partyism, separate territorial policies . . . with people lining their own pockets when they should have been engaged in organizing and expanding various fields of production and with people scraping up wealth at the public expense."

In much the same way that parliamentary democracy was gradually promoted from being just an unsatisfactory system for Indonesia to being the root cause of most of the country's current woes, so did other shifts occur in the course of the drive toward guided democracy. In the initial stages of his campaign, the President put heavy emphasis on the transitional nature of guided democracy. It would be, he said, "an implemental democracy, a *karja* (working) democracy. . . . What is it that it seeks to implement? It seeks to implement what has been aspired to by the Indonesian nation, primarily in the social field—specifically the creation of a just and prosperous society."[9] To achieve this goal, he explained, requires

> an architect, and as this architect I have in mind a National Planning Board . . . composed of experts in the development and planning of a just and prosperous society. . . . We must give this National Planning Board the important and clear task of drawing up a blueprint for a just and prosperous society. . . . And after we have this blueprint, brothers, we must implement this blueprint, because the blueprint will have become the national plan. Our sole task is to implement it. Of course, in implementing it, we may still conduct consultations, but these consultations should be restricted to the implementation of the blueprint. . . . Guided democracy is a democracy to implement this blueprint and in implementing this blueprint there should be guidance, the guidance of . . . really expert men. This is the essence of guided democracy.

This definition of guided democracy as a tool, and its corollary, that the system would only be a transitional stage, was repeated by the President and echoed by his chief supporters for some time. Democracy, Premier Djuanda told the elected Parliament in March, 1959," must have discipline and must have guidance. In the meantime, democracy is an instrument and not a goal."[10] But

9 *Ibid.,* p. 15.
10 Djuanda, *Keterangan Pemerintah Mengenai Pelaksanaan Demokrasi Terpimpin Dalam Rangka Kembali Ke U. U. D. 1945: Diutjapkan oleh Perdana Menteri H. Djuanda dalam Rapat Pleno Dewan Perwakilan Rakjat pada hari Senen tanggal 2 Maret 1959 mulai djam 19.30* (Djakarta: Kementerian Penerangan R. I., 1959), p. 4.

even while his aides were representing guided democracy as only a beginning stage in a much longer process, the President was shifting his ground slightly but significantly. In his appeal to the Constituent Assembly to adopt the 1945 Constitution, although Sukarno defined guided democracy as "a means, not an end," the rest of that official definition and the speech in which it was embedded gave little other indication that guided democracy might be dispensed with in the foreseeable future. Rather, the government's definition of the system, which the President gave in full in his speech, leaves the impression of an elaborate structure intended to function for a long time to come.

The government's definition of guided democracy, as presented by the President to the Constituent Assembly, is one of the most comprehensive statements of the new system. It consists of twelve points:

1. Guided democracy is democracy or, in the words of the 1945 Constitution, "democracy led by wise guidance in consultation by representatives."

2. Guided democracy is not dictatorship: it differs from centralist democracy as well as from the liberal democracy we have practiced up to now.

3. Guided democracy is a democracy which harmonizes with the personality and the outlook of the Indonesian Nation.

4. Guided democracy is a democracy in all affairs of the State and Society covering the political, economic and social spheres.

5. The substance of leadership in guided democracy is consultation; however, it is that kind of consultation which is "led by wise guidance" (*dipimpin oleh hikmat kebidjaksanaan*), not one which is led by "debates and manoeuvres, ending in a trial of strength and the calculation of the figures for and against." The outcome of "representative consultations led by wise guidance" is then submitted for implementation to a President, who, incidentally, is also elected by way of these consultations. To carry into effect the results of these consultations, the President appoints good and capable persons as his assistants, but the President remains

individually (not collectively with his assistants) responsible to the Consultative Body of People's Representatives (Madjelis Permusjawaratan Perwakilan Rakjat). Further, in the day-to-day conduct of State affairs (whose outlines are defined by that Consultative Body) the President must work together with the People's Representative Council, the Parliament (Dewan Perwakilan Rakjat). Such cooperation must also be practiced by means of "consultation led by wise guidance," and must not give priority to debates and manoeuvres which may lead to the dissolution of an entire Cabinet—things which are not possible under the 1945 Constitution.

6. Opposition in the sense of expressing sound and constructive opinions is a necessity under guided democracy; the important thing is the manner of deliberation in the representative consultations led by wise guidance.

7. Guided democracy is a means, not an end.

8. The object of implementing guided democracy is to arrive at a just and prosperous society, full of material and spiritual happiness, in harmony with the ideals of Indonesia's Independence Proclamation of August 17, 1945.

9. Since it is a means, guided democracy also recognizes freedom of thought and of expression, but within certain limits, i.e., the limits imposed by the safety of the State, the interest of the people at large, the national identity, morality and responsibility to God.

10. A just and prosperous society cannot but be an ordered and guided society, bound by the dictates of justice and prosperity, and recognizing guided economy. The implementation of Article 33 of the 1945 Constitution within the framework of guided economy still leaves economic sectors open to private enterprise.

11. A pattern is needed to realize a just and prosperous society. This pattern will be prepared by the National Planning Council (*Dewan Perantjang Nasional*) established under Act No. 80 of the year 1958. Guided democracy, in its turn, is needed to carry that pattern into effect, so that guided democracy is actually an implementation democracy or a work democracy.

12. The consequences of implementing the principle of guided democracy are as follows:

(a) Political parties as weapons in our struggle and realisers of the ideals of the Indonesian Nation must be brought to proper order and regulated in a Political Parties Act, with the main object of safeguarding the Indonesian State and People as decided by the National Conference in September 1957. This will also prevent the occurrence of a multi-party system which, in point of fact, unfavourably affects political stability in our State.

(b) Functional groups as dynamically developing and active national potentials in our society must be effectively canalized in representative bodies to smoothen the operation of administrative affairs and stabilize political conditions.

(c) A system is needed to give a better guarantee for the continuity of a Government capable of realising its programme, which forms a major part of the pattern for nationwide construction.[11]

Neither in the government's definition quoted above nor in the many official elucidations of guided democracy was there any explicit answer to the question of where ultimate authority would lie under the new system. The explanations had made clear who were to be the elders, who was to do the guiding: the President's hand-picked assemblies. But what provision, if any, had been made for occasions when these deliberative bodies were unable to reach agreement, when the principle of consensus failed to function? The answer to this was given by the President in mid-1960 as he installed the *gotong-rojong* Parliament he had selected:

I call upon you to concentrate in your deliberations upon one thing, namely, the realization of Indonesian Socialism. In your discussions, do not talk too much against each other but try to direct all discussion towards the realization of that Socialism. I even hope if possible the debates will not end in voting. You all know that I have never liked the system of "half-plus-one is always right." . . . Let us cling to our own characteristics, let us cling to the only right standpoint for

11 *Res Publica! Once More Res Publica!*, pp. 13-14.

Guided Democracy, namely no voting. . . . Wherever possible, the decisions should be reached through *musjawarah* and *mufakat*. I say "if possible." . . . *If, at a certain time, with regard to a certain question, a situation arises where no agreement can be reached because opinions are too widely different, I ask the leadership of the Gotong-rojong Dewan Perwakilan Rakjat to call upon me in my capacity as President-Supreme Commander to make a decision* based on all the opinions expressed by the members of this Gotong-rojong Dewan Perwakilan Rakjat. In this way we will be able to work effectively. In this way we will be able to work as a House of People's Representatives which truly is a tool for the realisation of socialism. As I said earlier, socialism can not be realised without leadership.[12]

The Constitution of 1945

However much the President was determined to institute his chosen system, he was equally determined to have some legal foundation for his regime. A suitable basis for the system of government he sought was ready at hand in the country's original Constitution drawn up in 1945.[13] The arguments the President used while urging the adoption of the 1945 Constitution tell us a good deal about his views on the nature of the state.

At the inauguration of the Constituent Assembly on November 10, 1956, a few days after his demand for the dissolution of political parties, Sukarno made clear that he sought a document that would provide a legal basis for guided democracy, though at this time he did not urge returning to the 1945 Constitution. After cautioning the members of the Constituent Assembly to move rapidly because the struggle of the people was going on outside their doors and "will take its course with your participation if possible, or, if not, over your honorable heads," the President exhorted the members to remain loyal to the Independence Proclamation of August 17, 1945, by drawing up a constitution for a

---

[12] *Indonesia 1961*, p. 23. My italics.

[13] The 1945 Constitution was replaced first by a provisional constitution, which was part of the Hague Agreement of 1949, and then by a provisional constitution drawn up in 1950 to provide for the return to a unitary system of government instead of the federal one agreed to at the Hague.

unitary state. He also reminded them that "the constitution which you are about to draw up is intended for the people of Indonesia and that therefore their soul, character and identity should be reflected in this constitution as the full moon is reflected in the placid waters of a lake." To give expression to this Indonesian identity, he continued,

> I personally feel it necessary that the weaker group should be protected from the stronger or, in other words, the use of democracy by the stronger group should be limited. This means that our democracy, for the time being, should be a democracy that sees to it that one group should not be exploited by another. This means that our democracy, for the time being, should be a guided democracy, a directed democracy which, therefore, does not stand on the principles of liberalism. If, later, economic emancipation and social emancipation shall have spread throughout our country, and the majority of our people have become able to use democracy as a weapon in their respective sectors of life, the nature of our democracy can again be adjusted in the future, to these conditions.[14]

Despite the President's warnings about the urgency of their task, the members of the Constituent Assembly were largely preoccupied for the next two and a half years with debating whether Pantja Sila or Islam should be the basis of the state. During this time, the Assembly took three decisions: The flag of the country was to be the red and white banner first adopted in the 1920's; the language was to be Indonesian; and the national anthem was to be *Indonesia Raya*.

When Sukarno returned to address the Assembly in April, 1959, he did not trouble to hide his dissatisfaction with its achievements. He reminded his listeners several times that "Today it is exactly two years, five months and twelve days since I officially opened the first session of this honoured Constitution Making Body." [15] Recalling the suggestions he had made on that earlier occasion,

14 Speech to Constituent Assembly, Bandung, November 10, 1956. (Broadcast over Radio Indonesia Home Service, Djakarta).
15 *Res Publica! Once More Res Publica!*, p. 1 and p. 4.

including the injunction that "this body was not a field for antithesis but a body for synthesis," he then put forward his own proposal for the adoption of the 1945 Constitution.[16]

Returning to the 1945 Constitution, the President said, was "a necessary historical step both in the journey of our National Revolution . . . as well as in the history of the Indonesian nation which, God willing, will continue eternally." But for the past years, he continued, the 1945 Constitution had been relegated to a kind of showcase, worshiped but not understood or followed. The result has been "deviations in the fields of Government and social life. Deviations in the field of politics. Deviations in the military field. Deviations in the social-economic field. Deviations, deviations, deviations, almost continuously for the past ten years."

What the President proposed to the Assembly was more than the mere adoption of the 1945 Constitution. He asked them also to endorse measures he outlined for the procedure of returning to the 1945 Constitution and to agree to the inclusion of representatives of functional groups within the elected Parliament. He even provided the Assembly with a new draft document, to be known as the Bandung Charter and to be signed by the Assembly's members. The Bandung Charter was to contain the following decisions: (1) recognition of the Djakarta Charter of June 22, 1945, as an historical document; (2) the handing over to the government of all results achieved by the Constituent Assembly; (3) the decision that the government shall immediately form a state committee to review all current legal rules and the existing state institutions that have to be made to conform to the Constitution of 1945. By signing the proposed Bandung Charter, the President explained, the Constituent Assembly would be fulfilling its obligation under Article 137 of the Provisional Constitution of 1950 to "declare the Constitution with Majesty." The signing of the Bandung Charter would also provide for the power

---

[16] This proposal had been unanimously approved by the Cabinet on February 19, 1959, officially approved by the President on February 20, and submitted both to the Parliament and the Constituent Assembly on February 21. Written explanations had also been given to both bodies by the Prime Minister in early March.

of government to be held by the President in accordance with the Constitution of 1945. The working cabinet would have to return its mandate to the President; meanwhile the working cabinet would present to the elected parliament a draft political party law and a draft law to perfect the 1953 electoral law. General elections would then be held, and there would be presented to the newly elected parliament draft bills on the setting up of the Supreme Advisory Council and of the People's Consultative Body. Thereafter, elections would be held for the President and the Vice-President. But the issue on which the President temporarily ran aground was his final proposal: the regulation of political parties by a new law "in order to make the party system sound and the parties simplified and more modest." Political parties would not be dissolved, he hastened to assure his audience, but "the Government considers it necessary to make the situation in our political parties suited to the atmosphere of Guided Democracy." The President then detailed the method by which representatives of functional groups would be selected, and outlined his plan for the establishment of a National Front.

Not all the members of the Constituent Assembly were enthusiastic about the President's plan. Indeed, a substantial minority indicated their unwillingness to endorse a plan that, in effect, left the President free to set the ground rules for the political party system.[17] As noted above, the required two-thirds majority could not be found to approve the plan. The circumstances surrounding the subsequent death of the Assembly were symptomatic of the new techniques of political strategy coming into vogue with the approach of guided democracy. The supporters of the President's plan, led by the PKI and the PNI, refused to attend any further sessions of the Assembly. This left the Assembly without a quorum, and so it ceased to meet.[18] Thus, the

[17] See *Inti Sari Pidato-Pidato Para Anggauta Konstituante,* May, 1959.

[18] Abdulgani, *Pendjelasan Manipol dan Usdek,* pp. 14-15. The President referred only to "the impossibility of the Constituent Assembly holding more sessions," "Penemuan Kembali Revolusi Kita" (hereafter referred to as the Manipol Speech), reprinted in *Dari Revolusi sampai Resopim,* pp. 391-431. The phrase quoted here is on p. 414.

President's decree of July 5, 1959, dissolving the Assembly had a certain internal logic if not the legal foundation he had sought.

The President maintains—and official sources repeatedly assert —that the July 5 decree was neither unconstitutional nor dictatorial. His action, the President said, "was based upon the will of the majority of the People, a will which was overflowing; . . . the existence of the emergency situation . . . the force-majeure for the President/Supreme Commander to save the Republic of the Proclamation." [19] As since elaborated in official exegeses of the text, these justifications are that "it is a contradiction in terms to speak of an act which brought about the changes desired by the majority of the People of Indonesia as a 'dictatorial' act" and "it is the duty of the President to assume control under conditions endangering the safety of the State, as is laid down in the laws governing the state of emergency and state of war which were then in force." [20] Finally, official sources point out, subsequent to the July 5 decree, the elected Parliament voted unanimously to continue working under the 1945 Constitution. This unanimous endorsement presumably endowed the decree with the necessary legal basis, in official eyes. But Parliament had bought itself only a very brief reprieve. Less than a year later it, too, vanished when the President waved the same magic wand that had solved the question of Indonesia's Constitution.

Guided Economy

The ideas and slogans of guided economy are, predictably, very closely tied to those that inform its collateral doctrine, guided democracy. The country's economy must express the national identity and be based on Pantja Sila. Guided economy is to be part of a wholesale retooling of Indonesian society that will "make the whole national economic structure the stepping-stone toward a just and prosperous economy to be realised in the future." In this reordering, there is no room for a liberal economy

[19] *Ibid.*, pp. 414-15.
[20] *Manipol/Usdek in Question and Answer*, p. 9.

"in which every individual has the opportunity to scoop up wealth at the public expense." But place must be found for those funds and forces that "have a progressive character and thus are not reactionary nor anti-revolutionary."

Like guided democracy, guided economy has had at its disposal a series of Presidential messages to guide it and a cluster of Presidentially-appointed councils to carry it out. The chief result has been a National Over-all Development Plan spelled out, with appropriate symbolism, in 17 volumes made up of 8 books containing 1,945 paragraphs and totaling 5,100 pages.[21] If magic formulas could speed up economic development, Indonesia's guided economy had been launched with a head start.

The National Over-all Development Plan was the product of the National Planning Council, which the President installed on August 15, 1959, two days before his historic Political Manifesto.[22] What had hampered Indonesian development in the past, the President explained to the new Council, was the lack of guarantees for the execution of the many plans drawn up. This "socio-economic phase of the Indonesian Revolution" required "over-all planning and firm leadership." The latter was now guaranteed with the advent of guided democracy; it only remained for the Council to provide the over-all plan for this firm leadership to carry out.

In his initial Development Message to the Council, the President stressed the four key requirements for them to bear in mind:

1. the necessity for over-all planning with blueprints based on the Indonesian identity, the essence of which is *gotong rojong* and the family system;

[21] The draft plan was submitted to the President on August 13, 1960. The 8 books of 17 volumes and 1,945 paragraphs represent, of course, August 17, 1945; the number of pages in the plan has no symbolic significance.

[22] The Dewan Perantjang Nasional or National Planning Council was established by Presidential act in 1958 but not installed until August 15, 1959. Its members were appointed as representatives of political, functional and regional groups; Mohammad Yamin was its chairman. The Council functioned with three special committees for Population, National Income, and Indonesian Socialism.

2. the connection between development and guided democracy and guided economy, which are basic elements in the Political Manifesto;

3. the factors which promote development like price stabilization, export drive, cooperatives and the like;

4. vigilance against elements which have obstructed efforts at development since 1950, including liberalism with its political instability, remnants of colonialism, and sabotage and subversive activities by anti-national elements. All of these had to be re-tooled.[23]

The National Planning Council even had its own officially designated set of historical documents to draw upon in drafting its plan: the 1945 Constitution, the Political Manifesto, and the President's Development Message of August 28, 1959.[24]

For the Council, the pertinent section of the 1945 Constitution (apart from the Pantja Sila, the part most often invoked in Presidential messages to the Council) was, of course, Article 33. In his Political Manifesto, the President explained that the true meaning of Article 33 was that "the economy shall be organized as a joint effort based on the family principle." In further explanation of Article 33, the President warned "vulture capitalists," whether Indonesian or foreign, that branches of production that are important to the state and that dominate the necessities of life of the people at large would be controlled by the state and not run by private entrepreneurs. For the benefit of potential foreign investors, he emphasized that any foreign non-Dutch capital that played "negative roles" would suffer the same fate as the expropriated Dutch.

Not only predatory Western capitalism but also many Western economic theories were rejected by the President. Indonesia's rev-

[23] Speech to the National Planning Council, August 28, 1959. Summarized in *Indonesia 1961*, pp. 78 ff.

[24] In a unanimously adopted decision on November 19, 1960, the MPR declared that the President's Speech of Counsel of August 28, 1959, was to be the main lines of the Development Policy. See *Handbook on the Political Manifesto: Two Executive Directions of Manipol* (Djakarta: Republic of Indonesia, Department of Information, 1961), Special Issue 73.

olution, he asserted, was not a revolution of rising expectations, the description assigned it by many Western students of contemporary economic development. The aspirations for which the Indonesian people fought, starting long before August 17, 1945, were fixed; their objective, the President said, had always been and remained a just and prosperous society. Indonesia's nationalism might be part of a wave of nationalism flooding all of Asia and Africa, but Indonesia's economic revolution was not to be equated with the developments taking place in other new countries that did not share Indonesia's socialist tradition.

One of the more specific elements in the President's plans for the retooling of Indonesia's economy was the vital role assigned to land reform. Land reform, the President declared in his 1960 Independence Day address, was an absolutely essential part of the Indonesian Revolution. Without land reform, the revolution "is just like a building without a foundation, just like a tree without a trunk, just like big talk which is empty." His aim was twofold: "the abolition of all foreign rights and colonial concessions over land and the gradual termination of feudal exploitation" on the one hand, and a "strengthening and extension of land ownership for the entire Indonesian people" on the other. The intention of the first part of his aim was clear: eliminating the large, foreign-owned plantations. "Land is for the farmer. Land is for those who really till the soil. Land is not for those who, seated at ease, become fat and corpulent through exploiting the sweat of the people whom they order to till that soil." But it was less clear what strengthening and extending land ownership would mean in Indonesia, where large-scale indigenous landholdings have never been a prominent feature of economic life and where the amount of arable land currently available is sharply limited.

Property rights, the President made clear, would continue to be recognized; people could still own hereditary lands. Only the extent of this property, a maximum and minimum size for landholdings, was to be regulated. But these property rights would be officially declared to have a social function, and, more significant, "the state and lawful social units have *greater powers* than private property rights." [25]

Just what this land reform was to mean in practice for the Indonesian farmer has gradually become less obscure as a series of agrarian laws and regulations have unrolled since October, 1960. Landholdings are to be no smaller than two hectares and, depending upon the number of dependents in a given family, may be as large as twenty hectares. While landholdings of this size are adequate to support farm families, difficulty arises because, in Java, the only part of the country for which this redistribution would be significant, the total available arable land, if parceled out in this fashion, would still provide for scarcely more than half the rural population.[26] Consequently, the heralded land reform has brought little discernible change for most of Java. At the same time, the President is apparently aiming past the redistribution of land to a still vaguely defined program of collectivization for rice production. Apparently, this would take the form of developing cooperatives for agricultural production on a much broader scale and with far more centralized control than the present, rather casual cooperative organization.

Land reform is but one feature of the Over-all Eight Year Plan, which was ceremoniously inaugurated on January 1, 1961. The Plan calls for a total investment of 240 billion rupiah or $5,300 million to be spread among eight fields: Mental and Spiritual; Research; People's Welfare; Government; Special Development, including security; Production; Distribution; and Finance. The largest investments are to be made in Production (45 per cent of the total), which includes industry, foodstuffs, clothing, and

---

[25] "Laksana Malaekat jang Menjerbu dari Langit Djalannja Revolusi Kita" (hereafter referred to as Djarek speech), reprinted in *Dari Revolusi sampai Resopim*, pp. 435-77. The excerpts quoted above will be found on pp. 456-66, *passim*.

[26] Two hectares of land are the equivalent of 4.9 acres. For an analysis of the land-reform program and of the Eight-Year Plan in general, see Bruce Glassburner and Kenneth D. Thomas, "The Swing of the Hoe: Retooling Begins in the Indonesian Economy," *Asian Survey*, I (June, 1961), 3-12; and Selo Soemardjan, "Land Reform In Indonesia," *Asian Survey*, I (February, 1962), 23-30.

pharmaceuticals; Distribution (25 per cent), including communications; and Special Development (12.5 per cent). The next
largest share, some 7.5 per cent, is allocated for the educational
and cultural projects listed in the Mental and Spiritual field.[27]

One of the most interesting features of the highly detailed
plan[28] is the proposed system of organization for both public and
private enterprise. State enterprises are to come under more direct control of the appropriate ministries. Both state and private
enterprises engaged in the same fields are to be grouped together
in organizations on the basis of specific products. Since in most
instances the private firms in any of these corporate-type groupings will be overshadowed by the much larger state enterprises,
it is clear that the decisions taken within each group can be expected to reflect the government's views. Article 33 of the Constitution of 1945, it is evident, is to be carried out to the fullest.

Indonesian Identity

Official definitions and elucidations of guided democracy,
guided economy, Indonesian socialism, and the Constitution of
1945 are dotted with references to the fifth component of Usdek:
kepribadian Indonesia or Indonesian identity. Although, comparatively speaking, Indonesian identity has received somewhat less
attention on an individual basis than its sister doctrines, it has
by no means been neglected. Indonesian identity, too, has figured in Presidential speeches, received its share of explanatory
pamphlets,[29] and been defined, elaborated, expanded, and, on

27 Some of the projects planned in this field include the establishment of
a national museum and a national art gallery in Djakarta; nautical schools in
Medan, Makassar, and Ambon; and the perfection and expansion of existing
universities and colleges.

28 For the basic features of the plan, see Paauw, "From Colonial to Guided
Economy," especially pp. 220-30; Guy J. Pauker, "Indonesia's Eight-Year De-
velopment Plan," *Pacific Affairs*, XXXIV (Summer, 1961), 115-30; and Donald
D. Humphrey, "Indonesia's National Plan for Economic Development," *Asian
Survey*, II (December, 1962), 12-21.

29 See, for example, Roeslan [Ruslan] Abdulgani, *In Search of an Indonesian
Identity* (New Nusantara Publishing Co., n.d. [probably Spring, 1959]).

occasion, slightly altered to suit the particular situation for which it was invoked.

In his Political Manifesto of 1959, President Sukarno stated that the essence of the true nature of the identity of the Indonesian nation was *gotong rojong* or mutual assistance. He reminded his listeners that in his speech of June, 1945, on Pantja Sila, he had defined Pantja Sila as the embodiment of the Indonesian identity and had reduced the five principles of Pantja Sila to the single, all-encompassing principle of *gotong rojong*. But *gotong rojong*, he explained in Manipol, was not "static, as is 'brotherhood' alone, but *gotong rojong* which is dynamic, *gotong rojong* with our sleeves rolled up, *gotong rojong* 'one, two, three, heave!'" *Gotong rojong*, the President stated, was firmly embodied in the setting up of the new advisory and consultative bodies which he was then in the process of establishing. The National Front, especially, would be established to "build up and channel everything to do with the people's *gotong rojong*."

The following year, referring in his Independence Day address to his dissatisfaction with the progress made in retooling the revolution, President Sukarno felt the need for being "clearer and firmer with regard to *gotong rojong*." He then proceeded with a clarification in which *gotong rojong*, now reduced to being but one characteristic of the Indonesian identity, was interpreted to mean unqualified and unquestioning unity in political life as in other aspects of national life. The target on this occasion was the continuing opposition of some political parties, then making their last feeble objections to the imposition of guided democracy. Only parties supporting the Political Manifesto could be permitted to exist, the President said. "A party can only be one of two things: either prohibited, or pro the Political Manifesto/ Usdek." Seeking to link support for guided democracy with Indonesia's highly valued cultural tradition of tolerance, the President pointed out that "there is no nation which is as tolerant as the Indonesian nation in its religious life." But, he then charged, "neither is there any nation which sometimes betrays the principles of *gotong rojong* in its political life as the Indonesian nation does." Specifically, he stated, one of the "crimes" of the government regulation of November 3, 1945, which laid the basis for a multiparty system, "was, in fact, that it betrayed this spirit of *gotong rojong,* because with the establishment of political parties, sprouting like mushrooms in the rainy season, political tolerance entered its grave and the devil of hatred bared its teeth everywhere."

What was needed, indeed a "must" in Indonesia's "struggle against imperialism and capitalism" was *"gotong rojong* in the political field . . . unity between the Moslems, the Nationalists and the Communists." This unity was an essential part of the 1945 revolution and to be faithful to the revolution, the President said, demanded that one be faithful to this unity, for "one of the characteristics of a person who is truly revolutionary is the oneness of words and deeds." Thus, Nasakom, the slogan coined for this phase of the march toward guided democracy, became an expression of *gotong rojong* and, by definition, of Indonesian identity. This call for unity among Indonesia's three "revolutionary powers," Moslems, nationalists, and Communists, even had the advantage of a suitable historical background. For, as the President pointed out, some thirty years earlier he had not only urged but "proved that unity was possible between Islam, Nationalism, and Marxism." [30]

What the President here referred to as unity, it was quickly made clear, was not mere mutual tolerance of differing political viewpoints. Unity as an extension of Indonesia's identity, *gotong rojong,* was to mean nothing less than total acquiescence in the government's pronouncements of doctrine as well as in its programs. The Law of Revolution, which the President propounded in this same speech, demanded not only one revolutionary leadership but "one National Ideology and Concept which is revolutionary, clear, firm, delineated." Like Manipol and the Development Message of 1959, the entire contents of this August, 1960, speech were given the cachet of official adoption as one of the two

[30] The President referred here to a series of articles he had written in 1926 for the nationalist journal *Suluh Indonesia Muda.*

Executive Directions of the Political Manifesto (the other Executive Direction was the President's speech of September 30, 1960, to the United Nations General Assembly) and an official elucidation that was "to become a uniform interpretation of the contents of these speeches, and thus to guarantee an orderly implementation of same." [31] In a preamble to the official handbook containing these Executive Directions of Manipol, the President, acting in his capacity as President, Supreme Commander, Prime Minister, and Chairman of the Supreme Advisory Council, gave his full endorsement to this elucidation of his speeches prepared by the Supreme Advisory Council.

More and more, Indonesian identity was equated with complete and unquestioning agreement with the government's—i.e., the President's—dictates. Demands for unity of thought, word, and deed and for absolute adherence to authorized interpretations of the slogans of guided democracy became an increasingly familiar obbligato accompaniment to official enunciations of doctrine. A leading spokesman of the current regime, Ruslan Abdulgani, when introducing his series of explanatory radio talks on Manipol/Usdek, gave as a primary reason for the broadcasts that "it is not possible to ignore the fact that signs are beginning to appear in our community of subjective interpretations and meanings of these two terms [Manipol and Usdek], whether this is being done consciously or not." [32] Agreement with the President had to be wholehearted and entirely free of voluntary or involuntary reservations. Indonesian authorities might not have at their disposal the necessary resources for the Correct Handling of Contradictions, but if exhortations alone could curb deviations from official doctrine, there would be little chance of any Hundred Flowers Blossoming or any Hundred Schools of Thought Contending in the Indonesian national garden.

Further light is shed on the concept of Indonesian identity by examining those patterns of behavior and modes of thought that the President has rejected or denounced as antithetic to the

---

[31] See *Handbook on the Political Manifesto*, pp. 3-4.
[32] *Pendjelasan Manipol dan Usdek*, p. 5.

national character. The President has defined as non-Indonesian all "Dutchified groups, reformist groups, conservative groups, contra-revolutionary groups, chameleon and cockroach groups." [33] It was these groups, he claimed, who were responsible for the dilution of the revolutionary spirit that resulted in the Hague Agreement of 1949. More than that, these groups had failed to recognize that the compromise embodied in the Hague Agreement was merely a tactic, not an objective; they mistakenly thought that Indonesia was obliged to abide by the agreement. Such people, he declared in his Manipol speech, were "possibilists, persons who in principle are not dynamically revolutionary, but are even possibly contra-revolutionary. At the least, individuals like that are rigid . . . people whose souls have stopped short." Such people, who have poisoned the spirit of the nation since 1950 with their poison of reformism, he said, are found in the first place among the intellectuals.

Intellectuals have been a frequent target of the President's attack. The intellectuals on whom his scorn is heaped are those accused of *Hollands denken* (Dutch thinking). Textbook thinking, especially when based on Western texts, had no place in the new Indonesia. University students were cautioned against pursuing "reflective wisdom"; their goal, the President said, should be the pursuit of practical knowledge, primarily applied science.[34]

The youth of the country were urged to eschew what the President terms cultural imperialism. The 1945 Constitution stipulates that "the government shall develop national culture." Somewhat plaintively, the President asked Indonesian youth: "Why is it that among you many like to read foreign writings which are clearly cultural imperialism?" The government, he said, would protect the national culture, but the youth of the country "must also join actively in protecting and developing our national culture."

The expression of Indonesian identity ranges from such mat-

---

[33] *Tjutjunguk*, the Sundanese word for cockroach, was used in the nationalist movement to refer to a spy for the Dutch.

[34] Speech at Gadjah Mada University, May 28, 1958, p. 5.

ters as spelling reform—a government regulation has replaced the Indonesian system of spelling, derived from the Dutch, with one that will "reflect the national identity"—to leisure-time occupations—Western social dancing, rock and roll music, and similar examples of Western decadence have been outlawed. Indonesians must seek cultural guidance in their own traditional roots.

Indonesian identity has thus come to mean a curious amalgam of extreme nationalism, abjuration of deviations from official dogma and an embrace of "centralist" thinking.

Indonesian Socialism

"Socialism," President Sukarno has said, "is an effort to achieve happiness for all men . . . justice among men, no exploitation of man by man and all equally happy. That is what is called socialism." There are varieties of socialism, he frequently tells his audiences; "there is religious socialism, there is utopian socialism, there is nihilistic socialism, there is scientific socialism. There is communism. All that falls under the term 'socialism.' " [35]

Since Indonesian socialism is an essential component of the new Indonesian form of government and since President Sukarno is the author of this new philosophy of state, to understand what is meant by Indonesian socialism one must examine the President's views on this subject.[36]

[35] Speech at the opening of the First Conference of the Department of the Attorney-General, Surabaya, October 30, 1960 (Djakarta: Republic of Indonesia, Sekretariat Negara, 1961), pp. 2-3. Referred to hereafter as Surabaya speech.

[36] Although other Indonesian spokesmen have written extensively on the subject, their works are, by and large, only a re-statement of President Sukarno's views on Indonesian Socialism. See, for example: Abdulgani, *Perkembangan Tjita-tjita Sosialisme di Indonesia: Kuliah Umum Sdr. H. Roeslan Abdulgani di Perguruan Tinggi Malang pada hari Saptu tanggal 2 Djuli 1960* (n.pl., n.d., mimeographed text); and *Tentang Ketegasan Sosialisme Indonesia: Landjutan Kuliah Umum Wakil Ketua Dewan Pertimbangan Agung H. Roeslan Abdulgani di "Universitas Malang" pada hari Senen tanggal 13 Pebruari 1961* (n.pl., n.d., mimeographed text). See also J. K. Tumakaka, *Sosialisme Indonesia: disusun berdasar kepada adjaran Bung Karno—Bapak*

The President frequently defines Indonesian socialism as marhaenism and marhaenism, he has said, "is Marxism practiced or applied in Indonesia. . . . Those who call themselves marhaenists but do not practice Marxism in Indonesia . . . are only pseudo-marhaenists." A true Marxist, the President explains, is a radical revolutionary; thus, those who call themselves radical revolutionaries but are not Marxists "are not radical revolutionaries and are therefore only pseudo-Marxists." Finally, "a true Marxist does not suffer from Communist-phobia." [37]

The President continually cautions his countrymen to remember that socialism is not equivalent to Communism; rather, there are the varieties of socialism mentioned above, of which Communism "as outlined by Lenin" is one "trend." That is so, the President explains, because Communism, like socialism, "demands justice, no exploitation, and happiness." In the Surabaya speech, the President outlined his criteria for determining who is and who is not a socialist: those who believe in justice among people, no exploitation of man by man, and everyone equally happy are socialists. Those who meet these standards and whose names are frequently invoked by the President include, in addition to Marx, Engels, and Lenin, such figures as his boyhood teacher, Hadji Tjokroaminoto; the Christian Socialists Félicité de Lamennais of France and Domela Nieuwenhuis of the Netherlands; the Utopians Louis Blanc and Charles Fourier; Jean Jaurès, to whom the President frequently refers as "the man I revere"; and Mikhail Bakunin. Not all socialists meet with the President's approval. Among the varieties of socialism that he deplores is that of Schermerhorn, the Dutch advocate of what the President terms "personalistic socialism." Schermerhorn, the President says, believed that "socialism cannot be carried out un-

---

Sosialisme Indonesia (Djakarta: Republic of Indonesia, Departemen Penerangan, 1961).

[37] *Setia Kepada Marhaenisme Sedjati: Amanat Presiden Sukarno pada Kongres Partindo di Gedung Olah Raga, Djakarta, 26 Desember 1961* (Djakarta: Republic of Indonesia, Departemen Penerangan, 1962), pp. 3-4.

less mankind has a pure heart" and therefore advocated that "first everyone should clean his heart. It is the same," the President remarks, "as the case of those among our leaders who were not yet revolutionary, who said that if we wanted our independence we all should be educated first." [38] Although it is important for the realization of socialism that the leaders be pure at heart, the President explains, socialism cannot await the moral improvement of all men any more than independence could await the education of all Indonesians. At the same time, the President places great stress on the moral content of socialism, saying that "socialism in its essence is a morality, a morality of high standards which demands that men should not quarrel among themselves, that all men should live like brothers, that all men should taste happiness. That is the essence of socialism and that is the essence of our identity, the essence of our Constitution. . . . I could even say that this is the essence of the Message of the Sufferings of the People."

As for the means of achieving socialism, the President says, in spite of the fact that Marx and Engels said that socialism was an historical inevitability, it is wrong to assume that socialism will presently come about all by itself. "Marx himself said that was wrong, Engels also said that is wrong. And especially the Communist leaders have said that that is wrong." Islamic leaders like Tjokroaminoto who also demanded socialism, notes the President, were aware that "the Islamic religion, too, firmly maintains that socialism cannot fall from Heaven like dew during the night." The instrument for carrying out socialism is the state, for the state is a "super instrument" and not merely "an idea which has become a reality."

> The state too is the result of a development. . . . [T]he state is an instrument of power, the state is an organization of power. I therefore maintain that the state has two functions: a function to suppress, to oppose, to annihilate, to destroy anything which threatens to harm

[38] This and the following quotations are from the Surabaya speech.

our life as a nation, our existence as a country, our existence as a state, and so on and so forth; that is one side of it. On the other hand, the state is a creative element, a creative tool to build, to reconstruct, to create, create, create. On the one hand, destroying; on the other hand, creating. Two acts which are inseparable.

Since the state is an instrument, officials in the state actually form a real organization "and there is no one organization which can function without leadership." That is why, in the new Indonesia, so much emphasis is placed on the term "guided" because "the state—in itself guided—is guiding . . . in carrying out socialism, the economy should be guided, guided along the lines already stipulated by the state, the state which is the instrument to carry out socialism."

The passage just cited is one of the President's relatively infrequent references to the economic content of socialism. While his statements on Indonesian socialism are replete with attacks on capitalism, imperialism, and colonialism, they rarely contain anything more concrete with respect to the economy than the assertion that it should be a guided one, in conformity with Indonesian socialism. Other spokesmen have, on occasion, attempted to clarify the economic aspect of Indonesian socialism. The Speaker of the elected Parliament, Sartono, for example, explained in the first years of guided democracy, that the socialism which Indonesia seeks "on the basis of her Constitution is not an extreme socialism. Indonesian Socialism is the kind implied in the Pantja Sila; the Indonesian Constitution provides for 'control' over economic activities in order to obtain social justice but does not provide for 'ownership.' . . . It is different in Communist countries where not only the means of production are state-owned but other enterprises as well. Cooperatives are one phase of Indonesian Socialism. . . . Socialism in Indonesia is very different from that in countries where extreme socialism prevails and where cooperatives are considered as transitional measures, after which everything is to be made collective property."

The Indonesian Constitution, Sartono pointed out, stipulates that citizens are allowed to own means of production but that control must come from the state.[39]

Indonesian socialism, as defined by the President, has, of course, its proper legal foundation. Since the Indonesian Constitution of 1945 is a socialist constitution, the President observes and official spokesmen repeat, putting the Constitution into practice means the application of Indonesian socialism. And, like the other component parts of the new state doctrine, Indonesian socialism also has its limits set by that wellspring of contemporary Indonesian philosophy, the Pantja Sila. Indonesian socialism, no less than guided democracy, guided economy, Indonesian identity and the Constitution of 1945, is just as Indonesian as appeals to Indonesian slogans can make it.

[39] *Information on Indonesia,* No. 76/5 (December 5, 1958), p. 5. (Publication of the Permanent Mission of the Republic of Indonesia to the United Nations, New York.)

11

Guided Democracy in Action

UNDER THE PRESIDENT'S PLAN AS INITIALLY PRESENTED, only two new organs of government were required for the establishment of guided democracy: a cabinet representing all parties with a defined minimum number of seats in the elected parliament, and a National Advisory Council representing functional groups in society. The elected parliament has since disappeared from the scene but the country is not suffering from any dearth of national governing bodies. As of 1962 there were nine such officially designated organs of state. Six of these derive their authority directly from the Constitution presently in force. In their official rank order, they are: the Madjelis Permusjawaratan Rakjat (hereafter MPR) or People's Assembly for Deliberations; the President; the Dewan Perwakilan Rakjat (hereafter DPR) or Council of People's Representatives; the Mahkamah Agung or Supreme Advisory Council; the Supreme Court; and the Badan Pemeriksa Keuangan or State Comptrolling Council. In addition to these six, three other bodies have been created "in the framework of implementing Guided Democracy and Guided Economy." They are the Dewan Perantjang Nasional or National Planning Council; the Badan Pengawas Kegiatan Apparatur Negara or Body for Controlling Activities of the State Apparatus; and the Front Nasional or National Front. These nine are the state's legitimate wielders of power.

On official charts of organization, the MPR takes precedence on the grounds that since it is "the embodiment of the whole of the Indonesian people" and "sovereignty is in the hands of the

people and is exercised in full by the MPR . . . the MPR, therefore, is the highest authority of the state." [1] The MPR is carefully
distinguished from the legislative body proper, the DPR, the latter
being incorporated into the MPR. In addition to all members of
the DPR, the MPR is made up of delegates appointed for each
region and representatives of such functional groups in society
as farmers, workers, businessmen, intellectuals, and the military.
The MPR is required to meet at least once every five years, and
has as its primary task setting the broad lines of policy of the
state and the government.[2] It is also empowered to elect the President and Vice-President who are responsible for implementing
that policy. While the stated intention is for members of the
MPR to be chosen by national elections, under the special laws
governing the state of war and emergency currently in force the
President has provisionally appointed its members, as he has
those of the other organs of state.

The powers of the President under guided democracy are extremely broad. Elected for a term of five years and eligible for
re-election, he is nominally responsible to the MPR but bears
full authority and responsibility for carrying out the administration of the state, following the broad lines of policy set down by
the MPR. The Ministers of State, whom he appoints and dismisses,
are responsible only to him. He is supreme commander of the
armed forces and enjoys the usual prerogatives of a head of state,
sharing with the DPR the power to make war and conclude trea-
ties with foreign states.

The relationship between the President and the DPR has a
certain ambiguity. The President is not responsible to the DPR
but neither can he dissolve it. Instead, working side by side, without being dependent upon each other, the President and the DPR
share the power to make laws. In many ways, this is the most

---

[1] *Indonesia 1961*, p. 45.

[2] An elucidation of the Constitution of 1945 provides that "in view of the
dynamic of society, once in every five years the Madjelis reviews everything
which has happened and considers all trends at that time and determines what
policies it desires to be used for the future." See *Manipol/Usdek in Question
and Answer*, p. 89.

direct translation of the village system of political organization to the national level; it parallels the pattern of the headman acting with the concurrence of the village elders. All legislation must have the concurrence of the DPR, which sits at least once a year. The DPR may also submit draft laws that must be ratified by the President, just as draft laws submitted by the President must be ratified by the DPR. In the unlikely event of disagreement between the hand-picked DPR and the President (or, as officially phrased, in situations where harmony may not prevail), the President has the power of determining Government Regulations in Lieu of Statutes. These Regulations must be ratified by the DPR at its following session and, if not approved, can be revoked. In practice, however, such lack of harmony has not thus far hampered the legislative machinery of state.

The provisional DPR has a total membership of 282, consisting of 130 representatives of political parties, 151 representatives of 20 functional groups, and 1 representative from West Irian.

The Supreme Advisory Council or DPA, in keeping with its title, is a purely advisory body that is obliged to submit its views on issues raised by the President. The DPA also has the right to submit proposals to the government but its proposals are not binding on the government. The President is Chairman of the DPA, which has 12 representatives of political parties, 8 regional representatives, and 24 representatives of functional groups plus a Vice-Chairman who has ministerial rank and is a member of the cabinet.

The Supreme Court, the highest judicial organ of the state, still functions on the basis of the prewar Dutch legal code with modifications introduced during the Japanese occupation and further alterations made in the years since 1945. A basic law for the reorganization of the legal system is still in the drafting stage.

The State Comptrolling Council operates temporarily on the basis of slightly refurbished prewar statutes. As the organ in charge of control over the accountability of public finance, it enjoys investigative powers and presents its findings to the DPR.

Of the three supplementary bodies specifically created to carry out guided democracy and guided economy, the National Planning Council has been described in Chapter 10. The second of these new organs, the Body for Controlling Activities of the State Apparatus, commonly abbreviated to BAPEKAN, is, as its name indicates, essentially a watchdog committee. It was installed in office on August 15, 1959, with five members, one of whom serves as its chairman. BAPEKAN's authority extends to both the central and regional governments and it is charged with receiving and considering complaints from the general public as well as from governmental institutions on matters that hamper the efficiency of the state machinery or in any way lower the authority and prestige of the government. BAPEKAN channels these complaints to the proper authorities for action, submits proposals and recommendations in some instances, and, on occasion, reports directly to the President.

Finally, and perhaps most important of all these organizations, is the Front Nasional or National Front. Described as a "mass organization of vertical structure, to encompass the whole of the nation," the National Front's assigned tasks match the breadth of its proposed structure; the National Front is to "mobilize the revolutionary forces of the people and to stimulate the potentials of all layers of society toward completion of the national revolution." More specifically, the National Front is instructed to direct its energies to activities in the field of development and reconstruction.

Deriving its legal basis from the same series of Presidential decrees that authorized the President to ban or dissolve political parties,[3] the National Front's Constitution was enacted by Presidential Directive No. 165/1960 and its Central Executive Board is presided over by the President "in his capacity as Leader of the Revolution." A preparatory committee, consisting of the chairmen of the major parties and such nonparty figures as Chairul Saleh, Mohammad Yamin, Erningpradja, Hanafi, and Pandu Wiguna,

---

[3] Series of decrees promulgated at the end of December 1959 and publicly proclaimed in early January, 1960.

was installed on March 28, 1960; its 70-member Central Executive Board was installed the following September, and the National Front itself was sworn into office on January 20, 1961. Within three days, the National Front had absorbed the West Irian National Liberation Front[4] and, by March 23, was setting up the first of its regional branches.[5] In practice, the National Front has taken over some of the functions earlier performed by political parties.[6] It has also proved to be the President's favored instrument on many occasions. This, coupled with the organization's size and increasingly well-articulated structure, has led many observers to consider it a potential counterweight to the only other organization with similarly widespread local units and tight-knit structure, the PKI. However, the PKI in its turn has not overlooked the possibilities offered by the apparatus fashioned for the National Front, and the present chairman of the PKI Secretariat has reportedly been zealous in his attempts to infiltrate local branches of the National Front.

Given the nine official sources of national power just described, and the somewhat ambiguous functions and responsibilities assigned to some of these bodies, it is logical to inquire where ultimate authority is lodged under the present system. The answer to this question is neither simple nor static,[7] and is necessarily couched in rather tentative terms. Nevertheless, from the availa-

4 An organization established under General Nasution's chairmanship in 1958 to replace the Action Committee for the Liberation of West Irian, which had been led by radical nationalists and the PKI.

5 For purposes of daily administration, the National Front is run by a Daily Executive Board composed of ten members aided by a secretariat headed by a secretary-general with four deputies. Regional boards and branch boards have been set up in all territorial regions.

6 Individuals affiliated with the banned political parties were barred from holding office in any of the regional committees by a decision of the Standing Committee of the Central Executive Board of the National Front taken at its second session on February 23, 1961. Individuals with such affiliations had, of course, been excluded from membership in the central body of the organization.

7 Indeed, the pursuit of this elusive answer has encouraged the development of an exercise which, with due apologies to those who speculate about Soviet affairs, might be termed Istanology (for the Presidential palace or *istana*). Like his counterparts studying Soviet-bloc countries, the Istanologist finds his path cluttered with red herrings, *wajang* shadows, and similar distractions. On the

ble evidence it is possible to conclude that, in spite of the elaborate superstructure of state provided by the other eight authorized repositories of power, the reins of authority under guided democracy are held by President Sukarno. It is he who makes the decisions and it is he who thus far retains the initiative in all significant spheres of action.

While the present Indonesian regime is in many respects authoritarian, it is not at present a dictatorship. Nor, in spite of the plethora of purely consultative (i.e., endorsing) official bodies at the top so reminiscent of the trappings of modern totalitarianism, is it a totalitarian state. The panoply of official councils at the apex of the pyramid has yet to be matched by an equally elaborate organization at the base, nor is power wholly centralized in the President's hands. In reaching decisions, President Sukarno is still obliged to take into consideration the views and the strength of the competing sources of power. It is in his remarkable capacity for balancing these contending forces against each other that the President has demonstrated his unique political talents. Of the forces that the President must take into account, two are of major consequence: the Army and the PKI. There are two other, lesser elements in the situation: the religious conservatives and the group that Arnold Brackman has characterized as "that curious collection of irrational ultranationalists, the 'national Communists'"[8]; but neither of these are of anything like the same order of importance as the Army and the PKI. The religious conservatives have a large but in-

---

other hand, unlike the Kremlinologist, he does not have at his disposal those useful photographs of the participants in major public ceremonies, for Indonesians tend to be something less than punctilious about arriving at social or official engagements. Thus, the absence of a major figure from an important event may mean no more than that the man in question arrived too late for the photographers. Judgments about Indonesian developments, therefore, have to be based on somewhat more traditional data, such as the statements issued by leaders and their organizations, the behavior of leaders and groups where visible, and, for those events that are partly or almost wholly submerged, the sifting of innumerable rumors, comments, and reports of varying degrees of bias.

[8] *Indonesian Communism*, pp. 274-75.

choate following organized in only the most rudimentary fashion. The national Communists, including both the official leaders of Murba and such figures as Chairul Saleh, are heavily dependent upon their personal ties with the President. The role played by the palace clique will be dealt with below. First, let us examine the two prime contenders for power, the armed forces and the PKI.

The Armed Forces

The Indonesian armed forces are composed of a variety of units that sprang up during the revolution in response to the special requirements of that era. These units were nominally tied to a central military command but in practice they were largely accustomed to operating on their own. The exercise of local initiative is a prime requisite for successful guerrilla action, the kind of military operation in which Indonesia's revolutionary army excelled.

Part of the heritage of this revolutionary experience is the loyalty of many troops to their wartime leaders, a loyalty usually unencumbered by any personal political convictions on the part of the troops involved. The lack of a tradition of firm central command of the armed forces and the inability of the government to provide enough facilities to restore surplus troops to civilian life made it easy for several political parties to capitalize on the discontent of various military units. The Army remains an oversized and unwieldy organization although its structure and administration have been considerably tightened up since the mid-1950's. Earlier efforts to cut down the armed forces to a workable peacetime force, as originally attempted by the Sultan of Jogjakarta when he was Minister of Defense, became political footballs, and even today any reorganization of the armed forces takes on highly political overtones. Inevitably, many Army officers succumbed to the temptation to engage in politics, and the military history of independent Indonesia has been marked by rebellions of regional commanders and their troops, struggles within the high command, and independent action casually taken by local Army leaders. At the same time, opportunities for military dabbling in nonmilitary matters have increased markedly in recent years. The expansion of the armed forces into many spheres of what is normally civilian life has been one of the most important developments of the past few years in Indonesia. Not only the expropriated Dutch properties but many other economic enterprises are managed by the Army. Army officers and to a lesser extent officers of the other branches of service have increasingly been assigned to key posts in all ministries. The growth of Army influence and the spotting of Army officers in strategic positions throughout the government have proceeded much faster than the modernization of the armed forces as a whole.

Much of the modernization of the Army which has taken place was accomplished through the efforts of Major General Abdul Haris Nasution, Army Chief of Staff from 1950 to 1952 and again from 1955 to 1962, and currently Minister of National Security.[9] Nasution's continued leadership of the armed forces has dispelled some of the confusion about the dominant political orientation of the Army; Nasution himself, while not at all reluctant to purchase arms and equipment from the Soviet Union, is very strongly opposed to any expansion of the PKI on the domestic political scene. However, while there is no question about the sincerity of Nasution's anti-Communist views, there is no equivalent clarity about the content of any political views he may hold of a more positive nature.[10] Nasution's failure imme-

[9] For details on the circumstances surrounding Nasution's return to active military life and his reappointment as Chief of Staff in 1955, see Feith, *Decline of Constitutional Democracy*, pp. 442-44. In June, 1962, Nasution was replaced as Army Chief of Staff by Major General Achmad Jani. Jani has long been an influential, if somewhat shadowy figure in political-military circles and is generally regarded as less hostile to the Communists than Nasution is.

[10] General Nasution's political leanings and affiliations through the years are too complex for detailed consideration here. However, it should be noted that he was one of the founders of the political party IPKI, League of Upholders of Indonesian Independence, established during the period when Nasution had withdrawn from active military service. IPKI, whose leadership always included a number of military and paramilitary figures, later shifted

diately to suppress the Democratic League, an organization formed in March, 1960, under Masjumi-PSI leadership and representing the moderate and right-wing parties, appeared to be tacit support on his part for the League's campaign against the President's march toward guided democracy.[11] However, both before and after the founding of the League, Nasution bore down heavily on Masjumi, PSI, and other center organizations, their leaders and their publications. He has, of course, been equally vigorous in his moves against PKI leaders, groups, and papers.

Adding to the confusion about where the Army stands are such factors as Nasution's relations with the palace and his relations with other Army figures. Over the past five or six years, Nasution and the President have drawn very close together but there is ample evidence that the President, at least, does not regard his former Army Chief of Staff as an uncritical supporter.[12] In some measure, Nasution is engaged in a tug of war with the President for the loyalty of the other key figures in the Army, for the officer corps is still far from being a cohesive body united in support of its commander. Several officers, formerly close to Nasution, at present enjoy better relations with the palace than does their chief. In any showdown between the President and Nasution, there is little doubt that these officers would side with the Presi-

---

its position and by the time of the second Ali cabinet, in which it participated, reflected the views of those Army leaders opposed to Nasution.

11 The Democratic League (Liga Demokrasi) was established on March 24, 1960, during one of the President's absences on a foreign tour. Led by prominent members of Masjumi and PSI, it included representatives of the Protestant and Catholic parties, IPKI, and, indirectly, NU, Perti, and PSII, whose participation is presumed on the basis of the presence of the chairman of the Moslem League in which all three of these parties were represented.

The League flourished briefly, aided by the tacit—and, in some regions, the open—support of several Army leaders. The Army even ignored a Presidential order sent from abroad to arrest certain leaders of the League. But as soon as the President returned to Djakarta, any Army support for the League collapsed and the League's power dwindled rapidly.

12 The inclusion of General Nasution as well as PKI leader Aidit in the President's entourage during Sukarno's trips abroad in recent years is widely interpreted in Indonesia as the President's way of preventing any coup in his absence either by the military or by the PKI.

dent. In addition to this clique, there are other cliques within the upper reaches of the Army. Several of them appear to have some leanings toward, if not identifiable ties with, the PKI; others have had a series of fleeting affiliations with a variety of parties of all possible political colorations. There is still a handful of officers whose loyalties remain with the Sultan of Jogjakarta; for others, the closest identification they retain is with their regional ties outside Java. Complicating the situation still more is the Communist orientation of much of the leadership of both the Air Force and the Navy. In short, the Indonesian armed forces can hardly be regarded as a monolithic organization. Quite apart from what is apparently the standard rivalry among the different branches of the armed forces, there are the splits within the Army leadership, the lack of a strong chain of command from top to bottom, and the many questions about the political orientations of different factions within the Army. For these reasons, the frequent attempts by some observers in recent years to equate Indonesia's armed forces and military leadership with their counterparts in Burma and Pakistan were a misreading of the data. So, too, were the conclusions drawn by many foreign observers that General Nasution represented a bulwark of moderate, anti-Communist sentiment backed up by substantial armed might. Undeniably, Indonesia's armed forces have been playing an increasingly important role in current political and economic life but there is little reason to expect that this power will necessarily be exercised either in unison or in behalf of moderate, pro-Western standpoints. Certainly the behavior of the Army, as one of the most vociferous exponents of *confrontasi* with Malaysia, suggests the opposite. Initially a bit reluctant to follow the President's lead on Malaysia, the Army shifted its position when it realized that it was being outmaneuvered by the PKI, and attempted to seize the leadership in the attack on Malaysia.

PKI

The other major contender for power that President Sukarno must take into account is the PKI. As indicated earlier, by the time the President proclaimed his concept of guided democracy, the PKI was one of the strongest elements on the scene, for all that it was not strong enough to maintain a position in defiance of the President. The PKI is still not strong enough to defy the President outright but the party's leaders and their rivals are keenly aware of the fact that, together with its affiliates, the PKI controls the largest, best-organized mass support in the country. The result has been that the PKI has entered into a kind of competition with the President to take over and control the direction of guided democracy. Thus it was always the PKI that organized the largest and most militant mass demonstrations in support of the President's program as it unfolded, and today Aidit, Njoto, and other PKI leaders couch their public statements in the slogans of guided democracy, repeatedly affirming their own adherence to Manipol and asserting that those who support Manipol must support Nasakom and Resopim.[13]

It was the President who vigorously campaigned for the inclusion of the PKI in the postelection cabinet, repeatedly insisting that he would not ride a three-legged horse, meaning a government that represented only three of the four chief victors in the elections: PNI, Masjumi, and NU. And it was the President who placed two thinly-disguised Communists in the Djuanda cabinet of 1957. But more recently the President's championship of the PKI has diminished somewhat in vigor, as it has become increasingly clear that his onetime protégé is consistently gaining on him. Nevertheless, for all that the President is uneas-

13 To fulfill the requirements of the January, 1960, law on the Conditions and Simplification of the Party System, the PKI has altered its constitution to include adherence to Pantja Sila and to the present form of guided or *gotong rojong* democracy. In further compliance with the law, the PKI on February 4, 1961, turned over to the authorities a list of party members including addresses, position in the party, and date of entry into the party.

ily aware that the day could soon come when their positions would be reversed, he has continued to rally to the support of the PKI whenever the party has been subjected to heavy attack. Thus, Army bans on the activities of the PKI or its front groups have been counterbalanced by the President's prompt denunciations of Communist-phobia.[14]

In striving to maintain its footing in the curiously complex and delicately balanced framework constructed by the President, the PKI has been particularly conscious of its lack of a strong military arm. PKI maneuvers to justify the arming of some of its large front organizations are woven through the pattern of party programs for the past decade. Meanwhile, party activists have been busily fishing in the well-stocked waters of the armed forces seeking ambitious dissidents.[15]

Frustrated in its efforts to increase its leverage through military support, the PKI in recent years has devoted increasing attention to building up its peasant support. Since 1959, the party has energetically campaigned for land reform, attacking the "deplorable conditions of the peasants" and the "feudal"

---

[14] There have been flurries of Army-sponsored demonstrations against the PKI and numerous crackdowns on PKI leaders by the Army in the past few years, especially in August, 1959, August, 1960, and again in the fall of 1961. For the President's efforts to redress the balance, including heavy attacks on those guilty of "Communist-phobia," see his speeches to the Ninth Congress of the PNI, July 25, 1960, and to Partindo, December 26, 1961.

[15] See above, Chapter 8, on the party's demand to the Ali cabinet for the arming of volunteer units to fight DI. During the heightened campaign for West Irian in the late 1950's, the PKI was obviously hoping that mobilization would mean the arming of the Pemuda Rakjat (People's Youth), with a million members, which was incorporated into the party officially at its Sixth Congress. Thus far, however, government regulations on mobilization have made it clear that recruits called up will operate under the control of the Army.

Donald Hindley, analyzing the alliance between the President and the PKI, writes that the PKI has gained very little support among Army officers and that since 1956 Nasution has gradually weeded out the few pro-Communist Army officers from positions of power. See "President Sukarno and the Communists: The Politics of Domestication," *American Political Science Review,* LVI (December, 1962), 915-26. However, not only is it extremely difficult to estimate the extent or intensity of pro-Communist sympathies among Indonesia's Army officers but also the substitution of Jani for Nasution as Army Chief of Staff may well have introduced new elements into the picture.

practices still obtaining in the villages. In October, 1959, the BTI representative in the elected Parliament demanded that peasant farmers receive 60 per cent of the harvest, and noted that, through the "tireless struggle" of his organization, tenant farmers in some areas were receiving as much as 70 and 80 per cent of the crop.[16] The following month, Parliament passed a bill providing for a 50-50 division of crops, with the expenses of production, including seed and fertilizers, to be borne by the landowners. Thereafter, following the dissolution of Parliament and the expansion of the institutions of guided democracy, the BTI moderated its demands to such statements as "The target of land reform must be determined in conformity with the target of the revolution as defined in President Sukarno's Political Manifesto," and shifted its attack to the special land concessions granted, "foreign monopoly capital." [17] An interesting aspect of the PKI's heightened campaign for peasant support has been the emphasis it now gives to organizing the country's millions of fishermen. In the view of one observer, the PKI's new concern for the fate of Indonesia's fishermen suggests that the PKI may be seeking a hospitable coastline that could serve as an escape hatch, provide a useful supply and communications line and possibly even an active sanctuary, should the need arise.[18]

The PKI has also been experiencing some internal problems, difficulties which have been exacerbated by the dispute within the Communist bloc. The PKI is currently suffering the familiar problems of a Communist Party that has identified itself with the nationalist slogans of the regime in power. The PKI's vast membership, both in the party itself and in its many affiliates, has been attracted by a combination of promises of plenty,[19] of attacks

[16] See the party monthly, *Review of Indonesia,* VI (November-December, 1959), 34 ff.

[17] Asmu, "The Question of Land Reform," *Suara Tani* (March-April, 1960), reprinted in *Review of Indonesia,* VII (July, 1960), 30-32.

[18] Brackman, *op. cit.,* pp. 264-65.

[19] In the 1955 elections, the PKI's campaign promises—largely of the specific material goods that would follow a PKI victory—were notable for their extravagance even in that campaign of wild promises by the competing parties. The party's failure to make good on these promises did not prevent it from

on the other parties as the authors of the corruption and upheaval besetting the country since independence, and of vociferous endorsement of the President's popular slogans of radical
nationalism. With this program, which is designed for popular
appeal,[20] the party has not merely held its own but continued to
grow. But for Communists as for other politicians, there comes
a day of reckoning. Promises must one day be redeemed. That
day is not yet upon the PKI, but it has had to contend with dissatisfied and increasingly restless elements among its supporters.
There has been ample evidence for some years of dissension
within the party high command. Chairman Aidit's efforts to hold
in check the revolutionary ardor of the party's left wing, headed
by Lukman and Sudisman, seemed in late 1961 to have succeeded. As the split between Moscow and Peking has widened,
however, Aidit has become correspondingly anxious about the
necessity for maintaining unity within his party. This urgent desire
to restore party unity at home was reflected for a time in the efforts
of the PKI leadership to heal the breach between Moscow and
Peking.[21] It is also reflected in the repetitious calls for unity within
the Indonesian Communist movement by Aidit, his principal
lieutenant Njoto, and others of their faction.[22] At the same time,
in response to the pressures exerted by the party's left wing,
Aidit has stepped up his public campaign against the Army and

---

substantially increasing its support at the polls in the provincial elections a
few years later. PKI campaigners made it clear that their exclusion from the
government absolved them of responsibility for the continuing economic disabilities afflicting the voters.

[20] The party's official program at present is summarized as the Three
Banners: democracy, unity, and mobilization.

[21] Aidit has several times called for a world Communist meeting to resolve
the differences within the bloc and demonstrate bloc unity. See, for example,
his speech of January 6, 1963, in *NCNA*, January 11, 1963. It was not until the
latter part of 1963 that the PKI's leaders openly and clearly ranged themselves
on the side of the Chinese in the Sino-Soviet split. Even then, however, their
tone has tended to be more moderate than that employed by other supporters
of Peking.

[22] See, for example, Njoto's statement in *Harian Rakjat*, April 2, 1963,
which indicates his faction's sensitivity to charges that the party is harsh in
its stand on the enemies of Communism abroad but moderate in its stance
at home.

specifically against Army-imposed restrictions on the activities of PKI front organizations.[23] But, however great the pressures exerted by the party's left wing, Aidit, whose faction still dominates, clearly has no intention of abandoning his strategy of seeking power by way of the palace. To get a more complete view of the relative position of the PKI under guided democracy, therefore, we shall have to turn—as we must inevitably turn, whatever the question—to the palace and President Sukarno.

The President and the Palace

The single most important figure in contemporary Indonesia is President Sukarno. For twenty years and more, he has dominated the Indonesian scene. His personal prestige far transcends that of any other political figure. To many Indonesians, apparently, he symbolizes Indonesia. His face and his name evoke virtually the same emotions as the country's flag and national anthem. A gifted orator of remarkable skill, he has the capacity for expressing the hopes, the latent aspirations, and the dreams of past glory and of future greatness of the average man in phrases that fire the imagination.[24] His magnetic platform personality and his undeniable ability to arouse and channel the passions of his audience assure him of a firm base of popular support. In spite of the

[23] See, for example, Aidit's political report to the PKI Central Committee Plenum, February 10, 1963, NCNA, February 15, 1963.

[24] It is an illuminating, and somewhat chastening experience to watch one of Sukarno's vast audiences under the spell of his oratorical powers. He quite literally holds his audience in the palm of his hand. He tells them: "Together we will say 'Merdeka' (independence)," or perhaps the word for the day is 'Manipol' or 'Nasakom.' Then he raises his hand. There is utter silence from the throng of several hundreds of thousands of people massed on the field before the speaker's platform. Then he sweeps his hand down swiftly, and in unison the crowd shouts 'Merdeka!' They repeat this again and again, at the tempo selected by the President. Most interesting of all is to observe the effect of all this on Sukarno. These public appearances before huge, enthusiastic audiences seem to reassure him. He beams at the response of the crowd and, on occasion, when some of the guests seated beside him on the platform are known to be something less than enthusiastic about his ideas, he will turn to the skeptical, between these controlled responses of the crowd, in a manner that all but says, "Do you doubt my ability to convince these people of anything?"

fact that in some circles his halo has become a bit tarnished in recent years, it is clear that as long as he chooses to do so, he can retain his hold on the mass of the people. There are groups that have defied him, but not for long; there are circles that detest him, but never dare attack him openly. Those few political figures who have opposed him publicly have soon regretted their tactical error: It is they, not he, who have ended up losing popular support.

Given the President's virtually unassailable position, much of the politics of independent Indonesia has consisted of efforts to curry favor with him, and of his manipulation of different groups for his own ends. Examples of the latter include the brilliant fashion in which the President in 1952 utilized the October 17 affair to achieve a firmer grasp on the Army and once again place himself in a role above the petty internecine warfare of the parties, while all the time denying vigorously that he sought to become a dictator. Subsequent incidents involving the armed forces have all been resolved in much the same fashion. The President, as some Indonesians have remarked (in whispers), invariably ends up with the best of both worlds. He allows one faction to gain ground at the expense of another, and then, just when he seems to be preoccupied elsewhere, he swiftly moves in and throws his weight behind the underdog of the moment, thereby redressing the balance. In all these abrupt reversals of position, he has never lost his balance; to some of his weary and more critical compatriots, it seems that he never even appears in danger of losing his footing, or risking any substantial part of his popular following. Nothing seems to damage his prestige with the masses, and this, of course, is the key to his role as the most important factor in Indonesian politics. Whatever he does, whatever sectors of the population he offends, he is still the idol of the masses and his personal backing is far more valuable than any number of armed divisions or any substantial sums of money.

The PNI, although it is not the heir to the nationalist party of the same initials that Sukarno headed in the early 1930's, capitalized heavily on this apparent link to Sukarno.[25] Even when some of the right-wing PNI leaders became uneasy over the President's rapidly growing ties to the Communists, they had the option of sacrificing their personal political futures or swallowing their misgivings. The Army too has learned that the President can be pushed just so far and then will swing back in the other direction, catapulting from power those who were too zealous in trying to foist a course of action upon him. General Nasution, for example, has learned that a cabinet post and a chief of staff's insigne are of less value than having the President's ear. When Nasution has become too militant in his attacks on the PKI, he has found some of his more malleable junior officers usurping his seat at the President's side.

The President's relations with the PKI have been among the most intricate and delicately performed of all these maneuvers. As is evident from the quotations from Sukarno's writings and speeches cited in Chapters 6 and 10, the President's own intellectual background and resources have drawn heavily upon a variety of socialist sources and indicate a substantial interest in Marxist-Leninist thought. But, as is also evident from his behavior over the years, the President's single deepest commitment is to his nationalist views. This may explain in part why, despite Madiun and the history of the PKI which preceded that event, the President, like so many of his countrymen, apparently assumed that with Communists as with any Indonesian, nationalism would come first, and that any political ideology that sought to supersede nationalist goals would be a poor second. Or perhaps Sukarno, again like so many other Indonesians, simply never considered it possible that the PKI any more than any other political group could ever achieve a status that might challenge the prestige of the President. Whatever the reasons—and they doubtless included Sukarno's early recognition of the natural appeal that the Communists' slogans had for most Indonesians—when the PKI began its postwar march back to power, Sukarno chose not to oppose this reviving Communist force.

25 See Kahin, *Major Governments of Asia,* p. 539.

Rather, not only did he appropriate many of its slogans for himself, but also, operating from his then totally undisputed position of power, he apparently felt secure enough to encourage
the PKI as another group to play off against the Masjumi, the PSI,
and any other critics of his policies. By the time of the first Ali
cabinet, 1953-55, the President seemed to have entered into a
tacit alliance with the PKI as well as with the left wing of the
PNI. Despite growing uneasiness in many circles close to the palace, the President continued to respond amiably to the wooing of the PKI, even when the Communists' tone, keeping pace
with their expanding strength, gradually changed from one of
entreaty to one of demand. When the 1955 elections showed that
the PKI was the fourth largest party in the country, it was the
President who championed the Communists' right to participate
in the new Ali government, and later it was the President who
made room for the Communists in the cabinet he selected to succeed Ali's in 1957.

Should one assume that the President's vigorous backing of
the PKI and his frequent and heated denunciations of "Communist-phobia" mean that he has wholeheartedly embraced Communist doctrine and committed himself to full support of the
PKI? Or does Sukarno's apparent enthusiasm for the PKI reflect
an accommodation on his part to the realities of the situation,
a carrying-out of the old adage, If you can't lick 'em, join 'em?
While there is evidence to support both of these possibilities, the
record shows that Sukarno, the master strategist, has not allowed
the situation to be reduced to a simple confrontation of Communists and anti-Communists. Whatever his possible miscalculations
in the early 1950's about the Communists' capacity for growth,
Sukarno more recently has demonstrated that he no longer
doubts the PKI's potential as a rival. Like a gifted puppeteer,
with one hand he continues to manipulate the contending forces
of the PKI and the Army while with the other hand he has
been busily building up his own counterforce, which for purposes of identification we might refer to as the palace guard.

This palace guard is not, on the surface, a particularly homo-

geneous group. It includes a now-dwindling number of old nationalist figures who were long-time friends of the President; the
most prominent of these men, until his death in late 1962, was
Mohammad Yamin. It also includes several Army officers, somewhat hostile to Nasution, the best known of whom is Colonel
Isman. Finally, the largest group in the palace guard is made
up of Murba leaders and those closely identified with Murba and
with several earlier Tan Malaka-oriented groups, among whom
are Chairul Saleh, Sukarni, and Adam Malik. On the fringes of
the palace guard are such figures as Ruslan Abdulgani of the
PNI, and Idham Chalid of NU. All these elements in the palace
guard have two things in common: Although many of them
have achieved national prominence in their own right, none of
them commands any really substantial popular support beyond
that which they currently derive from their link to the palace,
and all of them are committed to a vaguely defined but aggres-
sively expressed radical nationalism.

Since the identifiable elements in the philosophy of the palace guard most closely resemble the views of Tan Malaka, the increasingly important role assigned to this group has been a
source of worry to the PKI. Apparently, this is what Sukarno has
intended. In spite of the ease with which Tan Malaka's men have
been known to drift in and out of alliances with the PKI in the
past, the President apparently feels that under the present circumstances he can rely on their support as a counterweight to
the PKI. Members of the palace guard have been placed in
pivotal positions in the official bodies of guided democracy; their
standing has been enhanced by such prestige appointments as
that accorded Adam Malik, who was made chief negotiator for the
final settlement of the Irian dispute, and a number of them have
been awarded key diplomatic appointments. In the case of these
diplomatic posts, it is illuminating that the President has selected his emissaries to the capitals of world Communism from
the national Communists in the palace guard. The roster of Presidential appointments on the home front is by no means as con-
spicuously weighted in favor of the Murba elements; rather, each

national Communist in the Supreme Advisory Council and the National Planning Council is balanced by a PKI figure appointed to an equivalent rank. But, given the impotence of these official bodies in practice, what comfort the PKI may draw from being represented in these councils is very likely outweighed by the Communists' dismay at sharing responsibility for a government policy that it cannot control.

The President is not by any means relying for support solely on the palace coterie. He continues to maintain a wide network of relations with figures from all groups, including leaders of several minor but occasionally useful parties. But in all these relationships, Sukarno retains the initiative, confident that, if need be, he can always reach over the heads of rival groups to the still-adoring masses, and confident too of his ability to keep rival factions ranged against each other and incapable of uniting in opposition to him. While contentious groups bicker among themselves, the reins of guided democracy remain in the President's hands and the government functions by Presidential decree.

The only official body popularly regarded as sharing any authority with the President is the ten-man inner cabinet, which Sukarno appointed on July 10, 1959, following his decree dissolving the Constituent Assembly and reinstating the Constitution of 1945. With himself as Prime Minister, a presidium of Deputy First Ministers consisting of the former Foreign Minister, Subandrio, the former Minister of Health, Leimena, and Chairul Saleh, and with Nasution as Minister of Defense and Security, both the inner cabinet and the full cabinet of twenty-six "junior" ministers, who include such figures as Iwa Kusumasumantri, Erningpradja, and Sadjarwo, are made up of men who, with the possible exception of Nasution, are not likely to give the President any trouble—and Nasution is obviously heavily outnumbered in this set-up. Nevertheless, membership in the cabinet and especially the inner cabinet is considered to be of genuine importance and the PKI, which is not represented in the inner cabinet, has expended considerable energy on trying to force its way into this body.[26] In practice, both the inner and outer cabinets have confined their activities to expressing their approval of Presidential decrees. Presumably, then, the real value of a cabinet post lies in the opportunity it offers for establishing bases of power within the ministry assigned to each cabinet member.

The parade of decrees issued with monotonous regularity from the President's office covers virtually every aspect of national life from establishing foreign-exchange ratios to regulating the sending and receiving of international cultural missions, from setting up the National Front to banning the Boy Scouts (headed by the Sultan of Jogjakarta) and replacing them with an organization called, significantly, *Pramuka* or Pioneers, with the President –Prime Minister–Commander-in-Chief–Great Leader of the Revolution also serving as Chief Pioneer.

The Boy Scouts was not the only private international organization to be decreed out of existence. The Masons, Moral Rearmament, Rosicrucians, and the Divine Life Society were all ordered to dissolve on March 1, 1961. Also on that date, a Presidential decree banned the Democratic League on the grounds that "the organization and its charter do not accept and support the Political Manifesto which has become the Broad Outline for the Course of the State." [27]

The inner cabinet is preoccupied with as broad a range of topics as is the President. For example, on one occasion, after approving one bill for the mobilization of all citizens between the ages of eighteen and forty in the interests of the defense and security of the state, a second Presidential draft bill for the establishment of a civil defense organization, and a third Presidential bill providing for preliminary training of a people's defense unit,

[26] Reportedly, in 1963 the President had decided against giving the PKI any seats in the inner cabinet and as a consequence felt that he must balance this blow to the Communists by refusing to release from custody the Masjumi and PSI leaders who were arrested in early 1962. However, in the fall of 1964, Njoto of the PKI was given the special post of Minister attached to the Presidium—a compromise that gave the PKI a position close to the top but one that could still not be regarded as full entry into the inner cabinet. Meanwhile, the imprisoned opposition leaders remain in custody.

[27] Radio Republik Indonesia, Home Service, Djakarta, March 2, 1961.

the cabinet turned its attention to a program introduced by its Minister of Social and Cultural Affairs and its Minister of Education to reform the spelling of the Indonesian language to bring it more in line with the national identity.

Other facets of Indonesian cultural life have been swept into the realm of government decrees. Those publications that continue to appear do so at the discretion of the government. The Indonesian press, once among the most articulate organs of expression in Asia, was slowly being throttled by a combination of Army takeovers and mob violence even before the advent of guided democracy. The emergency regulations put into force with the outbreak of the civil war in 1958 permitted the Army to order publication suspended by newspapers accused of fomenting public unrest or printing subversive material. Editors representing papers of an astonishing variety of views—from the pro-Masjumi *Abadi,* the pro-PSI *Pedoman,* the anti-Army, anti-PNI, and otherwise somewhat eclectic *Indonesia Raya,* to the PKI's *Harian Rakjat*—paraded in and out of jail as though marching through a revolving door. Extremist Moslem mobs attacked the plants of Communist publications, Communist mobs attacked the plants of Moslem publications, and moderate newspapers were periodically put out of commission by successive mob violence from both sides. In November, 1960, the Information Minister announced that only papers that supported the Political Manifesto would be allowed to appear. In regions where this new decree would mean that there would be no newspapers, the government planned to provide its own publication. Government control of the press was fully established by late 1962 when PIA—the Indonesian news agency established by a group of editors of antigovernment papers in an effort to compete with the professedly unofficial but government-subsidized news agency Antara—was dissolved and integrated with Antara.

In spite of a controlled press, arbitrary arrests, the banning of political parties and private organizations, restrictions on public meetings of all sizes, and a general atmosphere that many Indonesians consider reminiscent of the years of the Japanese occu-

and thereafter pushed back to the sidelines. But although they have withdrawn from the vortex of activity, they have neither settled back into their old patterns of life nor put down new roots. Aroused, apprehensive, increasingly restless, they remain alert for any leadership that promises the fulfillment of their still inchoate but ardently desired goals. To many of them, guided democracy has seemed to offer that leadership.

The ferment produced by these persistent conditions of instability at the base and violent but indecisive strife at the top was brought to a head by a series of developments: the rebellions in the regions outside Java, the palpable helplessness of the second Ali cabinet in the face of this and other challenges, the growing restlessness of the Army high command, and the increasingly aggressive posture of the PKI. Into this situation of crisis, guided democracy was introduced as a panacea both for the symptoms and the causes of the present catastrophe.

Guided democracy is represented not only as the answer to Indonesia's problems but also as the logical and indispensable substitute for a discredited system that had failed to work: parliamentary democracy. But the truth of the matter is that parliamentary democracy was never put into actual practice in Indonesia. The underlying conditions that give meaning to parliamentary government—an informed, literate electorate with a widespread, however minimal, level of education, some comprehension of the role of government, and, above all, a sense of participation in government—were all lacking. What Indonesia had, from 1945 to 1957, were the external trappings of parliamentary democracy: cabinets, ministries, a legislature, a judiciary, a civil service, and, in the later stages, the selection of local and national representatives by vote. Many of those who took part in the functions of government made a genuine attempt to carry out their tasks in the spirit and the letter of constitutional democracy, but their activities were largely irrelevant. Both the events and ideas moving the mass of the people and the decisions reached and carried out at the top for the most part bypassed the constitutionally authorized organs of government. The parliamentary democracy that President Sukarno and others have condemned and rejected was never given the opportunity to function, nor were the conditions provided to encourage its development.

Under the circumstances, it is not surprising that the intiative passed into the hands of the one man who was both willing and able to exercise it, President Sukarno. At the outset, when he made his first tentative moves toward assuming power in late 1956, he was expressing a half-formed intention and not a prepared plan of action. But the reaction of the opposition groups was to continue their habitual bickering, meanwhile keeping a weather eye on the President's next moves. They did not offer any steadfast resistance. Unwilling to risk defying the President when he began his campaign for guided democracy, the political leadership soon found that it was too late to halt him; the President had moved too swiftly for them to recoup the initiative. The only group to make a firm stand against the President took the path of civil war. The strength of their convictions was clear enough but their capacity to back up those convictions with purposeful action was glaringly inadequate. Sukarno, finding his path to power so relatively unencumbered, was encouraged to take more positive action and build up his own bastions of support. Given his unchallenged popularity with the masses and the hesitant behavior of his opponents, it is small wonder that President Sukarno was able to fashion the system of personalized rule that he desired.

From our study of developments in Indonesia after 1956, we know that there is much dissatisfaction with guided democracy. How, then, does the system function? Whose interests does it serve? Whose interests does it oppose? And what values does it promote?

It might be said that guided democracy almost by definition serves the interests of the President and the palace clique. What these interests are, beyond the sheer desire for power, is less easily defined. Certainly, President Sukarno and many of his principal aides have a vision of the Indonesia they want: strong, independent, respected in the community of nations, its importance as the fifth most populous nation in the world given due recognition. They want a prosperous Indonesia, with a population enjoying the fruits of the vast natural resources of the land they occupy. They want a country faithfully living by its unique traditions and heritage and at the same time catching up with the modern world and enjoying the advantages of modern technology and science. In these respects, the Indonesia they seek is not very different from the goal of most of their countrymen or from that sought by most leaders of other emerging nations. It is in the values that they do not hold in common with some of the Indonesian opposition that the real difficulties arise. The men whose interests are most closely served by guided democracy do not regard representative government as an essential for their ideal state; they are not concerned to have a government of laws, but rather one of men.

While the President and the palace guard stand to gain most from guided democracy, they are not the only ones whose interests are served by the present regime. The Army finds much that is to its advantage in the current system. To the extent that the Army high command has been able to insinuate itself into the different branches of government and build up its own centers of power within the framework provided by guided democracy, it has found the new regime useful. The Army enjoys a freedom under guided democracy that no military service achieves, even in time of war, under a parliamentary system. Answerable to no one but the President, often carrying out his commands in the light of their own arbitrary interpretations, Indonesia's military leaders exercise a broad range of authority that cuts across the fields elsewhere reserved for the executive, judicial, and legislative branches of government. As with the President and the palace guard, it is difficult to determine what the Army seeks beyond power for its own sake, but that it is busy expanding and deepening its power is very clear.

Another group that has learned to make the best of a situation it cannot for the moment change is the PKI. Guided democracy has had certain distinct advantages for the PKI. Like the Army, the Communists can profit from the absence of the restraints imposed by parliamentary government. Its activities under the present system are limited only by the degree of freedom it is able to wrest from the President and, far better than the Army, the PKI is equipped to function quietly and clandestinely beyond the President's range of vision. The PKI, too, has used the opportunities offered by guided democracy to establish its own network of supporters in key branches of government. Publicly, it has derived great benefits from its vociferous endorsement of the slogans of guided democracy. Its identification with the vastly popular President and his still more popular slogans has enabled it to augment its mass following through its own front organizations and through those of the President's new mass organizations, which the PKI is currently attempting to take over. As we have noted, the PKI also tends to suffer from its identification with a regime that remains unsuccessful in many important fields. Nevertheless, by its periodic *démarches,* demanding more vigorous action by the government, the PKI is able to some extent to retain its own, distinct identity in the public eye. Finally, the PKI, as long as it is not the responsible party in power, can expect to reap the long-range profits of a situation of continuing economic deterioration and ever-increasing social and political unrest.

These are the groups whose temporary or long-range interests are served by guided democracy. What of those whose interests are poorly served, or served not at all, by the current system of government? The opposition leaders who were jailed early in 1962, and the groups they represent, clearly feel that they have lost more than their freedom of movement and their right to engage in political activities. For those whose own commitment is to a form of representative government, the abandonment of the effort at parliamentary democracy and its replacement by an authoritarian regime has meant suspending their participation in public life. Their supporters have been shunted out of the mainstream of political activity; the likelihood of their return remains to be seen.

At the level of general mass interests, what role has guided democracy played? Its introduction has been accompanied by a series of economic plans and programs; it has also involved major shifts in the ownership and control of large-scale Dutch-owned enterprises and small-scale Chinese businesses. Both the economic plans and the expropriation measures were supposed to work out for the benefit of the public. Neither have been successful. The new political organs of government, the consultative bodies and the National Front, were presented as new and more meaningful forms of representation for the populace at large. There is no reason to assume that these hand-picked groups reflect popular views or desires any more accurately than the elected bodies they have replaced. Nor have these appointed bodies been given the freedom of action that would allow them to translate popular interests and goals into feasible legislation.

What, then, has guided democracy brought to the Indonesian people? What values does it promote that capture their imagination and win their support? Perhaps its foremost appeal lies in its encouragement of a lively sense of nationalism. In this sphere, at least, guided democracy has brought about tangible results. West Irian was restored to Indonesia under the present regime, a feat that no previous government of whatever political complexion was able to accomplish. Guided democracy also sets great store by appeals to egalitarianism. It is the *marhaen*, the little man, the have-not, who is the focus of presidential addresses, government pronouncements, even of economic plans. The appeal has apparently not yet worn thin; Indonesians who have seen such cataclysmic changes take place in their country in the space of a lifetime can understandably await—and expect—further miracles.

Now that we have seen how guided democracy functions, let us consider President Sukarno's assertion that his system represents a synthesis of Indoneian socialist thought. First of all, is guided democracy a socialist system? Although its slogans lay great stress on socialist doctrines, although its supporters reiterate its militant anticapitalism and its unqualified rejection of

political and economic liberalism, it can hardly be termed a socialist system. Politically, as we have seen, it is a form of personal
rule. In spite of its superstructure of official bodies, which most
closely resemble that found in Communist states, it is neither a
totalitarian nor a Communist system. Economically, a form of
corporate or state capitalism has evolved under guided democracy; in many respects, it resembles that of Mussolini's Italy. This
form of economic organization can not be defined as socialist. In
short, while its slogans draw largely upon socialist theories long
popular in Indonesia and contain many elements derived from
still older, indigenous customs, guided democracy in practice remains a weakly structured and poorly functioning attempt at
authoritarian rule.

Proponents of guided democracy emphasize its alleged derivation from Indonesian traditions. They have promulgated a myth
of a government operating on the basis of *gotong rojong,* mutual
assistance, and of *musjawarah* and *mufakat,* deliberations that result in decisions based on mutual consent. However often the
myth is invoked, it remains a myth. The Indonesian people do
not take part in decision-making under guided democracy. The
consultative bodies that are supposed to represent them have
been chosen by their leaders and not by the populace. Even if
these were genuinely representative bodies, with some freedom
to determine the scope within which they have the right to take
the initiative, would they be able to function effectively under a
system that requires that they reach their decisions by consensus?
Decision-making by consensus in a small, cohesive unit functioning under stable conditions has proved to be a viable system. But
the kinds of procedures that work at the village level are not
readily transferred to the process of decision-making at the national level. The structural demands of decision-making at the
national level, especially when dealing with national problems
that cannot be separated from international issues, are vastly different from those in a small, self-contained community. In spite
of the numerous appeals to the indigenous traditions that are
contained in the slogans of guided democracy, the Indonesian

people and the councils appointed to represent them are limited in fact to approving and supporting the decisions made by their leaders. The number of decrees suspending the consensus and concentrating power in the hands of the President or the Army Chief of Staff, and the variety of topics with which these decrees deal, offer a continuing flow of evidence contradicting the myth.

What of the views of the Religious Socialists, which guided democracy is also supposed to encompass? The Religious Socialists stood for a socialism free of any spiritual tie to Marxism, but guided democracy's marhaenist socialism is, in the President's words, "Marxism as practised in Indonesia." The Religious Socialists insisted on the inviolability of individualism, individual initiative, and individual responsibility. Guided democracy vigorously opposes individualism as an expression of the "free-fight" liberalism it condemns.

Where, then, are the Indonesian socialist doctrines—Marxist, traditional Indonesian, and religious—that guided democracy claims to subsume? Under guided democracy, the forms of socialism that flourished in Indonesia are retained in the vocabulary of the system's protagonists. The only socialist doctrines to which the system of guided democracy gives more than lip service are those backed up by centers of power too strong for the country's leader to ignore. Specifically, this means certain of the positions taken by the PKI, for the eclectic and vacillating socialism espoused by the representatives of Murba in the palace guard can hardly be viewed at the moment as forming a coherent doctrine.

If guided democracy is not a synthesis of Indonesian socialist views, what is it? Put bluntly, it is a cloak for a power struggle, a façade built out of myths and slogans to shield a system of autocratic personalized rule.

If the profusion of complicated details surrounding the system in Indonesia occasionally obscures the reality, it is much less difficult to recognize guided democracy for what it is if one observes the system in operation elsewhere. For President Sukarno has his followers abroad as well as at home, and the term guided democracy has been adopted by at least one other state, Cambodia. Prince Norodom Sihanouk has maintained for several years that his nation is operating under the system of guided democracy. In Cambodia, where the competing power forces are fewer in number and easier to isolate and define than in Indonesia, the scene is also much less cluttered with variant, splinter groups. It is therefore that much easier to observe that in practice there is virtually no decision of any consequence whatsoever that is not in the end made by a single individual. Cambodia is one of the few places in the modern world to which one can still apply the formula: *l'état, c'est moi*. In Indonesia, sheer size and diversity may blur the picture somewhat, but when reduced to its essentials the formula might well be said to be the same. Indonesia under guided democracy is functioning under President Sukarno's chosen doctrine and President Sukarno's rule. The situation contains restraints on his freedom of action. But, for the moment and possibly for as long as he can successfully continue to juggle these restraining forces, he is in command.

Guided democracy is, of course, only a variation on the one-man system of rule encountered in a majority of the new nations of today's world. One of the distinguishing characteristics of the Indonesian system is that Sukarno, unlike some of his counterparts in other states, does not have at his disposal a strong one-party set-up. Other features of his regime, however, are the familiar ones found in many parts of Asia, Africa, and Latin America: the rejection of majority rule in favor of a form of consensus, the heavy reliance on symbols and slogans, the appeals to indigenous traditions which are usually described as locally derived forms of socialism. And in Indonesia, as in so many of these other nations, the cement holding the system together is provided largely by the charismatic personality of the national leader.

This state of affairs suggests a further question that lies, perhaps, outside the scope of this study but is nonetheless of intrinsic interest. Can this system be expected to outlive President Sukarno? The available evidence suggests that guided democracy has never penetrated beneath the surface of Indonesian life.

It draws its strength in part from its appeal to slogans that are genuinely part of Indonesian life and customs; these slogans, which preceded guided democracy, will doubtless persist in their appeal whatever the fate of the present regime. But given its superficial and largely mythological character, it is difficult to imagine that this particular system, which remains in force because of the extraordinary political talents of one man, can survive without him. Guided democracy is President Sukarno. If tomorrow the President decided to renounce guided democracy and Manipol/Usdek in their entirety, and flung aside as well Nasakom and Resopim and all his current ideological paraphernalia in favor of a new and entirely different system, the new invention would very likely come into being without too much dislocation, as long as Sukarno remained at the helm. A new system, in any case, would undoubtedly be introduced through the medium of similarly appealing slogans drawn from equally familiar Indonesian terms and most probably from a new application of these same terms. It is also true that if Sukarno were to depart the scene tomorrow, the contenders for the succession would doubtless, for a time, invoke the same slogans and symbols he has popularized so widely, not because of the inherent appeal of these slogans but rather because of their identification with the long-time national hero. Power lies with Sukarno, not with the doctrine he expounds or the system he has installed. President Sukarno can, if he chooses, get along without guided democracy but guided democracy as it exists today cannot get along without President Sukarno.

Selected Bibliography

OFFICIAL PUBLICATIONS OF THE REPUBLIC OF INDONESIA

[ABDULGANI, RUSLAN]. *Manipol/Usdek in Question and Answer.* New York: Permanent Mission of the Republic of Indonesia to the United Nations, n.d. [probably Summer, 1961].

ABDULGANI, H. ROESLAN [Ruslan]. *Pendjelasan Manipol dan Usdek (Elucidation of Manipol and Usdek).* Djakarta: Departemen Penerangan R.I., 1960.

———. *Perkembangan Tjita-tjita Sosialisme di Indonesia: Kuliah Umum Sdr. H. Roeslan Abdulgani di Perguruan Tinggi Malang pada hari Saptu 2 Djuli 1960 (The Development of Socialist Ideas in Indonesia: Public Lecture by Brother H. Ruslan Abdulgani at Malang University, Saturday, July 2, 1960).* Mimeograph; n.pl., n.d. [presumably Djakarta: Department of Information, 1960].

———. *Tentang Ketegasan Sosialisme Indonesia: Landjutan Kuliah Umum Wakil Ketua Dewan Pertimbangan Agung H. Roeslan Abdulgani di "Universitas Malang" pada hari Senen tanggal 13 Pebruari 1961 (On the Explanation of Indonesian Socialism: Continuation of the Public Lecture by Deputy Chairman of the Supreme Advisory Council H. Ruslan Abdulgani at Malang University, Monday, February 13, 1961),* Mimeograph; n.pl., n.d. [presumably Djakarta: Department of Information, 1961].

DJUANDA, H. *Keterangan Pemerintah Mengenai Pelaksanaan Demokrasi Terpimpin dalam Rangka Kembali ke U.U.D. 1945: Diutjapkan oleh Perdana Menteri H. Djuanda dalam rapat pleno Dewan Perwakilan Rakjat pada hari Senen tanggal 2 Maret 1959 mulai djam 19.30. (Government Statement Concerning the Implementation of Guided Democracy in the Framework of the Return to the Constitution of 1945: Statement by Prime Minister H. Djuanda at the plenary session of Parliament, Monday, March 2, 1959, at 7:30 P.M.).* Djakarta: Republic of Indonesia, Kementerian Penerangan, 1959.

Handbook on the Political Manifesto: Two Executive Directions of Manipol. Djakarta: Department of Information, 1961.

Indonesia, 1961. Djakarta: Republic of Indonesia, Department of Foreign Affairs, April, 1961.

229

Inti Sari Pidato-pidato para Anggauta Konstituante Berkenaan dengan Amanat Presiden Tanggal 22 April 1959, "Res Publica! Sekali Lagi Res Publica!," dalam Pemandangan Umum Babak Ke-II Sidang Pleno Pertama Konstituante Tahun 1959, pada tanggal 25-26 Mei 1959 (Essence of the Speeches by Members of the Constituent Assembly in connection with the President's Mandate of April 22, 1959, "Res Publica! Once More Res Publica!," during the General Debate in the Second Part of the First Plenary Session of the Assembly for 1959, May 25 to 26, 1959). N.pl. [Djakarta]: Kementerian Penerangan, n.d. [1959].

KEMENTERIAN LUAR NEGERI (MINISTRY OF FOREIGN AFFAIRS). *Daily Press Cable.* Djakarta, 1950-59.

Kepartaian dan Parlementaria di Indonesia (Parties and Parliament in Indonesia). Djakarta: Kementerian Penerangan, 1954.

Keputusan Dewan Pertimbangan Agung Tentang Perintjaan Pedoman Pelaksanaan Manifesto Politik Republic Indonesia (Decisions of the Supreme Advisory Council Regarding the Breakdown of the Specifications for the Implementation of the Political Manifesto of the Republic of Indonesia). No. 1/Kpts/Sd./1/61. Djakarta: Republic of Indonesia, Dewan Pertimbangan Agung Republik Indonesia, n.d. [presumably February, 1961].

Lembaran Sedjarah (Pages of History). Jogjakarta: Kementerian Penerangan, 1950.

Sari Pers (Press Review). Djakarta: Kementerian Penerangan, 1945-48.

SUKARNO. *The Birth of Pantja Sila.* Djakarta: Ministry of Information, 1950.

———. *Dari Proklamasi sampai Resopim: Terbitan berisi Pidato Proklamasi Diutjapkan oleh P.J.M. Presiden Republik Indonesia pada tiap tanggal 17 Agustus sedjak tahun 1945 sampai 1961* (From the Proclamation to Resopim: A Book Containing the Proclamation Speech by His Excellency the President of the Republic of Indonesia each August 17 from 1945 to 1961). Djakarta: Departemen Penerangan, n.d. [probably 1962].

———. *Res Publica! Once More Res Publica!* New York: Republic of Indonesia, Permanent Mission to the United Nations, 1959.

———. *Setia Kepada Marhaenisme Sedjati: Amanat Presiden Sukarno pada Kongres Partindo di Gedung Olah Raga, Djakarta, 26 Desember 1961* (Faithful to True Marhaenism: Address by President Sukarno to the Partindo Congress at the Sport Stadium, Djakarta, December 26, 1961). Djakarta: Departemen Penerangan, 1962.

———. *Speech to the Eighth Congress of the Indonesian Republic Teachers Association, Bandung, October 30, 1956.* Bandung, Radio Indonesia Home Service.

———. *Speech to the Students at Gadjah Mada University, Jogjakarta, May 28, 1958.* Jogjakarta: Radio Indonesia Central Java Regional Service.

———. *Speech at the Opening of the First Conference of the Depart-*

ment of the Attorney-General, Surabaya, October 30, 1960. Djakarta: Sekretariat Negara, 1961.

TUMAKAKA, J. K. *Sosialisme Indonesia: Disusun berdasar kepada Adjaran Bung Karno—Bapak Sosialisme Indonesia (Indonesian Socialism: A Compilation Based on the Teachings of Bung Karno—Father of Indonesian Socialism).* Djakarta: Departemen Penerangan, 1961.

Vakbeweging (The Labor Movement). Djakarta: Kementerian Penerangan, May, 1947.

NEWSPAPERS AND PERIODICALS

Abadi (Eternal). Djakarta.
Antara Daily News Bulletin. Djakarta and New York.
Bintang Merah (Red Star). Djakarta.
Communist International. London.
Harian Rakjat (People's Daily). Djakarta.
Indonesia Merdeka (Free Indonesia; after 1937, Indonesia). Leiden.
Indonesian Affairs. Djakarta.
Het Inzich (Insight). Djakarta.
Pikiran Rakjat (People's Opinion). Bandung.
Review of Indonesia. Djakarta.
Voice of Free Indonesia. Djakarta, Jogjakarta.
World News and Views. International Press Correspondence. London.

BOOKS, PAMPHLETS, AND ARTICLES

ABDULGANI, RUSLAN. "Ideological Background of the Asian-African Conference," *United Asia,* VII (March, 1955), 43-5.
———. *In Search of an Indonesian Identity.* N.pl.: New Nusantara Publishing Co., n.d. [probably Spring, 1959].
ALKEMA, B. *De Sarikat Islam (The Sarikat Islam).* Utrecht: G. J. A. Ruys, 1919.
ANDERSON, BENEDICT R. O'G. *Some Aspects of Indonesian Politics Under the Japanese Occupation: 1944-1945.* ("Interim Reports Series, Modern Indonesia Project.") Ithaca: Department of Far Eastern Studies, Cornell University, 1961.
AZIZ, MUHAMMAD ABDUL. *Japan's Colonialism and Indonesia.* The Hague: Martinus Nijhoff, 1955.
BENDA, HARRY J. "The Communist Rebellions of 1926-1927 in Indonesia," *Pacific Historical Review,* XXIV (May, 1955), 139-52.
———. *The Crescent and the Rising Sun: Indonesian Islam under the Japanese Occupation 1942-1945.* The Hague: W. Van Hoeve Ltd., 1958.
———. "The Structure of Southeast Asian History: Some Preliminary Observations," *Journal of Southeast Asian History,* III (March, 1962), 106-38.
———, and MCVEY, RUTH T. (eds.). *The Communist Uprisings of 1926-*

1927 in Indonesia: Key Documents. ("Translation Series, Modern Indonesia Project.") Ithaca: Department of Far Eastern Studies, Cornell University, 1960.

BLUMBERGER, J. TH. PETRUS. *Le Communisme aux Indes Néerlandaises.* Paris: Monde Nouveau, 1929.

———. *De Communistische Beweging in Nederlandsch-Indie (The Communist Movement in Netherlands India).* 2d rev. ed. Haarlem: H. D. Tjeenk Willink, 1935.

———. *De Nationalistiche Beweging in Nederlandsch-Indie (The Nationalist Movement in Netherlands India).* Haarlem: H. D. Tjeenk Willink, 1931.

BONE, ROBERT C., JR. "The Future of Indonesian Political Parties," *Far Eastern Survey,* XXIII (February, 1954), 17-23.

BOUSQUET, G. H. *A French View of the Netherlands Indies.* London: Oxford University Press, 1940.

BRACKMAN, ARNOLD C. *Indonesian Communism: A History.* New York: Frederick A. Praeger, 1963.

BRUGMANS, I. J., et al. (ed.). *Nederlandsch-Indie onder Japanse Bezetting: gegevens en documenten over de jaren 1942-1945 (Netherlands-India under the Japanese Occupation: Data and Documents for the Years 1942-1945).* Franeker: T. Wever, 1960.

COLLINS, JAMES FOSTER. "The UN and Indonesia," *International Conciliation,* CDLIX (March, 1950), 115-200.

DUIJS, J. E. W. *De Vervolging Tegen de Indonesische Studenten Mohammad Hatta, Mr. Ali Sastroamidjojo, Raden Mas Abdul Madjid Djojoadhiningrat en Mohammad Nazir Pamontjak. Verdedigings-Rede, Gehouden in de Zitting der Arr. Rechtbankte s'Gravenhage op 8 Maart 1928 (The Prosecution of the Indonesian Students Mohammad Hatta, Mr. Ali Sastroamidjojo, Raden Mas Abdul Madjid Djojoadhiningrat and Mohammad Nazir Pamontjak. Defense Speech Given Before the Session of the Court, The Hague, March 8, 1928).* Amsterdam: Ontwikkeling, 1928.

ELSBREE, WILLARD H. *Japan's Role in Southeast Asian Nationalist Movements: 1940-1945.* Cambridge: Harvard University Press, 1953.

EMERSON, RUPERT. *From Empire to Nation: The Rise to Self-Assertion of Asian and African Peoples.* Cambridge: Harvard University Press, 1960.

———. *Malaysia: A Study in Direct and Indirect Rule.* New York: The Macmillan Co., 1937.

Encyclopaedie van Nederlandsch-Indie (Encyclopedia of the Netherlands Indies). 8 vols. The Hague: M. Nijhoff, 1917-39.

Ensiklopedia Indonesia (Indonesian Encyclopedia). 3 vols. Bandung: W. van Hoeve Ltd., 1954-56.

EUDIN, XENIA J., and NORTH, ROBERT C. *Soviet Russia and the East, 1920-1927: A Documentary Survey.* Stanford: Stanford University Press, 1957.

FEITH, HERBERT. *The Decline of Constitutional Democracy in Indonesia.*

Ithaca: Cornell University Press, 1962.

―――. *The Indonesian Elections of 1955.* ("Interim Report Series, Modern Indonesia Project.") Ithaca: Department of Far Eastern Studies, Cornell University, 1957.

FRANKEL, JOSEPH. "Soviet Policy in South East Asia," in MAX BELOFF, *Soviet Policy in the Far East, 1944-1951.* London: Oxford University Press, 1953.

FURNIVALL, J. S. *Colonial Policy and Practice: A Comparative Study of Burma and Netherlands India.* Cambridge: Cambridge University Press, 1948.

―――. *Netherlands India: A Study of Plural Economy.* New York: The Macmillan Co., 1944.

GEERTZ, CLIFFORD. *The Religion of Java.* Glencoe, Ill.: The Free Press of Glencoe, 1960.

GIBB, H. A. R. *Mohammedanism: An Historical Survey.* London: Oxford University Press, 1949.

GLASSBURNER, BRUCE, and THOMAS, KENNETH D. "The Swing of the Hoe: Re-tooling Begins in Indonesia," *Asian Survey,* I (June, 1961), 3-12.

HANNA, WILLARD A. "The Chinese Take a Second Look," in *Bung Karno's Indonesia.* New York: American Universities Field Staff, 1959.

HATTA, MOHAMMAD. *(Statement on) The Conception of the President.* N.pl., 1957.

―――. *Verspreide Geschriften (Selected Writings).* Amsterdam: C. P. J. van der Peet, 1952.

HENDERSON, WILLIAM. "The Indonesian Question, 1946-1949," *Pacific Settlement of Disputes.* New York: Woodrow Wilson Foundation, 1954.

HIGGINS, BENJAMIN. *Indonesia's Economic Stabilization and Development.* New York: Institute of Pacific Relations, 1957.

HUMPHREY, DONALD D. "Indonesia's National Plan for Economic Development," *Asian Survey,* II (December, 1962), 12-21.

ISAACS, HAROLD R. *The Tragedy of the Chinese Revolution.* Rev. ed. Stanford: Stanford University Press, 1951.

JONES, F. C. *Japan's New Order in East Asia: 1937-1945.* London: Oxford University Press, 1954.

KAHIN, GEORGE MCTURNAN (ed.). *Major Governments of Asia.* Ithaca: Cornell University Press, 1958.

―――. *Nationalism and Revolution in Indonesia.* Ithaca: Cornell University Press, 1952.

KAT ANGELINO, A. D. A. DE. *Colonial Policy.* 2 vols. The Hague: Martinus Nijhoff, 1931.

―――. *Staatkundig beleid en bestuurszorg in Nederlandsch-Indie (Political Leadership and Administrative Policy in Netherlands India).* 2 vols. in 3. The Hague: Martinus Nijhoff, 1930.

KAUTSKY, JOHN H. *Moscow and the Communist Party of India: A Study in the Postwar Evolution of International Communist Strategy.* New York: John Wiley and Sons, 1956.

KENNEDY, RAYMOND. *The Ageless Indies.* New York: The John Day Co., 1942.

KLERCK, E. S. DE. *History of the Netherlands East Indies.* 2 vols. Rotterdam: W. L. & J. Brusse, 1938.

KOCH, D. M. G. *Om de Vrijheid: De Nationalistische Beweging in Indonesia (Toward Freedom: The Nationalist Movement in Indonesia).* Djakarta: Jajasan Pembangunan, 1950.

KOL, H. H. VAN. "De Strijd der SDAP op Koloniaal Gebied," *Gedenkboek ter gelegenheid van het vijf en twintigjaarig bestaan van de Sociaal-democratische arbeiderspartij in Nederland* ("The Struggle of the SDAP in the Colonial Sphere," *Anniversary Book of the SDAP on the occasion of the twenty-fifth year of the Social-Democratic Workers Party in the Netherlands*). Amsterdam: Ontwikkeling, 1919.

McVEY, RUTH T. *The Calcutta Conference and the Southeast Asia Uprisings.* ("Interim Reports Series, Modern Indonesia Project.") Ithaca: Department of Far Eastern Studies, Cornell University, 1958.

———. *The Development of the Indonesian Communist Party and Its Relations with the Soviet Union and the Chinese People's Republic.* Cambridge: Massachusetts Institute of Technology, 1954.

———. *The Soviet View of the Indonesian Revolution: A Study in the Russian Attitude Towards Asian Nationalism.* ("Interim Reports Series, Modern Indonesia Project.") Ithaca: Department of Far Eastern Studies, Cornell University, 1957.

MOSSMAN, JAMES. *Rebels in Paradise: Indonesia's Civil War.* London: Jonathan Cape, 1961.

NATSIR, MOHAMMAD. "Gapi-Komisi Visman" ("Gapi and the Visman Commission"), *Capita Selecta (Selected Works).* Bandung: W. van Hoeve Ltd., 1954.

———. *Some Observations Concerning the Role of Islam in National and International Affairs.* ("Modern Indonesia Project," Data Paper No. 16.) Ithaca: Department of Far Eastern Studies, Cornell University, 1954.

NIEUWENHUIJZE, C. A. O. VAN. *Aspects of Islam in Post-Colonial Indonesia: Five Essays.* The Hague: W. van Hoeve Ltd., 1958.

PAAUW, DOUGLAS S. "From Colonial to Guided Economy," in RUTH T. McVEY (ed.), *Indonesia.* New Haven: Human Relations Area Files, 1963.

PALMIER, LESLIE H. *Indonesia and the Dutch.* London: Oxford University Press, 1962.

———. "Modern Islam in Indonesia: The Muhammadiyah After Independence," *Pacific Affairs,* XXVII (September, 1954), 255-63.

———. "Sukarno the Nationalist," *Pacific Affairs,* XXX (June, 1957), 101-19.

PAUKER, GUY J. "Indonesia's Eight-Year Development Plan," *Pacific Affairs,* XXXIV (Summer, 1961), 115-30.

Peaceful Settlement in Indonesia. ("U.N. Publications No. 1951/I/6.") New York: United Nations, 1951.

PLUVIER, J. M. *Overzicht van de Ontwikkeling der Nationalistische Beweging in Indonesia in de Jaaren 1930 tot 1942 (Survey of the Development of the Nationalist Movement in Indonesia from 1930 to 1942).* The Hague: W. van Hoeve, Ltd., 1953.

PRINGGODIGDO, A. K. *Sedjarah Pergerakan Rakjat Indonesia (History of the Indonesian People's Movement).* Djakarta: Pustaka Rakjat, 1949.

PURCELL, VICTOR. *The Chinese in Southeast Asia.* London: Oxford University Press, 1951.

PYE, LUCIAN. "The Politics of Southeast Asia," in GABRIEL A. ALMOND, and JAMES S. COLEMAN (eds.), *The Politics of the Developing Areas.* Princeton: Princeton University Press, 1960.

RALIBY, OSMAN. *Documenta Historica: Sedjarah Documenter dari Pertimbuhan dan Perdjuangan Negara Republik Indonesia (Historical Documents: Documentary History of the Growth and Struggle of the Republic of Indonesia).* Djakarta: Bulan-Bintang, 1953. Vol. I.

RUTGERS, S. J. *Indonesia: Het koloniale systeem in de periode tussen de eerste en de tweede wereldoorlog (Indonesia: The Colonial System in the Period Between the First and Second World Wars).* 2 vols. Amsterdam: Pegasus, 1947.

SACKS, MILTON. "The Strategy of Communism in Southeast Asia," Pacific Affairs, XXIII (September, 1950), 227-47.

SALIM, H. AGUS. *Djedjak Langkah Hadji A. Salim. Pilihan Karangan Utjapan dan Pendapat Beliau dari Dulu sampai Sekarang (The Path of Hadji A. Salim: Selections from his Writings, Speeches and Opinions from Early Times until the Present).* Djakarta: Tintamas, 1954.

SASTROAMIDJOJO, ALI. "Survey of the Indonesian National Movement," *Indonesian Life,* I (March-April, 1947), 6-9.

SCHRIEKE, B. J. O. *Indonesian Sociological Studies: Selected Writings of B. Schrieke.* The Hague: W. van Hoeve Ltd., 1955.

SEMAOEN (SEMAUN). *Hoe het Hollandsche Imperialisme het Bruine Millionen-volk Aanzet tot een Massamoord op Europeanen in Indonesia (How Dutch Imperialism Urges the Millions of Brown People to a Mass Murder of Europeans in Indonesia).* Amsterdam: Brochurehandel der C.P.H., n.d.

————. "International Imperialism and the Communist Party of Indonesia," *Communist International,* No. 17 (1926), pp. 75-82.

SITORUS, L. M. *Sedjarah Pergerakan Kebangsaan Indonesia (History of the Indonesian Nationalist Movement).* Djakarta: Pustaka Rakjat, 1951.

SJAHRIR, SUTAN. *Indonesian Socialism.* Rangoon: Asian Socialist Publishing House, 1956.

————. *Onze Strijd (Our Struggle)*. Amsterdam: Vrij Nederland, 1946.

————. *Out of Exile*. Translated by CHARLES WOLF, JR. New York: The John Day Co., 1949.

SMITH, WILFRED CANTWELL. *Islam in Modern History*. Princeton: Princeton University Press, 1957.

SNOUCK, HURGRONJE C. *Mohammedanism*. New York: G. P. Putnam's Sons, 1916.

SOEKARNO (SUKARNO). *Indonesie Klaagt Aan! Pleitrede voor den Landraad te Bandoeng op 2 December 1930, Gehouded door Ir. Soekarno (Indonesia Accuses! Defense Speech given before the District Court in Bandung, December 2, 1930, by Engineer Soekarno)*. N.pl.: Het Fonds Nasional der Federatie van Indonesische Politieke Vereenigingen (PPPKI), 1931.

————. *Marhaen and Proletarian: Speech Before the Indonesian Nationalist Party at the Party's Thirtieth Anniversary at Bandung, July 3, 1957*. ("Translation Series, Modern Indonesia Project.") Ithaca: Department of Far Eastern Studies, Cornell University, 1960.

SOEMARDJAN, SELO. "Land Reform in Indonesia," *Asian Survey*, I (February, 1962), 23-30.

SUPOMO, R. "The Future of Adat Law in the Reconstruction of Indonesia," in P. W. THAYER, (ed.), *Southeast Asia in the Coming World*. Baltimore: The Johns Hopkins Press, 1953.

TAJIBNAPIS, S. H. "De Laatste Tien Jaren voor de Japanese Bezetting" ("The Last Ten Years Before the Japanese Occupation"), *De Brug-Djambatan*, I (April, 1946), 10-14.

TAYLOR, ALISTAIR M. *Indonesian Independence and the United Nations*. Ithaca: Cornell University Press, 1960.

TEDJASUKMANA, ISKANDAR. *The Political Character of the Indonesian Trade Union Movement*. ("Monograph Series, Modern Indonesia Project.") Ithaca: Department of Far Eastern Studies, Cornell University, 1958.

TRAGER, FRANK N. (ed.). *Marxism in Southeast Asia: A Study of Four Countries*. Stanford: Stanford University Press, 1959.

VAN DEN BRINK, H. *Een Eisch van Recht: De Koloniale Verhouding als Vraagstuk Getoest (A Demand for Justice: The Colonial Relationship as a Test Case)*. Amsterdam: Kirchner, 1946.

VAN DER ZEE, DAAN. *De SDAP en Indonesie (The SDAP and Indonesia)*. Amsterdam: Arbeiderspers, 1929.

————. *De Wereld Vrij: Socialistische Beschouwingen over het Koloniale Probleem (The World Free: Socialist Opinion on the Colonial Problem)*. Amsterdam: Arbeiderspers, 1931.

VAN NIEL, ROBERT. *The Emergence of the Modern Indonesian Elite*. The Hague: W. van Hoeve Ltd., 1960.

VERDOORN, J. A. *The National Movement in Indonesia*. Jogjakarta: Republic of Indonesia, Ministry of Information, n.d. [probably late 1947].

VLEKKE, BERNARD H. M. *Nusantara: A History of the East Indian Archipelago.* Cambridge: Harvard University Press, 1945.

VON ARX, ALEXANDRE. *L'Evolution Politique en Indonesie de 1900 à 1942.* Fribourg: Artigianelli-Monza, 1949.

WANG MING. "The Revolutionary Movement in the Colonial and Semi-Colonial Countries and the Tactics of the Communist Parties," *Communist International,* XII, Nos. 17-18 (September 20, 1935), 1323-33.

WERTHEIM, W. F. *Indonesian Society in Transition.* The Hague: W. van Hoeve Ltd., 1956.

WILMOTT, DONALD E. *The National Status of the Chinese in Indonesia.* ("Interim Reports Series, Modern Indonesia Project.") Ithaca: Department of Far Eastern Studies, Cornell University, 1956.

WOLF, CHARLES, JR. *The Indonesian Story: The Birth, Growth and Structure of the Indonesian Republic.* New York: The John Day Co., 1948.

"X." "The Revolutionary Movement in the East," *Communist International,* Nos. 18-19 (1926), pp. 97-115.

Index

Abadi (newspaper), 132n, 214
Abduh, Mohammed, 16n
Abdulgani, Ruslan, 6, 128, 186, 211
Action Committee for the Liberation
  of West Irian, 197n
adat law, 12
Aidit, 143n, 156, 203, 206–7
Ali-Baba firms, 121
Ali cabinet, *see* Sastroamidjojo, Ali
Alimin, 31, 32, 39, 40–41, 90, 143n,
  154
All-Indonesia Central Labor Organi-
  zation, *see* SOBSI
Al-Manar (periodical), 16n
Ambon, 100, 183n
Antara Daily News Bulletin, 157n,
  214
Anwari, Ir., 57n
Army of Indonesia, 4, 160n, 199–202,
  208–9, 211–12, 221
Asrama schools, 145n
Association of Indonesian Workers,
  see SKBI
Association of Railway Workers
  (VSTP), 25n
Atjeh, 28n, 131n

Baars, A., 24n, 34, 36, 82n
Bakunin, Mikhail, 7, 189
Bandjermasin, 28n
Bandung, 100, 156n
Bandung Charter, 176
Bandung Conference (1955), 153
BAPEKAN (Badan Pengawas Kegi-
  atan Apparatur Negara), 193, 196
Batuah, Datuk, 35
Benda, Harry J., 31n, 70n
Bergsma, P., 24n, 36

Bintang Merah (Red Star), 146n
Blanc, Louis, 189
Body for Controlling Activities of the
  State Apparatus, *see* BAPEKAN
Boven Digoel, 33–34
Brackman, Arnold, 40n, 198
Brandsteder, J. T., 24n, 36
Brunei, 155
BTI (Barisan Tani Indonesia), 109,
  111, 145, 205
Budi Utomo, 43, 61
Bukharin, 40, 42n, 96
Bulganin, 153
Burma, 3, 74, 92n, 93n, 153, 202

Cairo, 15
Calcutta Conference (1948), 93n
Cambodia, 225–26
Catholic Party, *see* Partai Katholik
Chalid, Idham, 211
China, 41, 49, 69; *see also* Chinese
  People's Republic
Chinese, in Indonesia, 120–21
Chinese Communist Party, 7
Chinese Foreign Ministry, 153
Chinese Nationalists, 132n, 154n
Civil Servants' Association (Persatuan
  Pegawei Binnenlandsche-Bestuur
  [PPBB]), 64n
Cochran, Merle, 94, 96n
Cominform, 88, 92n, 136, 144
Comintern, 25–26, 32, 35–36, 38–41,
  47, 49–51, 52, 54, 59–60, 63–69, 77,
  89, 91, 146n
Communist Party of Holland (CPH),
  24n; *see also* Communist Party of
  the Netherlands
Communist Party of India, 92n–93n

Communist Party of Indonesia, *see* PKI

Communist Party of Malaya, 93*n*

Communist Party of the Netherlands (CPN), 24*n*, 36, 37–38, 39*n*, 48, 49, 68, 90

Communist University of the Peoples of the East, 60*n*

Communist University of the Toilers of the East, 36

Communist World Federation of Trade Unions, 98*n*

Constitution of 1945, 121–23, 141–42, 162, 164, 171–72, 174–78, 183, 187, 192, 194*n*, 212

Consultative Body of People's Representatives (Madjelis Permusjawaratan Perwakilan Rakjat), 172

Council of Indonesian Moslem Associations, *see* Masjumi

Council of People's Representatives (Dewan Perwakilan Rakjat [DPR]), 163*n*, 172, 193–95

CPH, *see* Communist Party of Holland

CPN, *see* Communist Party of the Netherlands

Cramer, 42–44

"Culture System," 19

Dahlan, Kaiai Hadji Ahmad, 17, 31

Danuwinoto, Asmoro, 158*n*

Darul Islam (DI), 102, 131, 151, 204*n*

Dekker, H. W., 24*n*

Democratic League (Liga Demokrasi), 201, 213

desa system, 12–13, 102

De Visser, 38–39

Dewan Perwakilan Rakjat, *see* Council of People's Representatives

Dewantoro, Ki Hadjar, 24

DI, *see* Darul Islam

Dimitrov doctrine, 63

Djakarta, 76, 77*n*, 101, 104*n*, 105, 106*n*, 112, 115, 131*n*, 132, 138*n*, 139, 153–54, 159, 161–62, 183*n*, 201*n*

Djakarta Charter, 163, 176

Djojohadikusumo, Dr. Sumitro, 84*n*, 119*n*, 124*n*, 138

Djojoprajitno, Sudijono, 141–42

Djuanda, Premier, 161*n*, 170, 203

DPA, *see* Supreme Advisory Council

DPR, *see* Council of People's Representatives

Dutch Social Democrats, *see* Indische Sociaal-Democratische Partij

Dutch Socialist Trade Union Federation (Nederlandsch Vakbeweging Vereeniging [NVV]), 53*n*

ECCI, 40–41, 42*n*

Effendi, Roestam, 39

Engels, Friedrich, 135–37, 189, 190

Erningpradja, 196, 212

Fascism, in Indonesia, 63, 65–68, 86–87, 89–90

FDR (Front Demokrasi Rakjat), 91–92, 98, 109, 148

Federation of Indonesian Political Parties, *see* Gapi

Federation of Revolutionary Trade Unions of Indonesia, *see* GASBRI

Feith, Herbert, 141

Fighting Front (Persatuan Perdjuangan [PP]), 97–98

First Radical Concentration, 43–45

Foreign Ministry of Indonesia, 212

Fourier, Charles, 189

Fourth Comintern Congress (1922), 28

Fourth International, 98*n*

Furnivall, J. S., 19, 42*n*

Gadjah Mada University, 168*n*

Gapi (Gabungan Politik Indonesia), 63, 66–67, 69

GASBRI (Gabungan Serikat Buruh Revolusioner Indonesia), 109*n*

Gerindo (Gerakan Rakjat Indonesia), 65–66, 69

Glodok, 104

gotong rojong, 12, 13, 15, 127, 160–61, 173–74, 184–85, 203, 224

"Gottwald Plan," 91, 95

Greater East Asian Co-Prosperity Sphere, 67

Green Association, *see* Sarekat Hidjau

GRR (Gerakan Revolusi Rakjat), 98, 140

guided democracy, description of, 3, 170–74

Hadi, Asmara, 158n, 196
Hague Agreement (1949), 100–101, 106, 174n, 187
Harahap, Burhanuddin, 124n
Harian Rakjat (newspaper), 143n, 206, 214
Harjono, 109, 110n
Hasjim, Wachid, 164n
Hatta, Mohammad, 48, 50, 54, 56n, 58, 59n, 62, 68, 77, 81, 83–84, 87, 90, 91, 94, 99, 127, 138, 148–49, 153, 164n
Hindley, Donald, 204n
Ho Chi Minh, 104n
Holst, Henriette Roland, 7

Independence Preparatory Commission, 122n
India, 3, 93n, 153
Indies Social Democratic Association (Indische Sociaal Democratische Vereeniging [ISDV]), 23, 24, 25, 42n
Indische Sociaal-Democratische Partij (ISDP), 38, 42–44, 45, 50, 69, 82n, 91n, 108n
Indonesia (periodical), 68
Indonesia Raya (anthem), 175
Indonesia Raya (newspaper), 214
Indonesian Aims and Ideals, 83
Indonesian Chinese Party, 143n, 154
Indonesian Christian Party, *see* Parkindo
Indonesian Communist Union, *see* PKI
Indonesian Labor Front (Barisan Buruh Indonesia), 109
Indonesian Labor Party, 109
Indonesian National Education Club (Club Pendidikan Nasional Indonesia), 58
Indonesian Nationalist Party, *see* PNI
Indonesian Peasant Front, *see* BTI
Indonesian People's Council (Madjelis Rakjat Indonesia), 63
Indonesian People's Movement, *see* Gerindo
Indonesian Republic Teachers Association, 157n
Indonesian Socialist Party, *see* PSI
Indonesian Students' Association, 56n
Indonesian Teachers Congress, 167n

Indonesia's Technical Assistance Agreement, 147n
Indonesie Klaagt Aan! (*Indonesia Accuses!*), 55, 81
Insulinde, 43
International Red Aid, 49
International Union of Students, 93n
Inzicht, Het (*Insight* [periodical]), 84–85
IPKI, 160n, 161n, 200n, 201n
Irian, 106, 107n, 155, 211; *see also* West Irian
Isa Anshary, Kiaji, 130–31
ISDP, *see* Indische Sociaal-Democratische Partij
ISDV, *see* Indies Social Democratic Association
Iskaq, Mr., 57n
Islam, 15–17, 27n, 28–29, 46, 47, 62, 63, 74n, 81, 82, 87–89, 96, 102, 129–30, 131–33, 160n, 165–66, 175, 185, 190, 214
Islamic Association Party of Indonesia, *see* PSII
Islamic Education Party, *see* Perti
Isman, Colonel, 211

Jamal-al-Din, 16n
Jani, 204n
Japanese Foreign Office, 72
Japanese Naval Intelligence, 76
Japanese Peace Treaty, 149
Jaurès, Jean, 189
Java, 15, 17, 18n, 19, 20, 38, 48n, 50n, 57n, 60, 71n, 72, 94, 95n, 104n, 119n, 130–31, 159, 182, 202, 219
Jogjakarta, 28n, 147n
Jogjakarta, Sultan of, 199, 202, 213
Jussuf, Mohammed, 90

Kahin, George McT., 32n, 60
Kamoe, K., 60n
Kautsky, 56
Kawilarang, Colonel Alex, 138
Khrushchev, Nikita, 153
Koran, the, 16, 87
Korean War, 104, 105
Kremlin, 40, 89, 93, 118
kromo, definition of, 57n
Kusumasumantri, Iwa, 98, 109, 150, 212

Lamennais, Félicité de, 189
Laski, Harold, 7
League Against Imperialism, see Liga
League of Nations, 52
League of Upholders of Indonesian Independence, see IPKI
Left Wing, see Sajap Kiri
Leimena, Dr., 212
Lenin, Nikolai, 7, 8, 58, 106n, 140–41, 189
Liga, 48–51, 54, 60, 68, 96n
Linggadjati Agreement, 100
Lukman, 143n, 206

McVey, Ruth T., 42n, 93n
Madiun rebellion, 28n, 90, 92–95, 98, 103, 109–10, 118, 143–44, 145n, 146–49, 150, 209
Maeda, Rear Admiral T., 76–77
Makassar, 100, 183n
Malang, 109
Malaya, 92n, 104–5
Malaysia, 154–55, 202
Malik, Adam, 59, 76, 211
Mangoenkoesoemo, Dr. Tjipto, 24, 56n–57n
Manipol, 162, 184, 185–86, 203
Manipol speech, 177n, 187
Manipol/Usdek, 158n, 162–63, 169, 186, 227
Mao Tse-tung, 106n, 154
Maramis, A. A., 164
marhaen, definition of, 57n
Marsoeki, 60
Marx, Karl, 7, 8, 27n, 106n, 135–37, 140–41, 189, 190
Marxism, definition of, 9
Masjumi (Madjelis Sjuro Muslimin Indonesia), 46, 87–89, 98, 110, 113, 116, 125, 126, 127, 129–34, 138, 143, 145, 149–50, 157n, 160n, 161n, 166n, 201, 203, 210, 214
Masons, 213
Massa Actie (pamphlet), 32
Mauawar, 56n
Medan, 183n
Menado, 131n
Minangkabau, 28
Ministry of Defense and Security, 150–51, 199, 212
    Education, 214

Finance, 124n
Foreign Affairs, 104n
Health, 212
Information, 84, 103n, 104n, 122n, 214
Labor, 108
National Security, 200
Social and Cultural Affairs, 214
Miradsi, 146n
Misbach, Hadji, 35
Modernist Islamic movement, 12, 15–17, 26, 45–46, 62, 81, 87
Mohammedijah, the, 17, 45, 67, 81, 129
Moral Rearmament, 213
Moscow, 32, 36, 38–41, 49, 54, 56n, 60n, 91, 92n, 93n, 96n, 98, 136, 141, 154n, 206; see also Russia, Soviet Union, and U.S.S.R.
Moslem League, 201n
Moslems, see Islam
MPR, see People's Assembly for Deliberations
mufakat, 13, 224
Mukarto, 150
Murba (Partai Murba), 59n, 61, 98–99, 109n, 110, 117, 126, 139–43, 148, 160n, 161n, 199, 211, 225
musjawarah, 13, 15, 224
Musjawarah Nasional, 14
Musso, 31, 32, 38n, 40–41, 42n, 60, 91, 93n, 95, 148
Mussolini, Benito, 224
Mutual Security Act, 96n, 149
Muzakir, Abdulkahar, 164n

Nahdatul Ulama, see NU
Nasakom, 163, 185, 203, 227
Nasution, Major General Abdul Haris, 150n, 197n, 200–202, 204n, 209, 211, 212
National Advisory Council, 160–61, 193
National Consultative Conference, 14, 161, 173
National Front (Front Nasional), 193, 196–97, 213, 223
National Over-all Development Plan, 179
National Peasants' Conference (1959), 145
National Planning Board, 170

National Planning Council (Dewan Perantjang Nasional), 172, 179–80, 193, 196, 212
National Unity Program, 146
National Youth Day, 157, 159n, 165
Nationale Indische Partij (NIP), 24
Nationalist Party of Indonesia, see PNI
Natsir, Mohammad, 67, 88n, 113, 129–34, 144, 146
Nazi-Soviet pact, 66, 69, 89
Netherlands East Indies Government, 18, 19, 36, 45, 50, 53n, 56, 67n
New China News Agency, 156n
New Guinea, 33
New York Times (newspaper), 159n
Nieuwenhuis, Domela, 7, 189
Nitimihardjo, Maruto, 76
Njoto, 156n, 203, 206, 213n
North Borneo, 155
North Korea, 105
North Sumatra, 124
NU (Nahdatul Ulama), 89, 114n, 116, 126, 128, 129–31, 160, 161n, 201n, 203, 211
NVV, see Dutch Socialist Trade Union Federation

"October 17 Affair," 150, 208
Oei Gee Hwat, 109, 110n
ontvoogding, 18n
Our Struggle, 85–86
Over-all Eight Year Plan, 182

Pakistan, 3, 202
Palar, L. N., 51
Pandji Islam, 67
Pandu Wiguna, 196
Pan-Islamism, 16, 96
Pantja Sila, 81–83, 87, 132–34, 175, 178, 184, 191–92, 203
Parkindo (Partai Kristen Indonesia), 160n, 161n
Pari (Partai Repoeblik Indonesia), 59, 63, 76, 98
Parindra, 61n, 63, 65, 67n, 68
Partai Buruh, 146
Partai Indonesia, see Partindo
Partai Katholik, 160n, 161n
Partai Murba, see Murba
Partai Rakjat Indonesia, 146

Partai Rakjat Sosialis, 134n
Partai Repoeblik Indonesia, see Pari
Partindo (Partai Indonesia), 54, 60–61, 66, 88n, 158n, 160n, 204n
Party of the Common People, see Murba
Pasundan, 61
Pearl Harbor, 67n
Pedoman (newspaper), 214
Peking, 106, 118, 141, 153–56, 206; see also People's Republic of China
Pemuda Rakjat, 145, 204n
People's Assembly for Deliberations (MPR), 162n, 193–94
People's Association, see Sarekat Rakjat
People's Democratic Front, see FDR
"People's Front" doctrine, 64, 68
People's Republic of China, 21, 153–54, 167; see also Peking
People's Revolutionary Movement, see GRR
People's Youth, see Pemuda Rakjat
Perdjoeangan Kita (*Our Struggle* [pamphlet]), 85–86
Perhimpoenan Indonesia (PI), 48–51, 54, 56n, 64, 68, 86n, 88n, 96n
Persindo, 51
Perti (Persatuan Tarbiah Islamijah), 160n, 201n
Pesindo, 145
Peta (Soekarela Tentara Pembela Tanah Air), 79
PI, see Perhimpoenan Indonesia
PIA, 214
Pioneers (Pramuka), 213
PKI (Partai Komunis Indonesia), 4, 24, 25–42 *passim*, 47–51, 54, 56n, 57, 59–61, 64, 66, 69, 75, 77, 89–99 *passim*, 103, 107, 108, 109, 111–12, 114n, 117–18, 121, 124–25, 126, 128, 130–31, 134, 135n, 137, 141, 143–56 *passim*, 158, 160, 161n, 177, 197, 198–99, 200, 201, 202, 203–7, 209–12, 213n, 214, 218, 219, 221–22, 225
PNI (Partai Nasional Indonesia), 54–58, 60, 61, 62, 66, 81, 110, 113, 114n, 117, 121, 126–29, 130–31, 134, 135n, 137, 141, 143, 145–46, 149–52, 158, 160n, 161n, 169, 203, 204n, 208–9, 211, 214
Political Manifesto (Sjahrir), 83

Political Manifesto (Sukarno), 162, 184, 186, 205, 213, 214
Political Parties Act, 173
Politiek dan Revolusi Kita (Politics and Our Revolution), 87
Popular Front, 64, 69, 76
PP, *see* Fighting Front
PPBB, *see* Civil Servants' Association
PPPKI (Permufakatan Perhimpunan Politik Kebangsaan Indonesia), 62–63
Prague, 109
Prambanan decision, 31–33, 39, 41
Prawiranegara, Sjafruddin, 87, 129, 131
Principles and Policy . . ., 136
Profintern, 40
Progressive Party, 150
PSI (Partai Sosialis Indonesia), 4, 61, 88–89, 90, 91, 110, 113, 114n, 117, 120n, 124–25, 126, 134–39, 142, 144, 150–52, 157n, 161n, 177, 201, 210, 213n, 214
PSII (Partai Sarekat Islam), 61, 62, 67n, 141, 146, 160n, 161n, 201n

Railway Workers' Union (Vereeniging van Spooren Tramweg Personeel [VSTP]), 108n, 109
Ratu Adil, 82
Red China, *see* Chinese People's Republic
Religious Socialists, 87–89, 126, 129–30, 225
Renville Agreement, 91, 100, 106
Resopim, 163, 203, 227
Rida, Sheik Rashid, 16n
Rum, Mohammad, 129
Russia, 7, 38n, 78; *see also* Moscow, Soviet Union, *and* U.S.S.R.

Sadjarwo, 212
Sajap Kiri (Left Wing), 90–91, 109, 134n
Sakirman, 151
Saleh, Chairul, 76, 196, 199, 211, 212
Salim, Hadji Agus, 26, 62, 82n, 87, 164
Samin, 20
Samsi, Dr., 57n

Sarawak, 155
Sardjono, 90, 109
Sarekat Hidjau (Green Association), 29–30
Sarekat Hindyu, 30n
Sarekat Islam (SI), 21, 25–30, 35, 43–44, 45, 60, 62, 81, 108; *see also* Islamic Association Party of Indonesia (PSII)
Sarekat Rakjat (SR), 30–32, 35, 56n, 61
Sartono, Mr., 56n, 66, 191–92
Sastroamidjojo, Ali, 116, 124n, 127–28, 131, 150–52, 160, 201n, 204n, 210
Sastrosatomo, Sudarpo, 84n
Schermerhorn, 189–90
SDAP, *see* Social Democratic Workers Party
SDP, *see* Sociaal-Democratische Partij
Second Comintern Congress (1920), 29
Second Congress of the Communist Party of India, 93n
Second International, 47
Second Radical Concentration, 43–45
Semarang, 35
Semaun, 25n, 35–36, 37, 41, 45, 48–49, 50, 56n, 108n
Serikat Sumatra, 61
Setiadjit, 109
Seventh Comintern Congress (1935), 52, 63, 67–68
Sharkey, Lawrence, 93n
SI, *see* Sarekat Islam
Siauw Giok Tjhan, 143n
Sidik, 150
Sihanouk, Prince Norodom, 226
Siliwangi Division, 147
Singapore, 93n, 155
Sixth Comintern Congress (1928), 35, 41, 49, 51, 56n, 63, 68, 96
Sjahrir, Sutan, 6, 33–34, 54, 58, 68, 75–77, 81, 83–86, 88, 91, 97, 113, 114n, 135–39, 151
Sjarifuddin, Amir, 66, 75, 88, 90, 91–92, 134n, 147
SKBI (Sarekat Kaum Buruh Indonesia), 60, 63
Sneevliet, H. J. F. M., 24, 35n, 36, 37n, 108n
SOBRI (Sentral Organisasi Buruh Republik Indonesia), 98n, 109n

SOBSI (Sentral Organisasi Buruh Seluruh Indonesia), 92, 98*n*, 109–11, 121, 124, 144–45, 151
Sociaal-Democratische Partij (SDP), 24*n*
Social Democratic Workers Party (Sociaal-Democratische Arbeiderspartij [SDAP]), 23–24, 38, 43*n*, 51–53
Social Democrats, Dutch, see Indische Sociaal-Democratische Partij
socialism, definition of, 9
Socialist Party of Indonesia, see PSI
Soediro, 35
Soedjadi, 57*n*
Soejoedi, Mr., 57*n*
Soekarno, see Sukarno
Soekra, 31
Soenario, Mr., 57*n*
Soenarjo, 60
Soetardjo, 64*n*
Soetardjo Petition, 64
Solo, 28*n*, 35
Soong, Ching Ling, Madame, 168
Soviet Union, 91*n*, 95, 98, 148, 200; see also Moscow, Russia, and U.S.S.R.
SR, see Sarekat Rakjat
Staatspoorweg Bond, 108*n*
Stalin, Joseph, 39, 40*n*, 41, 42*n*, 75, 89, 90, 98, 150*n*
State Comptrolling Council (Badan Pemeriksa Keuangan), 193, 195
Stokvis, 53
Student Quarters for a Free Indonesia (Asrama Indonesia Merdeka), 76–77
Subandrio, 212
Subardjo, Achmad, 96, 98, 149, 164*n*
Sudarsono, Major General, 98*n*
Sudisman, 206
Sudjatmoko, 84*n*
Sukarni, 59, 76, 211
Sukarno, President, accused of Fascism, 90;
attacked in "White Paper," 147–49;
charismatic appeal of, 207–8, 220;
Communist support of, 60–61, 144, 160, 203–7, 209–11, 221–22;
and the Constitution of 1945, 174–78;
control of news media, 214;

and guided democracy, 3–5, 13, 116, 160–64, 170–74, 217, 226–27;
guided economy of, 178–83;
impatience with parliamentary democracy, 161–70;
Indonesia Accuses! speech of, 55–57;
National Youth Day speech of, 157–59, 165;
organization of government under, 193–98, 212–14, 215;
and Pantja Sila, 81–82;
Political Manifesto of, 162, 184, 186, 205, 213–14;
political slogans of, 160–64, 165–66, 178–79, 184–87, 207*n*, 223–24, 227;
relations with army, 201–2, 208–9, 211–12, 221;
relations with Murba, 140–42;
relations with PNI, 127–29, 208–9;
relations with Tan Malaka, 97, 99;
socialist influences on, 181–92, 209, 225;
trip to Russia, 153
Sukiman, 62, 129–30, 146, 149
Sulawesi, 131*n*, 161–62
Sumatra, 28, 35, 53*n*, 72, 131*n*, 132, 138, 161–62
Sunda, 57*n*
Sun Yat-sen, Dr., 7, 82*n*
Suprapto, 98
Supreme Advisory Council (Mahkamah Agung [DPA]), 162, 177, 186, 193, 195, 212
Supreme Court, 193, 195
Surabaya, 60, 167*n*, 188, 189
Surabaya Study Club, 61
Suryaningrat, Soewardi, 24
Suripno, 91
Sutomo, Dr., 68

Tan Ling Djie, 143*n*
Tan Malaka, 28–29, 32–33, 35, 39, 40, 41, 42*n*, 54, 59, 76–77, 81, 96–99, 109, 140, 148, 211
Than Tun, 93*n*
Third International, 49, 53*n*, 54, 59
Tjoa Sik Ien, 143*n*
Tjokroaminoto, Hadji, 26, 189, 190
Tjokrosujono, Abikusno, 62, 98, 164*n*
Trager, Frank N., 92*n*–93*n*

Troelstra, 53
Trotsky, Leon, 9, 40n, 42n, 76, 96, 98n

Union of Political Associations of Indonesian People, see PPPKI
United Nations, 80n, 94–95, 101, 105, 121, 147n, 152, 154n, 161–62
General Assembly of, 95n, 162n, 186
Security Council of, 95
United Nations Commission for Indonesia, 94n
United States, 96n, 105, 132n, 167
University of Indonesia, 165
University Students' Association (Persatoean Mahsiswa), 76
Usdek, 162, 183–84; see also Manipol/Usdek
U.S.S.R., 153; see also Russia, Soviet Union, and Moscow

Van Mook, 147
Van Ravesteyn, 39
Vietnam, 103n, 104
Vietnamese Communist Party, 7
Visman, Dr. F. H., 67n
Visman Commission, 67
Volksraad, 42–44, 61, 64, 66, 67n
Volunteer Army of Defenders of the Fatherland, see Peta

VSTP, see Railway Workers' Union

Warsaw World Peace Conference, 143n
Waworoentoe, J., 60n
Wentoek, C., 60n
West Irian, 121, 155, 158, 161–62, 204n, 223; see also Irian
West Irian National Liberation Front, 197
WFTU, see World Federation of Trade Unions
"White Paper" on Madiun, 146–49
Wikana, 66, 77n, 145n
Wilopo, 113, 119n, 124n, 149
Winarno, 158n
World Federation of Democratic Youth, 93n
World Federation of Trade Unions (WFTU), 109
World War I, 18, 19, 20
World War II, 24, 57, 64, 70–79 passim, 91n, 96, 101
Wynkoop, 39

Yamin, Mohammad, 164n, 179n, 196, 211

Zeven Provincie, 52–53
"Zhdanov line," 91, 92n